PRESBYTERIAN POLITY
FOR
CHURCH OFFICERS

(Third Edition)

PRESBYTERIAN POLITY FOR CHURCH OFFICERS
(Third Edition)

JOAN S. GRAY
and
JOYCE C. TUCKER

Foreword by Cynthia M. Campbell

Geneva Press
Louisville, Kentucky

Scripture quotations are from the Revised Standard Version of the Bible, copyrighted 1946, 1952, © 1971, 1973 by the Division of Christian Education of the National Council of the Churches of Christ in the U.S.A., and are used by permission.

Permission is granted from the Office of the General Assembly, Presbyterian Church (U.S.A.) to use material from the following sources:

The Constitution of the Presbyterian Church (U.S.A.), Part I: *Book of Confessions* and Part II: *Book of Order,* and all earlier constitutions of the predecessor denominations now part of the Presbyterian Church (U.S.A.).

James E. Andrews, "We Can Be More Than We Are," Joint Committee on Presbyterian Reunion, *Resources for Studying the Plan for Reunion,* 1982.

"Church Membership and Discipline" (Atlanta: Office of the Stated Clerk, Presbyterian Church in the United States, 1979).

Robert Clyde Johnson, ed., *The Church and Its Changing Ministry* (Philadelphia: Office of the General Assembly, The United Presbyterian Church in the United States of America, 1961).

"The Nature and Practice of Ministry" (Atlanta: Office of the Stated Clerk, Presbyterian Church in the United States, 1981).

"Ordination to the Ministry of the Word" (Atlanta: Office of the Stated Clerk, Presbyterian Church in the United States, 1976).

Published by Westminster John Knox Press, Louisville, Kentucky

Printed in the United States of America
16 15 14 13 12 11 10 9

Library of Congress Cataloging-in-Publication Data

Gray, Joan S. (Joan Standridge), 1952-
    Presbyterian polity for church officers / Joan S. Gray and Joyce C. Tucker. —
3rd ed.
        p. cm.
    Includes bibliographical references and index.
    ISBN-13: 978-0-664-50018-4
    ISBN-10: 0-664-50018-8
    1. Presbyterian Church (U.S.A.).   Book of order.   2. Presbyterian Church
(U.S.A.)—Government.   3. Presbyterian Church—Government.
I. Tucker, Joyce C.   II. Title.
BX8969.6.P743G73   1999
262'.05137—dc21   98-42258

This book is dedicated to the sessions of
Oglethorpe Presbyterian Church
Atlanta, Georgia
and
John Knox Presbyterian Church
Marietta, Georgia
with thanks for our shared ministry

CONTENTS

Foreword by Cynthia M. Campbell   xi

Introduction   xvii

Chapter One—A Polity for the Church   1

    What Is Polity?   1
    Fundamentals of Presbyterian Polity   5
    The Powers and Responsibilities of Governing Bodies   10

Chapter Two—Calling to Office in the Church   12

    The Calling to Church Membership   12
    Church Membership as Ministry   14
    Calling to Office   15
    Qualifications of Church Officers   17
    Ordination to Office   19
    Freedom of Conscience and Its Limitations   21

Chapter Three—Election of Church Officers   23

    Commitment to Inclusiveness in the Election
        of Elders and Deacons   23
    The Nominating Committee   25
    Exemptions for Certain Congregations   27
    Inclusiveness with Exemptions   28
    Election, Examination, Ordination, and Installation
        of Elders and Deacons   29
    Calling a Pastor   30
    Presbyteries Working Together   32
    Ministers of the Word and Sacrament:
        Their Election, Ordination, and Installation as Pastors   33

Chapter Four—The Office of Elder   35

    Early Reformers   35
    The Church in Scotland   36
    Early Presbyterianism in America   38
    The 1788 Form of Government   38
    Advocacy for the Office of Elder   40
    Debates Surrounding the Eldership   42
    Parity in Governance   45

Chapter Five—The Office of Deacon   46

    The Office of Deacon in the Reformed Tradition   47

The 1788 Constitution 47
Encouraging Churches to Institute the Office 48
Changes in Understanding of the Office 50
Developments in the Presbyterian Church U.S. 51
Trends in the Presbyterian Church U.S.A. 53
Deacons in the United Presbyterian Church of North America 54
The United Presbyterian Church in the U.S.A. 55
Recovering the Essence of the Office of Deacon 56

Chapter Six—A First Look at the Session 60

An Overview of Responsibilities and Powers 61
Gathering the Community of Faith 63
A Continuing Responsibility for Members 67
A Continuing Responsibility for Church Officers 73

Chapter Seven—Ministers Serving Congregations 75

The Office of Minister of the Word and Sacrament 76
Continuing Members of Presbytery 77
Pastoral Relations with Congregations 79
Permanent Pastoral Relationships 79
Dissolving Permanent Pastoral Relationships 80
Designated Pastoral Relationships 80
Temporary Pastoral Relationships 81
Other Patterns of Leadership 83
The Distinctive Role of the Pastor 86

Chapter Eight—Officers and Staff Working Together 88

Pastors and Elders Working Together 89
Joint Responsibilities for Worship 90
Joint Responsibilities for Congregational Care 91
Joint Responsibilities for Governance 91
Pastors, Deacons, and Elders Working Together 92
Staff Relationships Within the Church 93
The Session's Personnel Responsibilities 94
The Important Role of the Educator 95

Chapter Nine—Leading the Church in Mission 98

The Nature of Mission 98
Facets of the Church's Mission 100
Beyond Polity 107
An Ecumenical Note 107

Chapter Ten—Presbytery, Synod, and the General Assembly 109

More Inclusive Governing Bodies 109
Presbytery 112
Synod 118

The General Assembly   120
Committees, Commissions, Agencies, and Councils   123

Chapter Eleven—Stewardship, Finance, and Property   126
The Grace of Stewardship   126
Presbyterian Stewardship   128
Stewardship Development and the Session   131
Stewardship and Financial Management   133
The Session and Church Property   139

Chapter Twelve—Meetings of Governing Bodies and of the   144
    Congregation
The Importance of Meetings   144
Consensus and Conflict   145
Types of Meetings   146
Moderators and Clerks   146
Parliamentary Procedure   148
Congregational Meetings   149
Meetings of the Session   152
Meetings of Presbytery   152
Meetings of Synod   154
Meetings of the General Assembly   155

Chapter Thirteen—Preserving Peace and Purity   158
Conflict in the Church   158
Ground Rules for Dealing with Conflict   159
Options for Disagreement—Dissent and Protest   162
What Is "Discipline"?   163
Judicial Process   164
Trials and Appeals   169

Chapter Fourteen—Leading the Church in Worship   171
A New Thing   171
What Is Worship?   173
The Elements of Worship   173
The Order of Worship   175
The Context of Worship   176
The Font and the Table   178
Worship on Special Occasions   181
Worship and Personal Discipleship   182
Worship and Ministry   183
Responsibilities for Worship   184

Notes   189

Index of Book of Order References   193

Index of Topics   197

FOREWORD

Why are things in the church the way they are and not some other way? This book seeks not only to describe the government of the Presbyterian Church but also to explain some of the reasons for things being as they are. In addition to history, tradition, and convenience, there are also reasons that grow out of our understanding of the nature of the Christian faith. Certain fundamental convictions derived from the reading of Scripture have helped to shape the *Book of Order* and the Presbyterian Church into what they are today.

Is this form of government taught in Scripture? Almost all churches look to Scripture to justify their particular forms and orders. Rather than trying to use Scripture to justify the particular provisions or even the offices of the church, it is more helpful to observe the ways in which some of the fundamental affirmations of the Reformed faith find expression in our church's government. It is difficult to decide which came first, theological understanding or form of government. In Calvin's own writing and work these two were very closely related. The development of this new way of being the church called "Reformed" can scarcely be separated from the development of a new system of theological reflection. Indeed, we can see influence flowing both ways: (*a*) Particular affirmations of faith are lived out in church order, and (*b*) the lived experience of Reformed Christians has shaped the theological stance. In what follows, I will suggest several convictions about God and the Christian life that find clear expression in the Presbyterian form of government. Others could have been chosen or added, but these form the core of a theological answer to the question: Why are things in the Presbyterian Church the way they are?

The Covenant. The idea of the covenant has long influenced the Reformed way of viewing God and God's relationship with humanity. Out of their conviction that what God began with Israel God completed in Jesus Christ, Calvin and others found in the covenants of the Old Testament the foundation for the Christian life. The covenant image was so powerful because it reminded Calvin that initiative in salvation, as in creation, lay entirely with God: It was *God* who called Israel, *God* who chose Abraham and Sarah, *God* who gave the law through Moses to the people. Each act was an act of grace, not done because any had deserved it; in each case it was God who sought out people with whom to have a relationship.

Such a notion of the primacy of divine initiative and grace lies at the heart of the Reformed understanding of the church. We do not "join" the church of our choosing; rather, we are called by God into relationship. In the language of faith, we are sought before we ourselves find. It is this conviction that undergirds the Reformed emphasis on "infant" baptism. As God made covenant with Abraham and Sarah and their offspring, so God elects or chooses us before we are conscious that there is a God to choose. As church members, then, we do not depend on our agreement with one another in matters of belief or practice to keep us together. We are together because we believe that God has called each of us and that therefore we can and should live together.

This conviction of being called to life together is the second aspect of the covenant theme. The covenants of the Old Testament created the people of Israel; in the New Testament the covenant sealed in the blood of Christ created the church. Individuals are called of God, but they are always called *into* community with one another. However much we would prefer to go it alone, the Christian life is always life together. While this is a conviction shared by almost all Christians, it has led Reformed Christians into particular ways of ordering church life.

Not infrequently you will hear people complain about the never-ending use of committees in the Presbyterian Church; frustrated members and pastors sometimes say, "If you want something done right, do it yourself." The notion that we are called to *be* together has led Presbyterians to conclude that this is how we should make decisions: not independently or unilaterally, but together. This is as true within the life of a local congregation as it is for the denomination as a whole. Decisions are shared among the various members or governing bodies for the good of the whole, because *together* we are the body of Christ.

The Law. As noted above, one of the highlights of God's covenant making with Israel was the gift of the law. The Ten Commandments and the laws that flowed from them gave form or shape to the nation of Israel. The law made life together just, humane, and possible. To be sure, the law was abused: not only was it violated, but also the keeping of the law was used to assure individuals of their worthiness or righteousness. Calvin joined Luther in asserting that human beings were made righteous (or set in right relationship with God) by God's grace alone and not by any human works, even by keeping God's law. Calvin, however, retained a rather more positive view of the law itself than did Luther. He saw it as a gift of grace that could provide an orderly means for people to live together under God. The order of law provided the environment in which people could grow together in grace.

Since an ordered life is crucial for growth, it is small wonder that various forms of government and order have played such a central place in the life of Reformed or Presbyterian churches. The *Book of Order* is *not* a manual of operations. It is a way of making Christian life in community possible. (It is not the only way, to be sure, but one that generations have found conducive to the nurture of faith.) *The Book of Order* is to be studied and learned by those who hold office in the church because of their responsibility to guide and guard that life together.

Included in the *Book of Order* are the Rules of Discipline. These are procedures to be followed when there is serious difficulty in the life of the church. The intention of these regulations, however, must be carefully noted: discipline in the church is to be exercised for "building up the body of Christ, not for destroying it, for redeeming, not for punishing" [D-1.0102]. The same could be said of the entire form of government: these provisions are gifts that can enable orderly and peaceful life together.

Sin. As Luther and Calvin both pointed out, one of the functions of the law of God was to convict humanity of its sin. Judged by that standard of righteousness, no one is innocent. This conviction of the pervasiveness of sin even in the lives of believers stands at the heart of the Reformed faith. Many who see this as a gloomy doctrine fail to recognize that it must always be held alongside the unshakable conviction that we *have been justified* by the redemptive work of God in Christ. But on this side of the fulfillment of the kingdom, the world, believers and unbelievers alike, will be subject to the consequences of human sin.

Such a theological affirmation has led to two convictions about the church and decision making that we experience every day as Presbyterians. First, the Reformers assumed that not even the church was immune from the effects of human sin. Because the church was made up of human beings and because all humans have sinned and fallen short of the glory of God, the Reformers held that it could and did make errors of judgment and worse. The Reformation itself was an attempt precisely to reform and purify the church of its more obvious abuses of ecclesiastical and political power. Those same Reformers were not so naive as to assume that the reformed church would not become subject to similar abuses in time. Thus came the motto first used in the Dutch Reformed Church: *Ecclesia reformata, semper reformanda*—the church reformed, always being reformed. This is a commitment to continual self-examination, to the recognition that good policies do not always produce good results and that "new occasions teach new duties." Reformations are never easy, and change always brings a certain amount of conflict. The *Book of Order* is one means of ordering change and conflict so that minority views are always heard and so that petitions to amend or to redress grievance can always be presented in a civil manner. These procedures for change allow the church to be reformed under the leading of God in each new day.

The second implication of the doctrine of human sinfulness relates to the corporate nature of decision making discussed above. Because it is assumed that all persons will be subject to personal and selfish interest, it is a hallmark of the Presbyterian order that power and decision making are never vested in individuals acting alone. The powers of a pastor acting alone are severely restricted; the power and authority in a Presbyterian congregation rest with the session of which the pastor(s) is a member. The reason that Presbyterians have always been skeptical about the office of bishop is the potential abuse that could result from vesting too much authority in one person. In contrast the presbytery is often called the "corporate bishop," because it is a representative body of constituent congregations and ministers that makes decisions concerning the life and mission of the church in a given area. The conviction that sin is both real and inevitable has led Reformed Christians to the conclusion that the decisions that we make together will most often be better than the decisions that any one of us could make individually.

Called to Serve. Having stressed the reality of human sin, Presbyterians have not found this sufficient reason for withdrawing from the world or from relations with others. Indeed, the effect of the justifying grace of God is precisely to lead persons into relationship with one another and into mission in the world. Those whom God has called have been given grace to amend their lives and the responsibility to serve God and others. Whether in sending evangelists to Korea or Zaire, sharing the poverty of Native Americans on various reservations, or building schools and colleges across the nation, Presbyterians have felt called to act out their faith in God's grace in the world around them. This has sometimes led to conflict in the church: What are the priorities for mission? Where does service end and political action begin? How much money should be spent for what?

The Presbyterian system of government is intended not only to enable life together in the church but also to facilitate the church's mission in the world. Each governing body has a unique role to play in determining the overall mission of the church as well as in developing its own form of service in the particular place in which it finds itself. Because of the corporate nature of the church, what is done by one is done in the name of all. This has led, to be sure, to significant differences of opinion in the church, but it has also enabled the church to act and speak as one in a world hungry for unity.

The Sovereignty of God. At its heart, any theological question is a matter of our understanding of God. Who God is and how we understand God's self-revelation is *the* issue from which all other affirmations of faith flow.

For the Reformed tradition, God's sovereignty and, in particular, the sovereign nature of God's grace have seemed most compelling. Sovereignty is a political concept, born in the days when power in the human world was exercised by rulers acting more or less independently and often with unchecked authority. Applied to God, the concept of sovereignty recognizes that God was not under any compulsion but, rather, freely chose to create the world and redeem humankind. Even more, God has created the world and saves individuals without assistance, not even from the individuals concerned.

If God is thus sovereign over both the creation and human destiny, God is likewise sovereign over the church. All authority in the church rightly belongs to God, working through the Holy Spirit; all other authority exercised by persons and groups is derivative. All Christians affirm, of course, that Christ is the head of the church, which is the body of Christ. For Presbyterians this affirmation implies that we can invest in no person or church council the kind of absolute authority or honor that belongs to God alone. Along with the conviction that the church, because it is human, will err, this view of God's sovereignty has led to healthy self-criticism and a general reluctance on the part of church leaders to assume that they are speaking for God.

Another implication of this notion of God's sovereignty is the principle that "God alone is Lord of the conscience" (Westminster Confession of Faith, XXII, 6.109). God alone, and not any church governing body or nation or any other human authority, has claim on complete human obedience. There are several things that this affirmation does *not* mean. It does not mean that we do not owe allegiance and loyalty to various human institutions; it does not mean that we are not subject to one another in the Lord; it does not mean that to be a Christian is to go off by oneself with Jesus, acting and believing as one wishes. The Christian faith is still to be lived in community with others, where the opinions of others and the will of the majority are to be respected.

The notion of God's sovereignty over human conscience affirms that God, as in days of old, continues to make God's will known directly to particular persons and communities of faith. The conviction that God's will is not confined to the traditions of the church, or even to traditional interpretations of Scripture, has far-reaching consequences. The decision by the Presbyterian Church to ordain women was the result of the conscience of some members convincing the whole church that a traditional interpretation of Scripture was in error and that, in fact, God does call both women and men to service and leadership in the church. Similarly, the conviction that God alone is authoritative in human conscience has led Reformed Christians to defy and/or seek to reform human governments when those governments claimed absolute authority or when their laws compelled

Christians to act unjustly (The Theological Declaration of Barmen is an example of the first; the stand of the church on the matters of slavery and sanctuary for refugees may be cited as examples of the second).

The sovereignty of God is finally an affirmation of the sovereignty of God's grace. The love, compassion, and mercy of God for humanity can never be frustrated and have already triumphed in the death and resurrection of Christ. In that alone is our hope—for ourselves, for this world, and for the Presbyterian Church. Confidence in the sovereign grace of God enables us to live together and work out our differences while we recall that the hope of the world does not rest on our shoulders. The government and discipline of the Presbyterian Church have at times become demonic: Procedures have taken precedence over people; supposed purity has led to schism and rejection of each other; order has been used as a club and not a guide. The only thing that can save Presbyterians from confusing the *Book of Order* with God is grace. Only a constant recollection of who made us and brought us together, only the continual affirmation that it is mercy alone by which we live, enable us to make of our form of government what it is: a way of being the church by the grace of God.

Which came first, the order or the theology? That's hard to tell. As Calvin wrote his first rules of discipline he continued to refine his theology. It is the experience of Reformed Christians living in the world under the Word of God that has brought both doctrine and order to the present day. The *Book of Order* is not finished yet, and neither is our task of being faithful to God.

Cynthia M. Campbell
President, McCormick Theological Seminary
Chicago, Illinois

INTRODUCTION

One of the responsibilities thrust upon officers in the Presbyterian Church (U.S.A.) is that of learning our system of church government. At first glance, this may seem rather daunting. To be handed a copy of the *Book of Order* and told that there will be an examination on its contents in a few weeks' time could even lead an elder-elect to reconsider his or her call! We have found, however, that to know Presbyterian polity is to love it. In essence, it is a very simple system: It assumes that Christians meeting in representative bodies can seek and know the will of God and that, through these bodies, the whole church can be governed in ways that are just, decent, and orderly.

This book is written from the perspective of the local church. It focuses on those aspects of Presbyterian polity that officers of a particular church—elders, deacons, and pastors—should know to carry out their ministry. It is the hope of the authors that it will prove useful to officers in training classes and continuing education and also to theological school students as they prepare for service in congregations. While we have tried to suggest the outlines of Presbyterian polity as expressed in the *Book of Order* of the Presbyterian Church (U.S.A.), this volume does not by any means exhaust the subject. It is intended, instead, to entice officers into a deeper study of the book itself.

References to the *Book of Order* or quotes from it are designated throughout the text by section numbers. For example, in the citation G-9.0103, "G" refers to the Form of Government, "9" locates the reference in Chapter IX, and ".0103" refers to a particular section. The designation ".0000" refers to the entire chapter. For example, G-9.0000 refers to the entire ninth chapter of the Form of Government. References beginning with the letter "W" can be found in the Directory for Worship, and those with the letter "D" in the Rules of Discipline. The *Book of Order* contains a large number of cross-references within the text of particular sections. For this reason, to avoid confusion, the cross-references will be enclosed by parentheses and the authors' citations from the *Book of Order* will be in brackets.

This is a time of continuing rapid constitutional change in our denomination. The information included here is intended to be correct through the amendments to the *Book of Order* reported to the 210th General Assembly (1998) as having been approved by a majority of the presbyteries. Readers should be aware, however, that there are changes, sometimes major ones, made in the *Book of Order* each year. Every officer should have a copy of the most recent edition and refer to it directly as much as possible.

The fabric of our polity is a tightly woven one. The various topics intertwine so closely that it is difficult to separate one from the other, even for purposes of discussion. For that reason, the reader may notice a certain amount of repetition and cross-referencing between chapters. We have tried to keep the repetition to a minimum; a certain amount seems necessary, however, in order for the individual chapters to stand alone with any sort of integrity.

Churches come in all sizes and shapes, and some particulars of church government vary depending on the complexity of each organization. We have tried to sketch the boundaries and outline the general pattern of Presbyterian polity, hoping that within these boundaries officers will find creative ways to make the system work in their own church. All the information given here may not apply to every congregation at a given time, but what is included is here because it may prove useful to some churches in certain circumstances.

We offer this book with thanks for the privilege of serving as officers in the Presbyterian Church (U.S.A.) and in the hope that in some small way it may be used to give glory to God and to build up the church of Jesus Christ.

Chapter One

A POLITY
FOR
THE CHURCH

Jill McLauren was looking over a list of classes for adults being offered by her church. Among the listings was a course called "Presbyterian Church Polity." "Polity," she mused. "I wonder what that is."

The session of Crosslake Presbyterian Church had spent more than an hour debating whether to permit persons to smoke in the church's fellowship hall. As time for adjournment drew near and no consensus was in sight, one of the elders moved that the question be put to the congregation for a vote. The moderator ruled the motion out of order, but several elders objected. "We have not been able to come to agreement about this, so why not let the congregation decide?"

The business meeting of the session of Springs Presbyterian Church was winding down. Stan Wasylkiv had just been elected commissioner to an upcoming meeting of presbytery. At this meeting several controversial issues were going to be debated. When the agenda was completed, the moderator asked for a motion to adjourn. "Wait a minute!" said an elder. "We haven't given Stan any instructions about how he should vote at the presbytery meeting. As our delegate he needs to know what we want him to do."

What Is Polity?

Although the church was founded by Jesus Christ and is uniquely spiritual in character, it is also a human organization. Organizations require structure and a system of agreed-upon rules in order to carry out their tasks. Every organized group functions under rules or bylaws of some sort, even though they may be informal and unwritten. The larger the organization and the more complex its task, the more important it is that its structure and rules be efficient and precise.

The system of rules that governs a church is called its "polity." While there is an almost endless variety of belief and practice among Christian churches today, church polities can be roughly divided into three basic kinds. These are congregational, episcopal, and presbyterian.

Congregational Polity. Direct government of the church by the people who make up the congregation characterizes the congregational style of polity. The final authority on any question is the vote of a majority of the members of that particular congregation. Each local church is autonomous; it functions without any outside control. No higher church body can tell a church with this kind of polity what to do or to believe. Each congregation has its own bylaws and is sovereign in dealing with matters within its fellowship.

While churches of this kind may belong to certain associations or conventions made up of like-minded congregations, they still guard their independence jealously. It has been said, for instance, that while there are many Baptist churches (holding generally recognized Baptist doctrine), there is no Baptist Church. Congregations may cooperate to support a theological seminary or send missionaries to foreign countries, but their unity is strictly functional and voluntary.

Congregational polity comes close to being pure democracy in action. Frequent meetings of the congregation are held in which the business of the church is transacted. The congregation votes on whether or not to receive new members and sets the conditions for their membership. The congregation hires and fires the minister and other staff members. The congregation approves the church budget and votes on significant unbudgeted expenses. All matters of policy are decided by the congregation. Most churches with congregational polity do have a board of lay people (often called deacons) who administer the will of the congregation and make recommendations to it, but finally it is the congregation that governs the life of the church.

Adherents to congregational polity point to the primitive church as their model. During the days of the apostles and for some years afterward, there was little or no formal connection between congregations. Individually they elected their own officers, ran their own affairs by the vote of the members, and engaged only in the very loosest sort of association with other churches. The personal and written contacts with the apostles and a common faith in the risen Christ held these early congregations together. Congregational church government also rests on the belief that the influence of the Holy Spirit shows itself in the church primarily through the views and opinions of individual members speaking within the context of the particular congregation. What one congregation hears the Spirit saying to it is not necessarily what is being heard by another; therefore, each reserves the right to do what seems appropriate in its own situation. Almost without exception all Baptist churches have a congregational form of polity. Other churches that are congregational to a greater or lesser degree are the Disciples of Christ, the United Church of Christ, and various Pentecostal denominations.

Episcopal Polity. This form of church government takes its name from the Greek word for bishop: *episkopos,* literally "shepherd." While congregational polity gives virtually all authority to the congregation, in episcopal polity power is lodged in the highest-ranking bishop and is delegated downward through the clergy.

One important facet of episcopal polity is the doctrine of "apostolic succession." Simply stated, this is the belief that those who are ordained as clergy stand in an unbroken line of authority reaching back to Jesus himself. The purity of the church's teaching and administration of sacraments is protected by a succession of laying on of hands in ordination that reaches back to the apostles. Christ empowered his apostles to carry on the ministry and teaching of the church. It is this power, derived from the church's founder, that the bishops exercise. According to this polity, those who stand in the unbroken line of orthodoxy have been given the authority to govern in the church.

Various rankings of clergy are also a facet of the episcopal system. In some churches, the office of bishop may be the only rank above that of ordinary clergy. A bishop is in authority over a number of congregations in a given area, often called a diocese. In other churches, such as the Roman Catholic, there are numerous ranks, including those of bishop, archbishop, cardinal, and pope. Power is apportioned according to rank in the church, with some functions also being reserved for certain officers. Bishops ordain clergy, for example. This apportionment of power and function provides for control of and uniformity among the various congregations. While there may be some latitude for local preferences, for the most part the liturgy, doctrine, and practice of congregations with strict episcopal polity vary little within the denomination.

Episcopal polity places a strong emphasis on the unity of the church. The apostolic succession of the clergy and the historic orthodoxy of its teachings are seen as concrete signs of this unity. In the episcopal system, individual congregations are not independent entities but rather parts of an indivisible whole: the body of Christ.

More Christians by far belong to churches holding to some form of episcopal polity than belong to either of the other two forms of church government. Included in their number are the Roman Catholic Church and the Orthodox churches. The Methodist, Wesleyan, and Anglican churches depart in a number of ways from strict episcopal polity, especially in giving more authority to laypersons. Their use of the office of bishop, however, qualifies them for inclusion in this category.

Presbyterian Polity. The name of our church, "Presbyterian," refers not to our doctrine or beliefs, but rather to how we govern ourselves. Presbyterian polity takes its name from the Greek word for elder, *presbuteros.* "Presbyter," an English word derived from this Greek term, refers both to ministers of the Word and Sacrament and elders as officers in the church. Each of our congregations is governed by a group of presbyters elected by the congregation and known as the session.

Presbyterians recognize that the Scriptures do not contain a detailed plan for church government; in spite of this, however, Presbyterians (along with other Christian churches) have always sought to base their polity on principles found in the Bible. The *Book of Order* states that "In the worship and service of God and the government of the church, matters are to be ordered according to the Word by reason and sound judgment, under the guidance of the Holy Spirit" [G-1.0100c].

In keeping with this idea, the offices of our church, presbyter (minister of the Word and Sacrament and elder) and deacon, are ones for which there is clear precedent in Scripture. Acts 6:1–6 tells of the origin of an office like that of deacon to meet a need in the early church. The Scripture establishes this office as one of service to those in need.

The New Testament also shows evidence of the use of the office of presbyter or elder. The writer of 1 Timothy gives detailed instructions as to the character and qualifications of those who would aspire to this office (1 Tim. 3:1–7; 5:17–22). The book of James instructs those who are sick in the church to call the elders to pray for them (James 5:14). First Peter 5:1–10 is an exhortation to the elders in several churches in Asia. Acts 14:23 speaks of Paul and Barnabas ordaining "elders for them in every church, with prayer and fasting."

Presbyterians believe that the New Testament uses the words "bishop" and "elder" to refer to the same office. This can be seen in Titus 1:5 and 1:7, as well as in Acts 20:17, 28.[1] Thus, there is no hierarchy of presbyters in the Presbyterian Church; ministers of the Word and Sacrament and elders differ only in the functions they are called to perform. When functioning together in governing bodies, they are equals. We do not have individuals serving as bishops as the episcopal system of church government does. At meetings of the church governing bodies, all presbyters stand on the same footing, and decisions are made by majority vote of the whole body. Even those elected to be officers of governing bodies, moderators and clerks, have no individual authority outside the body. Their only power is that which has been constitutionally assigned to them for their term of office by the governing body that elected them.

Another principle of our polity derived from Scripture is that power within the church is to be exercised by groups of officers rather than individuals. Both Old and New Testaments refer to gatherings of elders that exercised government over the people (Deut. 27:1; 2 Sam. 5:3; Acts 15:6).[2] We believe that the Holy Spirit speaks most clearly on matters of government through the prayerful deliberations of groups of presbyters. While the decisions of groups are also likely to be fallible, Presbyterian polity holds that groups are perhaps less likely to fall into error than are individuals. Therefore most decisions in our church are made by officers organized into groups called *governing bodies*.

Fundamentals of Presbyterian Polity

Presbyterian churches are found the world over, and the details of their polity differ somewhat to accommodate differences in culture and circumstance. There are, however, at least three fundamental characteristics without which a system of church government could hardly be called presbyterian. Ours is a polity that is representative, constitutional, and relational.

Representative. The Presbyterian Church (U.S.A.) is governed by groups of presbyters elected by the people. One of the rights of the Presbyterian congregation is that of electing its own permanent officers [G-6.0107]. Therefore, no higher governing body can instruct a congregation to install a particular man or woman in a permanent office against its will. This power is exercised under the oversight of the session and the presbytery, and in certain cases the session or presbytery can exercise a "veto power" over the congregation's decisions. If the congregation elects an elder who cannot pass the ordination examination given by the session or one whom the session finds morally unacceptable, the session can refuse to ordain that person. Also the congregation votes to call a pastor and establishes the pastor's terms of call, but the presbytery may refuse to approve either the person or the terms of call if it finds them unacceptable. This system of government by officers duly elected by the people is a primary difference between our polity and congregational or episcopal polity.

The congregation in Presbyterian churches governs in ways that are strictly limited. The congregation elects officers who govern the church. The session is responsible for making most decisions relating to the congregation's life and welfare. This is why, as in the situation outlined at the beginning of the chapter, it would not be advisable for the congregation to vote on whether smoking should be permitted in the fellowship hall. This is a matter of policy relating to the use of church property, and responsibility for making such policies rests with the session [G-10.0102o].

Officers elected by congregations or governing bodies to serve in more-inclusive governing bodies cannot be told how to vote. G-1.0100b says that "It belongs to Christ alone to rule, to teach, to call, and to use the Church as he wills, exercising his authority by the ministry of women and men for the establishment and extension of his Kingdom." Our officers must be free to listen for the word of Christ to his church. As *commissioners*, therefore, they are independent decision makers, and they cannot be bound to vote according to the wishes of those who elected them. A meeting of commissioners is a deliberative body open to the give-and-take of discussion and to the free working of the Holy Spirit. In contrast, those elected in other settings to serve as *delegates* may be instructed beforehand and are then obligated to act in accordance with their instructions. The outcome of a question before a meeting of delegates may be decided in advance, because delegates generally have no option except to vote as they have been instructed. Our church does not elect such delegates to serve in governing bodies. Presbyters are to seek the will of Christ for the church and not be mirrors reflecting only the will of the people [G-4.0301d]. They are finally responsible, not to the congregation, but to Christ, for the decisions they make.

Constitutional. Our church has a Constitution that seeks to put our beliefs and polity into writing. This Constitution has two parts: the *Book of Confessions* and the *Book of Order* [G-1.0500].

A confession, or creed, is an authoritative expression of the Christian faith, or some part of it, by Christians using the language of their own day.

> In these confessional statements the church declares to its members and to the world
>   who and what it is,
>   what it believes,
>   what it resolves to do.
> These statements identify the church as a community of people known by its convictions as well as by its actions. They guide the church in its study and interpretation of the Scriptures; they summarize the essence of Christian tradition; they direct the church in maintaining sound doctrines; they equip the church for its work of proclamation. [G-2.0100]

While Jesus Christ, as revealed in Scripture, is the most authoritative standard of our church, confessions are helpful in that they present the teachings of the Bible in relatively concise form. These subordinate standards give us interpretations of biblical doctrines as seen through the eyes of Christians from different times in history. The Barmen Declaration, for instance, was written by Christians facing subjugation by the Nazi movement in Germany.

Our *Book of Confessions* contains the following documents [see G-1.0501]:

The Nicene Creed
The Apostles' Creed
The Scots Confession

The Heidelberg Catechism
The Second Helvetic Confession
The Westminster Confession of Faith
The Larger and Shorter Catechisms
The Theological Declaration of Barmen
The Confession of 1967
A Brief Statement of Faith–Presbyterian Church (U.S.A.)

While officers are not required to agree with everything in these confessions, they are required to

> receive and adopt the essential tenets of the Reformed faith as expressed in the confessions of our church as authentic and reliable expositions of what Scripture leads us to believe and do and to be instructed and led by those confessions as they lead the people of God. [G-14.0207c]

Having a Constitution that includes creeds, confessions, and catechisms takes nothing away from the authority our church gives to the Scripture. Instead, these documents provide voices from the church's history that help us interpret the meaning of the Bible for our own day. They remind us that many Christians lived before us, and they call us to renew our commitment to the faith that is our heritage.

Whereas the *Book of Confessions* deals with what we believe, the *Book of Order* explains the workings of our polity. It seeks to collect and interpret biblical teachings about the church into a system of church government. Most organizations have a set of bylaws to govern the workings of the group. The *Book of Order* could be seen as our church's bylaws; it is one of the standards under which the church makes decisions and carries out its mission.

This part of our Constitution has three sections, each dealing with a different area of the church's life. They are the Form of Government, the Directory for Worship, and the Rules of Discipline. The basic principles and rules of our polity are outlined in the Form of Government. Among other things, this section deals with the responsibilities of sessions and other governing bodies, the way officers are elected and ordained, the church's use of its property, the rules for meetings of congregations and governing bodies, and our relationship to churches of other denominations. The Directory for Worship contains our standards relating to worship (including funerals and weddings), the sacraments, admission to membership in the church, and the church's service in the world. The Rules of Discipline deals primarily with handling conflict in the church.

To help readers with the task of interpreting our polity, in 1998 a portion of the Directory for Worship was moved to the Preface of the *Book of Order*. It states that:

> In this *Book of Order*
> (1) 'Shall' and 'is to be/are to be' signify practice that is mandated,
> (2) 'should' signifies practice that is strongly recommended,
> (3) 'is appropriate' signifies practice that is commended as suitable,
> (4) 'may' signifies practice that is permissible but not required.

The need for a Constitution stems in part from the representative nature of our polity. Officers are elected by the congregation to exercise authority on its behalf. A Constitution that details the precise boundaries of that authority keeps the officers from assuming powers they were never intended to have. The *Book of Order* is essential equipment for all church officers because it tells them not only the duties they must fulfill but also the powers they can exercise. Officers are elected by the congregation to exercise authority on its behalf only as stated in the Constitution.

Relational. This characteristic of Presbyterian polity is rooted in our belief in the unity of the church. Ephesians 4:5–6 reminds us that all Christians have "one Lord, one faith, one baptism, one God and Father of us all." First Corinthians 12 compares the church to a human body with its many parts, stressing that we are indivisibly bound together in Christ. One of the earliest documents of American Presbyterianism (still included in the *Book of Order*) states "That the several different congregations of believers, taken collectively, constitute one Church of Christ, called emphatically the Church" [G-1.0400]. Another term for this one church is the "church universal."

> The Church universal consists of all persons in every nation, together with their children, who profess faith in Jesus Christ as Lord and Savior and commit themselves to live in a fellowship under his rule.
> Since this whole company cannot meet together in one place to worship and to serve, it is reasonable that it should be divided into particular congregations. The particular church is, therefore, understood as a local expression of the universal Church. [G-4.0101–.0102]

The Presbyterian Church (U.S.A.), as a particular denomination of the church universal, tries to reflect this unity through participation in various national and international councils of churches. "It is our membership in the body of Christ that is the source of our ecumenical commitments" ("The Life and Mission Statement of the Presbyterian Church (U.S.A.),"

1985, par. 27.398). We join with other denominations in doing the work of God whenever possible. We invite all those who have been baptized [W-2.4011a] to partake of the Lord's Supper with us. Our Constitution provides for recognizing the ordination of ministers from other denominations who are called to work in our churches [G-15.0202, G-14.0508]. Presbyterian congregations may even join with congregations of other denominations to form federated or union churches [G-15.0204]. In all these ways we seek to make visible the oneness of Christ's body.

Within itself, our denomination reflects the unity of the church universal through a common system of beliefs and a common polity. These twin ties of faith and government bind particular churches together into the Presbyterian Church (U.S.A.). Our common faith is expressed in Scripture as interpreted by our *Book of Confessions*. Our polity is expressed in the *Book of Order*.

The unity of the church is reflected in our polity in a number of ways. First, there are no independent Presbyterian churches. The very words are antithetical. To be Presbyterian is to be in relationship with other congregations and under the authority of a presbytery. A congregation can hold to Reformed theology while electing to be independent. However, it would hardly be justified in calling itself "Presbyterian," because that word itself implies the relational character of our polity. Presbyterian churches are by nature involved in the life and mission of the wider church. They are called to listen to the voice of the wider church, to help fund its ministry, and to participate in the deliberations of its governing bodies [G-9.0404].

The relational nature of our polity is also clearly reflected in its structure of governing bodies. There are four of these: session, presbytery, synod, and the General Assembly [G-9.0101]. The session governs a particular congregation [G-10.0102]. A presbytery has authority over congregations and ministers within a certain district [G-11.0101]. A synod functions in relation to three or more presbyteries [G-12.0101], while the General Assembly has jurisdiction over those things that are of common concern to the whole church [G-13.0101]. It is one of the historic principles of our polity that

> a larger part of the Church, or a representation of it, should govern a smaller, or determine matters of controversy which arise therein; that, in like manner, a representation of the whole should govern and determine in regard to every part, and to all the parts united. [G-1.0400]

This means that more-inclusive governing bodies have the power of review and control over less-inclusive ones. It is the responsibility of a presbytery, for instance, to make sure that the congregations under its jurisdiction are acting in accord with the Constitution of the church. Synods have the same duty toward presbyteries. The General Assembly exercises the same authority over synods. This general oversight of a less-inclusive governing body by a more-inclusive one is called administrative review and is discussed more fully in G-9.0400.

Concerns and business also move upward from one governing body to another through the overture process. An overture is a request for consideration of a problem, for an action to be taken, or for a change to be made in some area of the church's life. Many changes to our *Book of Order* originate through the overture process. Presbyteries may send overtures to synod or to the General Assembly. Synods also may send overtures to the Assembly. Sessions may send overtures to presbytery about matters of interest to the wider church.

More-inclusive governing bodies have jurisdiction over cases of judicial process brought to them from less-inclusive ones. These judicial responsibilities of governing bodies are discussed in chapter 13 of this book.

A further implication of the church's unity is that the action of a governing body is the action of the whole church [G-9.0103]. When a presbytery examines a minister for ordination, it is doing so for the whole church. When a session accepts a person into the membership of the congregation, it is acting for the church at large. Elders are ordained, not just for a particular congregation, but for the denomination. The actions and pronouncements of governing bodies are those of the whole church unless or until they are reversed by a more-inclusive governing body. It is this intimate relationship that makes effective means of review and control necessary.[3]

The Powers and Responsibilities of Governing Bodies

The *Book of Order* says several important things about the power of governing bodies. First, any power that the church exercises rightfully comes from Jesus Christ. Christ alone is head of the church, and no human being or group should usurp his Lordship. The authority of governing bodies is "only ministerial and declarative" [G-1.0307]. This means that the pronouncements and rules of governing bodies should be based on the will of God revealed in Scripture. The governing bodies do not have power to require things that the Scripture does not require. As the Westminster Confession of Faith says:

> God alone is Lord of the conscience, and hath left it free from the doctrines and commandments of men [sic] which are in anything contrary to his Word, or beside it in matters of faith or worship. (XXII, 2)

Second, the power of the church is strictly that of moral and spiritual influence [G-9.0102a, G-1.0308]. It is the power of loving concern, not of punishment. There was a time when a person could be locked in the village stocks for religious offenses, but our polity clearly says that no civil penalties can be sought for religious wrongdoing.

Third, the particular powers of governing bodies are only those stated in the Constitution. A general outline of these powers is found in G-9.0102b. The session has no mandate to be a dictator in the congregation. It can only exercise the authority that has been given to it in the *Book of Order*. For example, sessions have the power to "determine occasions, days, times, and places for worship" [W-1.4004f], but they do not have the power to tell the minister what Scripture passages he or she shall read in the service. Presbyteries have the power to examine ministers for admission into the presbytery, but they do not have the power to refuse them admission purely on the basis of their race or sex. Each governing body has certain expressed powers, and only those powers, to exercise.

The principles outlined above help our churches to function in ways that are generally efficient, fair, and orderly.

The presbyterian system was formed out of a deep respect for the ability of church members to participate in their own government. It gives ultimate allegiance only to Jesus Christ. Its structures and polity are designed to further the mission of the church, to promote discipleship, and to build up the body of Christ.

Chapter Two

CALLING
TO OFFICE
IN THE CHURCH

Jane had been extremely active in Second Presbyterian Church. For years she had taught the junior high church school class, been a member of the choir, and served on the committee that visited newcomers to the community. When a member of the nominating committee asked if she was willing to serve as an elder, Jane's amazed response was, "But I don't feel called!"

David's experience was different. While still a relatively new member of the Presbyterian Church (U.S.A.), he was asked to consider serving as a deacon. He agreed to do so without much thought. He viewed the prospect of being a church officer in a very matter-of-fact way. There was a job to be done and he was willing to give it a try. After his election by the congregation, David began a series of study sessions with the other newly elected officers. When the pastor, who was leading the officer training classes, spoke of being called to office in the church, David was thoroughly confused.

Presbyterians have long emphasized the concept of God's call to church office, but we have sometimes been unclear as to what we meant by the term "call." Some, like Jane, have focused upon the "inner call," that special feeling that God does indeed have a special use for one's particular talents and abilities. Others have stressed the church's seeking out someone to fulfill a specific function—the call that comes as an unexpected "tap on the shoulder," to which the first response is often, "Who, me?" What do we mean when we speak of being called to church office?

The Calling to Church Membership

Calling to office must always be understood within the context of the calling to church membership. The beginning point is a faithful response to the good news of God's redemption of human life through the life, death, and resurrection of Jesus Christ. The sacrament of Baptism is the sign of entry into membership in the Christian church. In baptism, believers, or the parents of a child receiving the sacrament, acknowledge faith in Jesus

Christ as Savior, trust in God's grace, and commit themselves to a life of discipleship. Calling to church membership is essentially the call of Christ, "Follow me."

Those who respond in faith, together with their children, claim their church membership through the sacrament of Baptism. When a person makes a public profession of faith in Jesus Christ as Savior and Lord, that person accepts Christ's call to responsible involvement in the church's ministry and becomes an active member of a congregation.

The Presbyterian Church (U.S.A.) in adopting a new *Book of Order* placed a renewed emphasis on the meaning of church membership. Nine responsibilities of active membership are highlighted. The ideas are not new ones, but they take on a new forcefulness by the way they are now listed [G-5.0102]:

A faithful member accepts Christ's call to be involved responsibly in the ministry of his Church. Such involvement includes:

    a.   proclaiming the good news,
    b.   taking part in the common life and worship of a particular church,
    c.   praying and studying Scripture and the faith of the Christian Church,
    d.   supporting the work of the church through the giving of money, time, and talents,
    e.   participating in the governing responsibilities of the church,
    f.   demonstrating a new quality of life within and through the church,
    g.   responding to God's activity in the world through service to others,
    h.   living responsibly in the personal, family, vocational, political, cultural, and social relationships of life,
    i.   working in the world for peace, justice, freedom, and human fulfillment.

This listing includes both specific and general responsibilities. The more specific relate to the internal life of the church or to the life of the individual participating in the common life and worship of a congregation: praying; studying the Bible and the faith; giving of money, time, and talents in support of the work of the church; and participating in the governing responsibilities assigned to church members in the Form of Government.

The more general responsibilities relate both to life within the community of faith and to life beyond that community: proclaiming the good news; demonstrating a new quality of life; serving others in response to God's activity in the world; struggling for peace, justice, freedom, and human fulfillment within oneself, in the family, and around the world.

From the statements on the meaning of membership in the *Book of Order* it can be seen that membership in the church is no casual decision, no minor commitment. It is the testimony of the Presbyterian Church (U.S.A.) that when one responds to the call of Christ to discipleship and claims membership in the church, one is beginning a journey that affects all of life.

Church Membership as Ministry

Emphasis should be placed on the use of the term "ministry" in the section quoted above. All church members are called to ministry. Ministry is not limited to those functions performed by ordained persons. It is the work of the entire people of God. In the twenty-five years preceding Presbyterian reunion in 1983, both The United Presbyterian Church U.S.A. (UPCUSA) and the Presbyterian Church U.S. (PCUS) placed increasing emphasis on the ministry of all church members. Study books and General Assembly-approved papers, as well as church school curricula, tried time and again to reinforce the understanding of ministry as the work of the whole church.

Because of the extreme importance of this concept, it is helpful to take a look at three of the studies made by our predecessor denominations. The 170th General Assembly (1958) of the UPCUSA appointed a special committee on the nature of the ministry. In 1961 this committee issued a study book titled *The Church and Its Changing Ministry*. A major theme of this book is that ministry belongs to the whole church:

> From the moment that we transfer the responsibility for ministry to a selected or elected group, we have gone down a dead-end street. For although we may be deeply concerned to *have* an effective ministry, we will necessarily forget that we have been called, one and all, to *be* the ministry of Jesus Christ. We will be unable to understand the import of the simple statement which (perhaps more accurately than any other) describes the very being of the church: the church is the ministry of Jesus Christ.[1]

A similar point is made in the paper "Church Membership and Discipline," adopted by the 119th General Assembly (1979) of the PCUS and commended to the church for study:

> Ministry is both the privilege and responsibility of church members. The ministry of the church is a corporate as well as individual task committed not to the ordained clergy only but to every member of the church. Every member is a minister. To be a member of the body of Christ is to identify oneself with the mission of Christ. Christ did not draw disciples out of the world, but placed them in the world to carry out his purpose of new life for the world.[2]

In 1981 a Joint Task Force of the UPCUSA and PCUS presented its report on "The Nature and Practice of Ministry." The report indicated that the church was still struggling with ministry in relation to the whole church:

> Ministry also belongs to the community, to the people of God as a body. For it is the whole people who are the body of Christ, never one family or class or office. This reality implies interdependence of the exercise and practice of ministry, a collegiality between laity and clergy, a partnership in service. This lesson has been clearly taught in all the theological work of recent years but it has not been clearly learned, i.e., embodied in the life and practice of the church. We still tend to focus ministry in the clergy and to define ministry in terms of what the pastor does.[3]

The reaching out of any Christian person to another human being is a work of ministry. The witness of a congregation that takes a stand on an issue of concern in the community is a work of ministry. This understanding of ministry is essential to the faithfulness and integrity of the church. The church has been damaged far too long by the attitude of "Let the pastor do it," perhaps even without the help of the other church officers, much less the whole membership. How different it is when church members claim for themselves the full responsibilities of membership and of ministry!

The *Book of Order* also places accountability upon persons for fulfilling their responsibilities of membership. Those who accept membership in the church and thereby make a binding commitment to Jesus Christ are, with the encouragement of the session, to "review and evaluate the integrity with which they are involved in the ministry of the church and consider ways in which their participation in the worship and service of the church may be increased and made more meaningful" [G-5.0501]. Members are accountable to God and to the church for fulfilling the commitment of membership.

Calling to Office

The Presbyterian Church believes that certain responsibilities within the life of the church should be assigned to officers who have been called and ordained to fulfill these particular functions. Any person considering accepting a call to church office should review the responsibilities of church members and evaluate his or her own present involvement in the ministry of the body of Christ. Then that person can consider a call to perform specific leadership tasks.

How does the Presbyterian Church (U.S.A.) understand calling to church office? First, it is none other than the Triune God who calls to office in the church. God in Christ through the Holy Spirit calls by giving gifts and abilities to certain members which qualify them to perform special functions in the life of the Christian community.

How is this call known? The Reformed family of faith claims that God's call is known in three ways. One way is that the church seeks out those who give evidence of having the God-given gifts required for the job—such qualities as leadership ability, sensitivity to the needs of others, dependability, enthusiasm, theological awareness, and administrative skills. The congregation through its members takes the initiative to locate those persons within the church whom God may be calling into service as elders, deacons, or ministers of the Word and Sacrament. The church then challenges them to share their gifts by responding positively to the request to serve. The congregation further indicates its desire to have certain persons as its officers by actually electing them to office in a regularly called congregational meeting. The process of the election fulfills a fundamental principle of Presbyterian polity: namely, that no person is to be placed in any permanent office in a congregation without being elected by that body [G-6.0107].

Another way in which Presbyterians recognize God's call is through the inner experience of the person involved. How does the person feel about the possible new function? Is there a willingness to become involved? Does the person feel, in some way, that this new opportunity is in accordance with God's will for her or his life? The feelings of the person are significant, although the Reformed tradition has often considered them less important than the church's feelings about the suitability of the person for the particular task.

The candidate for church office may feel like the person in the Gospel account who responded to Jesus, "I believe; help my unbelief!" (Mark 9:24). Doubts about one's abilities and feelings of inadequacy for the task may well be very appropriate early responses to the call to office in the church. Think of the biblical stories of God's call in which persons argue with God, convinced that God has made a mistake, that God intends to be calling someone with more skills or someone more worthy. A person may well prefer to dismiss all thought of accepting office in the church and yet find that the idea will not go away. God's call may involve a certain wrestling with unwelcome challenges. It is in times of such struggle that the church's view that the person is indeed fitted for the office may well become a decisive confirmation of God's call.

A final way in which God's call is made known is through the "concurring judgment of a governing body of the church" [G-6.0106a]. In the case of those elected by the congregation to serve as elders or deacons, the governing body is the church session, which has the responsibility of preparing and examining those elected to office. The session must satisfy itself as to their personal faith; knowledge of doctrine, church government, and discipline as set forth in the Constitution; and understanding of the duties of the office [G-14.0205]. Only then is the service of ordination and installation conducted.

Qualifications of Church Officers

What are the qualifications for church office? The *Book of Order* states that the standard for all offices is the ministry of Jesus, and thereby one of service. Speaking of all officers, our Constitution [G-6.0106a] specifies:

> In addition to possessing the necessary gifts and abilities, natural and acquired, those who undertake particular ministries should be persons of strong faith, dedicated discipleship, and love of Jesus Christ as Savior and Lord. Their manner of life should be a demonstration of the Christian gospel in the church and in the world. They must have the approval of God's people and the concurring judgment of a governing body of the church.

Until 1997 the above quoted section was all that the Form of Government said about the personal qualifications required of all church officers. There were some additional particular characteristics needed for each of the three offices, but the qualities required in all officers were summarized in very few words: All must be persons of "strong faith, dedicated discipleship, and love of Jesus Christ as Savior and Lord."

Beyond those characteristics was a single sentence about the style of life that qualifies persons for church office: "Their manner of life should be a demonstration of the Christian gospel in the church, and in the world."

The only other requirements set forth were "the approval of God's people" and "the concurring judgment of a governing body of the church." In the case of elders and deacons, "the approval of God's people" was indicated by receiving the required number of votes in a congregational meeting to be elected. The "concurring judgment of a governing body of the church" was the session's decision to proceed with the ordination after a period of training and an examination.

In 1997 a new provision was added to the basic statement of qualification for all offices quoted above. G-6.0106 continues as follows:

> b. Those who are called to office in the church are to lead a life in obedience to Scripture and in conformity to the historic standards of the church. Among these standards is the requirement to live either in fidelity within the convenant of marriage between a man and a woman (W-4.9001), or chasity in singleness. Persons refusing to repent of any self-acknowledged practice which the confessions call sin shall not be ordained and/or installed as deacons, elders, or ministers of the Word and Sacrament.

This new provision, popularly known as Amendment B, was added to the Form of Government after twenty years of debate, study, and then more debate about the sexual standards that the church should require of its officers. The standard set in G-6.0106b applies to both heterosexual and homosexual persons. However, it should be said that the question which has most divided the church is: Can persons who live in a committed sexual relationship with another person of the same sex be living in such a way that their manner of life is a "demonstration of the Christian gospel in the church and in the world"? Amendment B answers this question in the negative.

G-6.0106 declares that "obedience to Scripture" and "conformity to the historic confessional standards of the church" require that all persons live "either in fidelity within the covenant of marriage between a man and a woman . . . or chastity in singleness." There is no other acceptable practice.

G-6.0106b also adds a sentence that both supporters and opponents of the amendment have found difficult and imprecise:

"Persons refusing to repent of any self-acknowledged practice which the confessions call sin shall not be ordained and/or installed as deacons, elders, or ministers of the Word and Sacrament."

The 209th General Assembly (1997) that heard the report of the vote of the presbyteries and declared that G-6.0106b had been enacted also had before it many overtures that sought to change the amendment. The assembly committee to which the overtures were referred, during its deliberations and consideration of possible wording changes, developed a new statement that moved beyond fine-tuning of G-6.0106b to changing its meaning significantly. The assembly approved and sent to the presbyteries a revision that became known as Amendment A. The sexual standard it called for was "fidelity and integrity in marriage or singleness, and in all relationships of life."

Once again the church found itself faced with a divisive debate. Amendment A was defeated by the presbyteries with a larger majority of presbyteries voting against Amendment A than had voted for Amendment B. In mid-1998 the constitution of the PCUSA is clear as to its sexual standard for its officers. G-6.0106b is in the Form of Government. The church, however, remains divided over the issue.

The Form of Government does list a particular qualification for the office of elder. Elders should be persons of good judgment, because of their responsibilities for governance and for the overall life of the particular church [G-6.0303].

The description of the office of deacon lifts up additional qualities that should be demonstrated in the lives of holders of this office [G-6.0401]:

The office of deacon as set forth in Scripture is one of sympathy, witness, and service after the example of Jesus Christ. Persons of spiritual character, honest repute, exemplary lives, brotherly and sisterly love, warm sympathies, and sound judgment should be chosen for this office.

These statements of the call to very high standards for officers can convince any prospective officer that he or she does not measure up. The persons that the Nominating Committee feels would make good officers need to listen carefully to what the committee says about their gifts and prayerfully consider the request. The church, led by its officers, moves forward in faith, trusting in God's grace to make us more than we are.

Ordination to Office

Ordination is the act by which the church admits persons to office, placing them within the "ordering" of the church's life. Those ordained are not *separated out* from the people of God but rather *placed into* special tasks within the people of God. In the words of the *Book of Order:*

> The existence of these offices in no way diminishes the importance of the commitment of all members to the total ministry of the church. These ordained officers differ from other members in function only. [G-6.0102]

The service of ordination includes the following elements: an appropriate sermon, a brief statement of the nature of the office or offices to which persons are being ordained, the answering of constitutional questions by those being ordained and by the congregation that elected them, prayer and the laying on of hands (with the persons being ordained kneeling, if able), a declaration of ordination, and a welcoming of those ordained to their new office. The whole service is to focus on Jesus Christ and the joy and responsibility of serving Christ through the church, its mission, and its ministry [G-14.0206–.0209].

It is important to consider the constitutional questions that must be answered in the affirmative by those being ordained to office. Many of the questions asked of ministers of the Word and Sacrament, elders, and deacons are identical; the only ones that differ are related to the specific responsibilities of each office. All those assuming any office in the Presbyterian Church (U.S.A.) make certain basic commitments as to their faith in Jesus Christ as Lord of all and Head of the church and in the Triune God, their acceptance of the Scripture as God's Word, and their adoption of the essential beliefs of the Reformed faith as expressed in the *Book of Confessions.* All promise to be instructed and led by the confessions in their leadership of the church, to be governed by the polity of the Presbyterian Church (U.S.A.), to abide by its discipline, and to work collegially in ministry. All promise to lead lives that seek to follow Christ, to love neighbors, and to work for the reconciliation of the world. All promise also to further the peace, unity, and purity of the church and to seek to serve God's people with energy, intelligence, imagination, and love. Elders and deacons are asked if they will fulfill their offices in obedience to Jesus Christ, under the authority of Scripture, and if they will be continually guided by the confessions. (This question is reworded slightly for ministers of the Word and Sacrament.) Each person being ordained as an elder is then asked, "Will you be a faithful elder, watching over the people, providing for their worship, nurture, and service? Will you share in government and discipline, serving in governing bodies of the church, and in your ministry will you try to show the love and justice of Jesus Christ?" [G-14.0207i].

Deacons are asked the following: "Will you be a faithful deacon, teaching charity, urging concern, and directing the people's help to the friendless and those in need? In your ministry will you try to show the love and justice of Jesus Christ?" [G-14.0207j].

The congregation is then asked to affirm the election of these new officers by agreeing to accept them, to encourage them, to respect their decisions, and to follow their guidance, in all these things serving Jesus Christ, the Head of the church [G-14.0208].

By answering the constitutional questions affirmatively, the newly ordained officer becomes more accountable to the Presbyterian Church (U.S.A.). The officer binds himself or herself more closely to the faith and polity of the church. At ordination the officer affirms that the faith of the Reformed confessions (that is, those in the *Book of Confessions*) is indeed one's own faith and that she or he will be led by the faith of the Reformed family in providing leadership to the church. The officer's commitment to Presbyterian polity and discipline is a more explicit one than that assumed by unordained active church members. An active member is defined as one who "has voluntarily submitted to the government of this church" [G-5.0202]. An officer promises to be "governed by our church's polity" and to "abide by its discipline" [G-14.0207e]. The officer's commitment involves greater intentionality. The officer also promises to live and work in such a way as to promote the peace, unity, and purity of the church. Implicit in this commitment is the agreement to accept the decisions of the session, board of deacons, presbytery, synod, or General Assembly even when one disagrees with the decision or has actively supported another point of view.

In the Presbyterian understanding, ordination itself confers no special gifts but rather recognizes those gifts already given by God in calling a person to office. There is no magic, no sudden difference in a person following ordination. Abilities are recognized, God's calling acknowledged, and prayers offered for God's blessing upon those ordained as they assume new responsibilities and undertake new tasks. In ordination some members of the body are being "set into" a disciplined and purposeful activity in the life of the church.[4] The purpose of ordination is to enable Christ's body, the church, to work together as a whole, in order that the ministry and mission of the church might be fulfilled.

The Presbyterian Church (U.S.A.) understands office as being perpetual. Elders and deacons may be elected for limited terms of active service, but they still hold their office when their active service ends. If reelected to the same office they are not reordained. Even if not in active service, elders and deacons can still serve the church in certain functions of office. Within the particular church, any ordained officer may serve the Lord's Supper to the people. (This privilege may be extended to any member upon the invitation of the session [W-3.3616d].) Elders not currently serving as session members may represent their church in presbytery and may serve as commissioners from presbytery to synod or the General Assembly [G-14.0203].

The Reformed understanding of how the church is ordered and of the functions fulfilled by its officers has been worked out over many centuries, in many countries, and in a great variety of situations. A look at the history of the Reformed church shows much growth, change, and adaptability in the Presbyterian system. From the time of John Calvin, Reformed Christians have emphasized the principle that persons other than ministers are to serve as church officers. Calvin envisioned four offices: pastor or minister, elder, deacon, and doctor. The doctor, in Calvin's concept, was a learned teacher who preserved and passed on knowledge but did not assume the responsibilities of preaching and administering the sacraments. (By the middle of the seventeenth century, the doctoral office was assimilated into that of pastor or minister.)[5] Calvin saw elders as those who, along with ministers, made the decisions of governance. Deacons exercised ministries of compassion. Calvin did not emphasize the ordination of officers other than ministers. That emphasis was to come later.

Freedom of Conscience and Its Limitations

It has been emphasized that ordination to church office makes persons more accountable to the church. This accountability includes accepting some limitations on the officer's freedom of conscience. The key passage is G-6.0108:

> a. It is necessary to the integrity and health of the church that the persons who serve in it as officers shall adhere to the essentials of the Reformed faith and polity as expressed in the *Book of Confessions* and the Form of Government. So far as may be possible without serious departure from these standards, without infringing on the rights and views of others, and without obstructing the constitutional governance of the church, freedom of conscience with respect to the interpretation of Scripture is to be maintained.

b. It is to be recognized, however, that in becoming a candidate or officer of the Presbyterian Church (U.S.A.) one chooses to exercise freedom of conscience within certain bounds. His or her conscience is captive to the Word of God as interpreted in the standards of the church so long as he or she continues to seek or hold office in that body. The decision as to whether a person has departed from essentials of Reformed faith and polity is made initially by the individual concerned but ultimately becomes the responsibility of the governing body in which he or she serves. (G-1.0301; G-1.0302)

Freedom of conscience in the interpretation of Scripture is recognized insofar as the exercise of freedom of conscience does not lead to serious departure from the essentials of the Reformed faith and polity as expressed in the church's Constitution, does not infringe on the rights and views of others, and does not obstruct the constitutional governance of the church. Freedom of conscience may not be used by an officer as a reason for holding beliefs contrary to the essentials of the *Book of Confessions*, infringing on the rights of other church members, or refusing to act in accordance with the *Book of Order*.

The Presbyterian Church (U.S.A.) affirms that God calls the church's officers by giving them the gifts necessary for fulfilling the task. This call is known through the church's seeking out of the person, the feeling of willingness on the part of the person, and the concurrence of a governing body. The church ordains those who have been called, acknowledging by that ordination the new responsibilities being assumed and the seriousness of the task. By affirming the constitutional questions of ordination, the officer places himself or herself in a position of greater accountability to the church. Through this whole process, the church "orders" its common life to enable the ministry of the whole people of God.

Chapter Three

ELECTION
OF
CHURCH OFFICERS

The nominating committee of Tall Pines Presbyterian Church was bogged down in a major debate between two members over the proper procedure for electing elders. The committee planned to nominate two persons for every vacancy and anticipated additional nominations from the floor. One committee member wanted to expedite the election by asking that the three persons receiving the highest number of votes be declared elected. Another member said that she thought the *Book of Order* requires each nominee to receive a majority of the votes cast to be elected. The other members of the committee could not provide any help.

The Frontier Presbyterian Church found itself without a pastor after twelve years of a very meaningful pastoral relationship. A pastor nominating committee was elected in accordance with the *Book of Order*. At their first meeting the members of the committee looked at one another and one voiced what most were feeling: "How do we know where to begin? Finding the right pastor for our church seems like an impossible task!"

A basic principle of Presbyterian polity discussed in chapter 1 is the right of every congregation to elect its own officers. This right is exercised when the congregation chooses some from among its members to serve as elders and deacons. It is also exercised when the congregation, with the approval of presbytery, calls a pastor, co-pastor, or associate pastor. The purpose of this chapter is twofold: first, to consider the principle of inclusiveness as it relates to the constitutional process for the election of elders, deacons, and pastors; and second, to explain that process.

Commitment to Inclusiveness in
the Election of Elders and Deacons

The present *Book of Order* places a major emphasis on the church as an inclusive community. Undergirding many specific provisions providing for inclusiveness are two foundational statements that establish the principle:

The Church is called . . .

b. to a new openness to its own membership, by affirming itself as a community of diversity, becoming in fact as well as in faith a community of women and men of all ages, races, and conditions, and by providing for inclusiveness as a visible sign of the new humanity. [G-3.0401]

> The Presbyterian Church (U.S.A.) shall give full expression to the rich diversity within its membership and shall provide means which will assure a greater inclusiveness leading to wholeness in its emerging life. Persons of all racial ethnic groups, different ages, both sexes, various disabilities, diverse geographical areas, different theological positions consistent with the Reformed tradition, as well as different marital conditions (married, single, widowed, or divorced) shall be guaranteed full participation and access to representation in the decision making of the Church. (G-9.0104ff) [G-4.0403]

The importance of these statements of principle should not be underestimated. Both are found in the early chapters of the Form of Government, Chapters III and IV. It is no overstatement to say that the principle of inclusiveness and full participation is a foundational one in the *Book of Order*. In at least twenty places in later chapters of the Form of Government, G-4.0403 is referred to either directly or indirectly.

One place where the general commitment of the church to openness and inclusiveness is made concrete is in the provisions for the election of elders and deacons:

> Every congregation shall elect men and women from among its active members, giving fair representation to persons of all ages and of all racial ethnic members and persons with disabilities who are members of that congregation, to the office of elder and to the office of deacon, or either of them, in the mode most approved and in use in that congregation. . . . [G-14.0201]

Having established the constitutional expectation that all congregations are to elect both men and women to the offices of elder and deacon (where deacons are used), the section becomes even more specific, suggesting concrete ways to do this.

First, there is a provision for limited terms of service of church officers (often referred to as the rotation system). The term of active service of an elder or a deacon serving on a board of deacons shall be no more than three years, with the possibility of reelection for an additional three years. Elders and deacons serving on boards are to serve for no more than six consecutive years. Anyone who has served for six years is ineligible for reelection to that office for at least a year [G-14.0201a]. Particular congregations may decide that an officer is ineligible to serve again after one three-year term (without at least one year's absence from active service).

In 1987 the *Book of Order* was amended to allow persons under twenty-five years of age to be elected as elders or deacons for one- or two-year terms of active service, as well as for a regular three-year term [G-14.0201a]. The purpose of this amendment was to encourage the service of young people who plan to be away from their home community to pursue additional education or military service. These young people could enrich the work of the session or board of deacons for one or two years when they might not see the way clear to make a three-year commitment.

One effect of all the provisions for a limited term of service is to enable more persons to serve as church officers. Each year a new class of officers is elected and installed. Those persons previously in active service on the session or board of deacons who have completed their year of ineligibility are not automatically renominated and reelected. Some churches have a tradition of renominating old officers, but the constitutional process is designed to enable congregations freely to choose the persons who the members believe are the best equipped to lead the congregation.

The provisions for rotation of officers clearly state that the session and board of deacons are to be divided into three classes as nearly equal in size as possible. The term of service of one class shall expire each year. Such an orderly system of completing terms and bringing on board newly elected officers assures both continuity of knowledge and fresh ideas. The terms of those serving on a session or board of deacons do not expire until new officers have actually been elected and installed (even though the designated term may have expired a few weeks earlier). The *Book of Order* assures an orderly transition [G-14.0201a].

In 1985 one exception to the requirement that elders and deacons be elected for limited terms of service was added to the *Book of Order*. G-14.0202a(3) states that churches may request a waiver of the requirement for limited terms of service if the church finds it "impossible because of limited membership to provide for the rotation of terms." The exemption is granted by presbytery for not more than three years at a time. The exemption can be renewed or revoked at any time by a majority vote of the presbytery.

The Nominating Committee

Another way in which the *Book of Order* attempts to assure greater inclusiveness in electing church officers is in the procedures set forth for nominating committees. Every congregation is required to use a nominating committee that is chosen annually. The makeup of this committee is carefully spelled out. Two members of the nominating committee are to be elders chosen by the session. One of these session appointees shall be currently serving on the session and shall be designated by the session to serve as moderator of the nominating committee. If the church has a board of deacons, then the board shall designate one of its members to serve on the committee. The remaining members of the nominating committee shall be elected by the congregation or chosen by organizations within the church designated by the congregation. A majority of the members of the nominating committee must *not* currently be members of the session or of the board of deacons. The minimum size for churches of seventy members or over is five persons—two elders appointed by the session and three persons chosen by the congregation or designated organizations and not serving on the session. If the church has a board of deacons, then the nominating committee must have a minimum of seven members—two session appointees, one member of the board of deacons, and four persons chosen by the congregation or designated organization and not actively serving on the session or board of deacons. If the church has a pastor, then she or he shall be an ex officio member of the nominating committee without vote. No member of the nominating committee, except the pastor, is permitted to serve more than three consecutive years. The committee must be representative, including "both women and men, giving fair representation to persons of all age groups and of all racial ethnic members and persons with disabilities who are members of that congregation" [G-14.0201b].

In 1986 a provision was added to the *Book of Order* to allow congregations of fewer than seventy members to vote to elect a "small church nominating committee" [G-14.0201c]. If the church does not have a pastor, the committee consists of three persons: a member of the session, appointed by that body, who will serve as moderator, and two members of the congregation who are not currently serving on the session. If the church has a pastor, then the pastor shall serve as an ex officio member without vote. The provisions for inclusiveness apply.

For all churches, regardless of their size, the provisions specifying that a majority of the members of the nominating committee not be currently serving on the session or board of deacons and that the committee itself must be representative of the congregation in terms of sex, age, racial ethnic groups, and persons with disabilities are intended to enable the congregation to have before it, at the time of the election, a slate of officers inclusive of the church's membership.

Two other provisions apply to the nominating process. The nominating procedures themselves are subject to the principles of participation of G-4.0403 (quoted earlier in the chapter) and G-9.0104. Also, any active member of the church shall always have the opportunity of making nominations from the floor.

The actual procedures that the nominating committee is to use are not specified. The committee's work is to be conducted "in the mode most approved and in use in that congregation" [G-14.0201]. Practice varies from congregation to congregation. Some committees nominate one person for every vacancy; others nominate one or two more persons than they have vacancies; still others nominate two or more times as many persons as vacancies. Some congregations have a tradition of rarely if ever making nominations from the floor, thus increasing the importance of the committee's work. One thing is clear, however: the opportunity for nominations from the floor *must always* be provided.

Exemptions for Certain Congregations

Because the predecessor denominations had followed different approaches as they moved toward increasing acceptance of women in ordained office, the Constitution allows different exemptions to the requirements for inclusiveness for congregations that were formerly part of The United Presbyterian Church U.S.A. and those formerly part of the Presbyterian Church U.S. The exemption clause that applies to former UPCUSA congregations is the same one that existed for them prior to 1983. It is found in G-14.0202a(1).

The PCUS had never taken steps that required every church to elect women and to provide fair representation to persons of all ages and of all racial ethnic groups within the congregation. While the pros and cons of such provisions had been discussed by PCUS women, such constitutional amendments had not even been proposed to the General Assembly. PCUS women had used a different approach to move into the total life of the denomination. At the time of reunion, three fourths of PCUS congregations did have women officers, but they reached this point without a constitutional requirement of electing women. The PCUS *Book of Church Order* stated that "both men and women shall be eligible to hold church offices" (*BCO* 9-2). Eligibility, rather than actual election, had been the operative constitutional principle.

Former PCUS congregations (not members of union presbyteries at the time of reunion) that choose to be exempt from the requirements of electing women to office follow the procedures of G-14.0202a(2). These congregations may also be exempt from the requirement of electing elders and deacons serving on boards of deacons for limited terms of service, since that requirement too was not a part of the PCUS Constitution prior to reunion. The process requires that the congregation consult with the presbytery of which it is a member. Presbytery could require that the consultation take the form of a congregational meeting at which representatives of presbytery would have the opportunity to explain the positions of the PC(USA) that women should be elected elders and deacons and that officers should be elected for limited terms of service. After consulting with presbytery, the congregation can then vote by secret ballot to be exempt from electing women to office or from electing officers for limited terms. The decision reached must be reported to presbytery. The exemption is granted on an annual basis. (The whole procedure has to be repeated the following year.) The vote to request exemption must be taken at a congregational meeting separate from the one at which officers are elected.

Former PCUS congregations that choose to be exempt from the requirements of electing women officers may not be exempt from the requirements of electing a representative nominating committee. G-14.0201b makes clear that the exemption is only from electing women, not from the requirements for the nominating process. A church that votes to be exempt from the requirement to elect women must still permit women to be nominated both by the nominating committee and from the floor.

The exemption provision that applies to former UPCUSA churches (and to all churches from union presbyteries) enables congregations to apply for a waiver of the requirement to elect both women and men as elders and deacons, but presbytery has to satisfy itself that the church is making an effort to move toward compliance. The exemption is not automatic (as it is for former PCUS churches) but is given and renewed by a three-fourths vote of presbytery. It may be given for up to three years. It may also be revoked at any time by a majority vote of presbytery.

Inclusiveness with Exemptions

The Presbyterian Church (U.S.A.) finds itself with two different systems for congregations that have difficulty accepting women as ordained officers. The UPCUSA exemption clause [G-14.0202a(1)] could have been amended at any time. The PCUS exemption clause [G-14.0202a(2)] could not be changed before 1998.

This complicated situation exists because the Presbyterian Church (U.S.A.) values two constitutional principles that are in tension with one another. It is important to maintain the historic principle of a congregation's right to elect its own officers, while at the same time respecting the right of the General Assembly and the presbyteries through the process of constitutional change to reform the church. The Presbyterian Church (U.S.A.) is committed to the inclusiveness described in G-3.0401 and G-4.0403. This is now as important a constitutional principle as that of a congregation's right to elect its own officers. The congregation must decide on the particular persons it wishes to lead it, but the congregation must not be permitted in the long run to deny to whole groups of people because of age, sex, race, marital status, or various disabilities their God-given rights to full participation in the people of God. By adopting exemption provisions for certain congregations, the Presbyterian Church (U.S.A.) has agreed to allow time for education, growth, and change. By establishing inclusiveness as a new constitutional principle, the Presbyterian Church (U.S.A.) has also made clear that it values all its members and their contribution to the wholeness of the church.

Election, Examination, Ordination, and Installation
of Elders and Deacons

The actual election of members of a church's session and board of deacons takes place at the regular annual meeting of the congregation or at a special meeting called for the purpose of electing officers. The procedure is found in G-14.0204. After the moderator explains the purpose of the meeting, he or she asks the congregation if it is ready to proceed with the election. Unless objections are raised or concerns expressed about continuing, the election proceeds. Every member present is given the opportunity to make a nomination from the floor. The voting is conducted, using a written ballot if the number of nominees is greater than the number of officers to be elected. If the number of nominees equals the number of positions to be filled, then the vote may be taken by voice or the show of hands. In order to be elected, a nominee must receive a majority of all the votes cast.

According to G-14.0205, the session confers with all those who have been elected as to their willingness to serve. In most congregations the nominating committee ascertains that a member is willing to serve before putting the name in nomination. Many moderators look for an indication of willingness from persons who are nominated from the floor. If, however, an active church member is nominated and it is not known whether that member is willing to undertake the responsibilities of the office, the moderator has no right to remove the member's name from consideration, even though that member might later decline to serve and thus make it necessary for the congregation to reconvene for the purpose of electing another elder or deacon.

Newly elected officers are expected to enter into a period of study and preparation, in order that they may faithfully fulfill the responsibilities of their office. The nature and extent of this officer training varies from church to church. At the very minimum it should include a careful look at the constitutional questions that must be answered by those being ordained or installed. In order to answer the questions affirmatively, certain basic knowledge is required. It is the responsibility of the session to determine if each person newly elected to office has the essential knowledge of the "doctrine, government, and discipline contained in the Constitution of the church" [G-14.0205]. The session also is required to examine those elected to office as to their personal faith and understanding of the office. A 1985 amendment to G-14.0205 clarified the procedure to be followed if a session does not approve the examination of one or more of the officers elected by the congregation: "The session shall report its action to the congregation's nominating committee, which shall bring nomination(s) to a special meeting of the congregation for any office(s) not filled."

Once the examination of newly elected officers has been approved, the session shall determine when the service of ordination and installation is to be held. "The service of ordination and installation shall focus upon Christ and the joy and responsibility of serving him through the mission and ministry of the church, and shall include a sermon appropriate to the occasion" [G-14.0206]. The constitutional questions asked of elders and deacons and of the congregation of which they shall be officers are discussed in the preceding chapter. It may be of value to review that discussion.

Calling a Pastor

In addition to electing elders and deacons to serve in leadership positions, Presbyterian congregations also elect ministers of the Word and Sacrament to serve in pastoral relationships. When a congregation elects (and thereby calls) a minister to serve in an unlimited or permanent pastoral relationship, that minister is installed by the presbytery to serve as pastor, co-pastor, or associate pastor of the congregation. Chapter 7 of this book discusses in detail the various types of pastoral relationships and the differences among them. Here it is important to understand the process for calling pastors by congregations and to see that process within the context of the election of all church officers.

Let us assume that the session has consulted with the presbytery's committee on ministry and received its permission for the church to seek a pastor. (The procedure about to be described would be the same if the congregation were seeking co-pastors or an associate pastor.) The next step is for the session to call a congregational meeting for the purpose of electing a nominating committee. The congregation shall be given public notice of the time, place, and purpose of the meeting at least ten days before the meeting, "which shall include two successive Sundays" [G-14.0502a]. The only specification about the makeup of the nominating committee is that it be "representative of the whole congregation." Once again the church's principle of inclusiveness is emphasized. How the nominating committee itself is to be nominated is not mentioned. The session may suggest the makeup of the committee and may even make nominations for the committee, or it may nominate a committee to nominate the pastor nominating committee (PNC). Of course, nominations must be permitted from the floor for any committee elected. The congregation may amend the session's proposal on any of the matters concerning the pastor nominating committee: its size, makeup, method of being selected, and the particular church members to serve on the committee. Because of the extreme importance of the work of the PNC, it is certainly in the interest of the congregation to make all decisions concerning this committee with care.

The *Book of Order* offers little guidance as to how a pastor nominating committee conducts its work. Two sentences come between the election of the committee and the committee's readiness to bring a potential pastor's name before the congregation: "The nominating committee shall confer with the committee on ministry as provided in G-11.0502d. . . . Care must be taken to consider candidates without regard to race, ethnic origin, sex, marital status, age, or disabilities" [G-14.0502b]. (If the PNC is seeking an associate pastor or a co-pastor, then the committee must also confer with the church's pastor or any co-pastor who is already in place [G-14.0502b].)

Conferring with presbytery's committee on ministry is a key that should provide access to a wide variety of helps. The committee on ministry will probably immediately appoint one of its members to serve throughout the search process as a liaison with the PNC. The liaison should meet with the committee as soon as possible to orient the committee to its work. In addition to the help that the liaison provides, the committee will almost certainly be introduced to a large number of resources that have been produced by presbyteries and by national offices. The PNC will learn how to work with the General Assembly Council's call/referral system office in developing a church information form that is used in the matching process. In this process a computer locates ministers or candidates for the ministry who have talents and interests similar to those requested by the particular church. Presbytery's committee on ministry helps a PNC understand how to make the best use of the sophisticated process available. It should be noted that a PNC is required to confer with the committee on ministry. The verb used in the passage quoted above [G-14.0502a] is "shall confer." In order to make certain that this step is not bypassed, the chapter on the presbytery contains the following provision:

No call to a permanent pastoral relationship shall be in order for consideration by the presbytery unless the church has received and considered the committee's counsel before action is taken to issue a call. [G-11.0502d]

The principle of inclusiveness is made specific in the second aspect of the search process highlighted in G-14.0502b. A PNC should seek a minister who has the skills, interests, and commitments to serve the church. The committee's search should not be limited to persons of a particular racial ethnic background, sex, marital status, or age. Candidates with disabilities should be considered. In other words, the committee should be open to finding a minister who may bring new perspectives and new insights to the church's ministry.

The *Book of Order* does give some additional guidance to aid a PNC in its work. It does this by guiding presbytery's committee on ministry as it works with the PNC [see G-11.0502d] and by indicating some of the specifics that should be included in the terms of call to a pastor [see G-14.0506]. When the PNC has located the person it hopes to call as pastor, it must work very closely with presbytery's committee on ministry and with the church's session in working out the terms of call and in seeing that all steps of the calling process are done properly. The PNC should not make commitments that the session is not willing to stand behind. Therefore, the timing of various steps in the process becomes extremely important.

Presbyteries Working Together

As the PNC completes its work, it often has a good opportunity to learn first-hand about the interdependence of presbyteries. If the minister or candidate for ministry whom the committee desires to call is under the jurisdiction of a different presbytery from the one of which the church is part, then the two presbyteries must work together in fulfilling their responsibilities.

In the case of a minister, the presbytery of which the minister has been a member must dismiss the minister to the presbytery in which the church is located (the presbytery of call) and, in the case of a minister who has been serving as a pastor, must dissolve the pastoral relationship between the minister and the church in which the minister has been serving. The presbytery of call must examine the minister for membership in that presbytery, seeking information as to the minister's "Christian faith and views in theology, the Sacraments, and the government of this church" [G-11.0402]. The presbytery must also approve the call to the minister.

In the case of a candidate, the presbytery that has supervised the candidate during the time of preparation for ministry must certify that the candidate has completed the required preparation and is ready to receive a call. The candidate's presbytery conducts a final assessment of the candidate's readiness for beginning ministry, making certain that all the steps required in both G-14.0305j and G-14.0310 have been completed. When the presbytery of preparation is fully satisfied as to the candidate's readiness to be ordained and to begin ministry of the Word and Sacrament, it certifies the candidate as "ready for examination for ordination, pending a call" [G-14.0310a]. Then ordinarily it is the calling presbytery that examines the candidate for ordination. The presbytery of preparation then ordinarily ordains the candidate. The system is designed to be flexible and to allow for the continuation of two different traditions that came into the PC (USA) at the time of the 1983 reunion. One part of the church felt that it was extremely important for the candidate to be ordained by the presbytery of preparation as the completion and culmination of the whole experience of seminary education and the candidacy process. The other tradition emphasized ordination as the beginning of ministry and insisted upon examination and ordination by the presbytery of call.

The question of which presbytery should ordinarily examine a candidate and which one should ordinarily ordain the candidate has been much debated since reunion. The answer has been changed by constitutional amendment several times. In 1997 the presbytery to conduct the examination was changed from the presbytery of preparation to the presbytery of call. The ordination itself remains with the presbytery of preparation [G14.0314].

The provision that presbytery must examine ministers and candidates seeking membership in the presbytery is an expression of another constitutional principle, namely, that a presbytery has the right to determine its own minister members. A congregation may not call a particular person to be its pastor, co-pastor, or associate pastor unless the presbytery accepts that person into membership. If the presbytery declines to receive the minister (or candidate), then the PNC must seek another person to nominate to the congregation and once again seek presbytery approval.

Presbyteries may delegate many of their responsibilities relating to the calling and examining of ministers and candidates for ministry to either the council of presbytery or presbytery's committee on ministry. When these responsibilities are delegated to the council or the committee on ministry, then the council or the committee actually acts on behalf of the entire presbytery. The council or committee on ministry must report its actions to the next stated meeting of the presbytery [G-11.0103v; G-11.0502g; G-14.0507c].

Ministers of the Word and Sacrament: Their Election, Ordination, and Installation as Pastors

The process of calling and conducting the congregational meeting for the purpose of electing a pastor, co-pastor(s), or associate pastor is carefully spelled out in G-14.0503. What to do when some members vote against extending the call is prescribed in G-14.0505. The session and the PNC should become thoroughly acquainted with these sections.

In many ways the ordination and installation of ministers of the Word and Sacrament parallel that of elders and deacons. Seven of the nine constitutional questions are identical, one varies by indicating that the office is minister of the Word and Sacrament, and one is the specific question that deals with the unique responsibilities of the office of minister. It is extremely significant that all three officers—elders, deacons, and ministers—make the same commitment in terms of belief and quality of service.

There are significant differences, however, between ordination and installation of ministers and of elders and deacons. Whereas the ordination and installation of elders and deacons is an act of the session, ordination and installation of ministers is an act of the presbytery. Ministers become members of a presbytery, accountable to it for their ministry in the congregation. Although pastors and associate pastors are officers of the particular church and members of its session, they are not members of the congregation.

The *Book of Order* includes a great deal of detail in setting forth the procedures for the election of church officers—elders, deacons, and ministers of the Word and Sacrament. These procedures are designed to enable churches to elect their own officers without undue influence from the session or any particular group within the church and to become more inclusive of the church's overall membership as they select their officers. The *Book of Order* envisions a church where persons with disabilities, persons of different racial ethnic groups, persons of various ages, both sexes, and different marital conditions, and persons holding differing theological positions consistent with the Reformed tradition share their gifts of leadership, as they serve together as ministers, elders, and deacons.

Chapter Four

THE OFFICE
OF
ELDER

The newly elected elders of Calvin Presbyterian Church were on a weekend retreat led by their pastor and a professor of polity from a Presbyterian seminary. The purpose of the retreat was to study those subjects in which newly elected officers must be examined before they are ordained and installed. The pastor encouraged all participants to share their stories of growth in personal faith and led a discussion of Presbyterian doctrine. The professor dealt with government, discipline, and the duties of the office of elder. One participant pointed out that Calvin Church would probably be run more efficiently if the congregation would hire two additional professionally trained ministers. Then the three pastors could meet together to make policy decisions. The session would have to meet only rarely, if indeed the church needed a session at all! The three pastors—each with an excellent theological education and a different area of expertise—could function as a management team. There would still be a corporate aspect to decision making. The seminary professor realized that these newly elected elders needed an overview of the office of elder and its importance for Presbyterians. She chose to begin with a look into the history of the office.

Early Reformers

The Reformed emphasis on the office of elder can be traced to several early Reformers, including John Calvin. When Calvin developed a polity for the governance of the church, he placed particular emphasis on the officers of the church. An early emphasis of the Protestant Reformation had been on discarding practices of the Roman Catholic Church which the Reformers felt to be opposed to the teachings of Scripture. With regard to governance, Protestant Christians first decided how the church was *not* to be governed. Then they undertook the positive task of designing a system of governance, seeking to follow biblical principles as they built. John Calvin was faced with the particular task of developing a church organization for the city of Geneva. Studying the New Testament, Calvin identified other offices in addition to that of minister which he considered to be permanent, that is, intended for the church in all times. One of these was the office of "government," that is, the office of elder. Calvin concluded that the New Testament envisions two kinds of presbyters. Some presbyters have the responsibilities of preaching and teaching the Word. The other type of presbyter does not have this responsibility for proclamation, but along with the minister shares the responsibility for governance within the church. Calvin placed particular emphasis on the discipline of personal conduct. Governance was almost synonymous with the correction of error or faults. Elders were charged with oversight of the daily behavior of the people. Calvin organized the ministers and twelve elders of the city of Geneva into one consistory—the forerunner of what we now know as a session. The consistory had responsibility for discipline. Its major concerns were that the people act according to the highest moral standards, that they participate regularly in worship, and that they become more knowledgeable of the Christian faith.

The influence of Calvin and the church at Geneva rapidly spread throughout Europe and Great Britain. Calvin encouraged his followers to adapt the system of church government begun in Geneva to their own particular situation.[1] Many variations on Calvin's system were developed. Churches throughout Europe developed written constitutions that systematized their ecclesiastical institutions. These constitutions were probably freely shared among the Reformed family. As Reformed leaders in one country attempted to solve their own problems of ecclesiastical organization, they kept a watchful eye on the solutions to similar problems advanced by reformers in other countries.[2]

The Church in Scotland

Because of the influence of Scotland on American Presbyterianism, it is important to pay particular attention to developments in polity in that country. The first Constitution of the Scottish Reformed Church was completed in 1560. The office of elder was fairly well developed in this *First Book of Discipline.* Elders were elected by the congregation after nomination by the retiring elders and deacons, with members of the congregation eligible to make further nominations. Twice the number of persons to be elected were nominated by the retiring officers, an indication that the congregation exercised a significant element of choice.

Elders and deacons, as well as ministers, were subject to strict discipline by the Scottish church. The church in Scotland differed from Calvin's church in Geneva with regard to the role of deacons. In Scotland, deacons as well as elders participated in governing responsibilities. The congregational court was called the consistory and was composed of ministers, elders, and deacons. Of more importance than their difference over the rightful responsibilities of deacons was the agreement between the church in Geneva and that of Scotland that officers other than ministers should be members of the consistory. The point of agreement was the participation of the elder. Besides the role of deacons, the consistory of the Scottish church differed from that of Geneva in another important way. In Scotland each congregation had its own consistory, since the Scottish church covered a much larger area than the city of Geneva.

The Scottish consistory had three major areas of responsibility. The consistory administered ecclesiastical discipline, managed the general affairs of the congregation, and took a leading part in the election of the ministers of the congregation. (In exercise of this final responsibility, the deacons were excluded from the consistory.)[3] It is interesting to note that the Scottish consistory exercised discipline over all church officers, including ministers, as well as over members of the congregation. In this respect the church in Scotland was more democratic than that in Geneva, which made a distinction between its discipline of office bearers and church members. Only ministers disciplined other ministers in the Genevan church.[4]

The *First Book of Discipline* attempted to serve an entire nation, but it soon became inadequate for its task. A revised constitution was drawn up between 1574 and 1578. This *Second Book of Discipline* introduced the court of the presbytery to meet the needs of a larger geographical area. The presbytery was to become the major contribution of Scotland to Presbyterian polity. The office of elder took on additional responsibilities with the introduction of presbyteries. The presbytery was composed of pastors, doctors, and elders representing each kirk session within the district of the presbytery. (Doctors, or teachers, were the fourth church office in Calvin's polity, and these were carried over into the polity of the Church of Scotland for a period of time. Deacons lost their responsibilities for governance under the *Second Book of Discipline*, and thus were not members of presbytery.) Although elders were members of presbytery and urged to attend its meetings, they were not as obligated to participate as were the pastors and doctors. The pastors and doctors apparently summoned the elders to attend particular meetings that dealt with important business. In fact, it was declared in 1582 that when the presbytery was exercising ecclesiastical discipline, the pastors and doctors must outnumber the elders.[5]

The duties of presbytery were many and varied: making certain that the preaching within the churches of its district was orthodox, seeing that the sacraments were rightly administered, overseeing financial affairs, maintaining ecclesiastical discipline, and seeing that the actions of the Provincial and General Assemblies were carried out. Presbyteries could also enact rules to maintain order in their congregations, as long as the presbytery notified its Provincial Assembly. Again, what is most significant to note is that the presbytery, when it conducted its most important business, was not made up of pastors and doctors alone but included the participation of elders representative of the churches. It is also of interest to note that the governing body of the congregation, previously called the consistory, was called the "Kirk Eldership" or the "Session" in the *Second Book of Discipline.* According to the new constitution elders were to hold office for life. Previously they had been elected annually.[6]

Early Presbyterianism in America

When Presbyterians came to America, they brought with them their basic understanding of the office of elder. There is evidence from as early as 1617 of at least one attempt to set up in the Colony of Virginia a church government with ministers and elders. Four elders were selected from among the membership of a parish.[7] One congregation in Maryland, after the death of its pastor in 1679, was held together by a ruling elder until the new minister arrived, probably several years later.[8]

The first presbytery in America was founded in 1706 under the leadership of Francis Makemie. The first meeting of the presbytery was attended by ministers only. Ruling elders joined in subsequent meetings, however.[9] This Presbytery of Philadelphia included congregations from Maryland and Delaware as well as from the Philadelphia area. Later, churches from New Jersey and Long Island joined the presbytery. Growth was so fast that a synod of four presbyteries was organized in 1717. In these early years of organized Presbyterianism in America, the ministers exercised the major leadership. However, the office of elder was clearly a part of American Presbyterian life from earliest days.

The synod, which became known as the Synod of New York and Philadelphia, determined in 1785 that a General Assembly consisting of elected delegates would be a more effective form of national organization than the existing synod, which was made up of all the ministers of the church and one elder from every congregation. The synod meeting in 1788 adopted a constitution including a Form of Government. It also organized a General Assembly with four constituent synods: New York and New Jersey, Philadelphia, Virginia, and the Carolinas. The first meeting of the General Assembly was called for May 1789.

The 1788 Form of Government

The Constitution adopted by the synod of 1788 became the Constitution of the new General Assembly. It is to this Constitution that we must look to find the foundational statements on the office of elder. This Constitution contains a brief chapter, titled "Of Ruling Elders," which remained unchanged for nearly one hundred years. It reads as follows:

> Ruling elders are properly the representatives of the people, chosen
> by them for the purpose of exercising government and discipline, in

conjunction with pastors or ministers. This office has been understood, by a great part of the Protestant Reformed Churches, to be designated in the holy Scriptures, by the title of governments; and of those who rule well, but do not labour in the word and doctrine. [IV]

Scriptural references accompany this chapter. First Timothy 5:17 and 1 Corinthians 12:18 are quoted in the notes. Two additional passages are cited: Romans 12:7–8 and Acts 15:25.

Another chapter of this Form of Government is titled "Of Electing and Ordaining Ruling Elders and Deacons." This chapter begins by stating that it is prescribing "the mode in which ecclesiastical rulers shall be ordained to their respective offices" [XII.1]. It is important to notice that the title of the chapter and the first section used the word "ordain." That word is not used, however, later in the chapter where the introduction into office is actually described. The chapter states that ruling elders are to be elected by the congregation "in the mode most approved and in use in that congregation" [XII.2]. Persons who are elected and indicate a willingness to accept the office take up their office during a service of worship. Following the preaching of the sermon, the newly elected elders answer constitutional questions in the presence of the congregation. The elders are then "set apart . . . by prayer" [XIII.4]. "An exhortation suited to the occasion" is to be given to the new elders and to the congregation [XII.4].

The 1788 Form of Government states clearly the membership of each judicatory and the requirements for a quorum. "The Church session consists of the pastor or pastors, and ruling elders, of a particular congregation" [VIII.1]. The presbytery is made up of all the ministers within the presbytery and one ruling elder from each congregation. It is interesting to note the quorum of a presbytery:

> Any three ministers, and as many elders as may be present belonging to the presbytery, being met, at the time and place appointed, shall be a judicatory, competent to dispatch of business, not withstanding the absence of other members. [IX.4]

Apparently it was not necessary for *any* elders to be present in order for the presbytery to meet. The synod is defined as a "convention of several presbyteries, within a larger district" [X.1]. The makeup of the General Assembly is defined as follows:

> The General Assembly shall consist of an equal delegation of bishops and elders from each presbytery in the following proportions: viz. each presbytery consisting of not more than six ministers shall send one minister and one elder, each presbytery, consisting of more than six ministers and not more than twelve, shall send two ministers and two elders. [XI.2]

The listing continues, with the number of representatives increasing as the number of ministers increased, but in every case a presbytery sends the same number of ministers and elders. It is interesting to note that for a quorum to be present at the General Assembly at least half of the quorum had to be made up of ministers. The Constitution does not say that half must be elders. Apparently the quorum could be composed entirely of ministers [XI.3]. The sections concerning representation and the quorum in various judicatories are significant because of the struggles that occurred over the next century concerning the whole question of parity between ministers and elders.

Advocacy for the Office of Elder

One of the early influential advocates for elevating the office of elder to its proper dignity and responsibility was Dr. Samuel Miller of Princeton Theological Seminary. In 1832 Miller published a book titled *An Essay on the Warrant, Nature, and Duties of the Office of the Ruling Elder.* This book contains Miller's thinking on the subject of the elder developed over a twenty-year period. In the introduction, in which the author states that his purpose is not to cause controversy but rather to benefit the church, Miller, referring to the office of elder, states that some details of his opinions have changed over the years, but he affirms "In reference to the Divine warrant and the great importance of the office for which I plead, my convictions have become stronger than ever."[10] As had been the custom of the Reformed tradition since its beginnings in the sixteenth century, Miller went into great detail to show the roots of the office of elder in both Old and New Testaments and throughout church history. After six chapters of evidence, Miller concluded that ruling elders are absolutely necessary in the church.[11] One advantage to having a group of elders exercising authority in a congregation is to protect the minister from succumbing to the temptation of assuming too much power and authority. Also, a church with a group of responsible elders can receive "all the principal advantages which might be expected to result from being under the pastoral care of four or five ministers," without having the disadvantage of having to support so many pastors.[12]

Miller distinguished between the corporate duties of the body of elders and those duties which fall upon the elder as an individual. In considering the corporate responsibilities he made a strong case for the equality of the elder with the pastor:

> In the Church Session, whether the Pastor be present or presiding or not, every member has an equal voice. The vote of the most humble and retiring Ruling Elder is of the same avail as that of his Minister. So that no Pastor can carry any measure unless he can obtain the

concurrence of a majority of the Eldership. And as the whole spiritual government of each Church is committed to its bench of Elders,
the Session is competent to regulate every concern, and to correct
every thing which they consider as amiss in the arrangements or affairs of the Church which admits of correction. Every individual of
the Session, is of course, competent to propose any new service, plan,
or measure, which he believes will be for the benefit of the congregation, and if a majority of the Elders concur with him in opinion, it
may be adopted.[13]

Because of his view of the nature and importance of the office, Miller
questioned the practice of calling ruling elders "lay-elders." To speak of
ministers as clergy and elders as part of the laity makes a distinction between these two classes of elders that is "out to convey an idea altogether
erroneous, if not seriously mischievous."[14] He went back through early
church history to show that the terms "clergy" and "clerical" were, in the
early centuries of the church's history, applied to all classes of church officers. Speaking of elders, Miller reasoned:

They are as really in office; they as really bear an office of Divine appointment, an office of a high and spiritual nature, and an office, the
functions of which cannot be rightfully performed, but by those who
are regularly set apart to it, as any other officer of the Christian
Church. They are as really a portion of God's lot; as really set over the
laity, or body of the people as the most distinguished and venerated
minister of Jesus can be. Whether, therefore, we refer to early usage,
or to strict philological import, Ruling Elders are truly entitled to the
name of Clergy, in the only legitimate sense of that term, that is, they
are as truly ecclesiastical officers as those who "labour in the word
and doctrine."[15]

Miller did not believe he could successfully redefine the word "clergy." He
did hope to succeed in discouraging the use of the term "lay-elder." He
concluded:

Let all necessary distinction be made by saying:—"Ministers, or pastors, Ruling Elders, Deacons, and the Laity, or body of the people."
This will be in conformity with ancient usage. This will be maintaining every important principle. This can offend none; and nothing
more will be desired by any.[16]

There is much more of Miller's important book that could be read with
great benefit by officers of today's church.[17] Miller advanced strong arguments for the practice of laying on of hands in the ordaining of elders. He
believed that elders should participate in the laying on of hands in the

ordination of both elders and deacons because ordination was an act of government, and elders participate in government. He could not, however, go so far as to argue for the participation of elders in the laying on of hands in the ordination of ministers. For Miller such a practice was "contrary to essential Presbyterian principle."[18] One additional quotation will have to conclude this discussion of Miller's important work on the subject of the elder:

> The design of appointing persons to the office of Ruling Elder is not to pay them a compliment; not to give them an opportunity of figuring as speakers in judicatories; not to create the pageants of ecclesiastical ceremony; but to secure able, faithful, and truly devoted counselors and rulers of the Church; to obtain wise and efficient guides, who shall not only go along with the flock in their journey heavenward, but go before them in everything that pertains to Christian duty.[19]

Debates Surrounding the Eldership

Later in the same decade in which Samuel Miller published his significant volume on the elder, the place of elders in the government of the Presbyterian Church became a significant topic of debate. At this time it was not yet established constitutionally that elders themselves should be ordained with the laying on of hands. The Form of Government still stated that elders were to be set apart through prayer. The Form of Government was silent as to the laying on of hands. The question that caused the biggest controversy was not the laying on of hands in the ordination of elders but whether elders might participate in the laying on of hands in the ordination of ministers. In the late 1830s, presbyteries in Kentucky began permitting elders to participate in the ordination of ministers. In 1843 the Presbytery of West Lexington overtured the General Assembly on the question. The General Assembly's answer was overwhelming: By vote of 183 to 9 the Assembly stated that elders were not authorized to participate in the laying on of hands in the ordination of ministers, either by the Constitution or by the practice of the church.[20] In that same year the General Assembly, in response to an overture from yet another presbytery, stated that according to the Form of Government it was not necessary for any ruling elders to be present in order to have a quorum for a meeting of presbytery. The battle was joined!

Dr. Robert J. Breckinridge and Dr. James Henley Thornwell took up the side of granting more authority to elders. They saw the presence of elders, the representatives of the people, as necessary for any meeting of a judicatory or court. The participation of elders was seen as essential to Presbyterianism. Because of their membership in presbytery, elders were entitled to participate in the laying on of hands in the ordination of ministers.[21] According to Thornwell and Breckinridge, the participation of the elder in the ordination of a minister grows out of the understanding of an elder as a presbyter. As a presbyter the elder is entitled to participate in all acts of presbytery and therefore entitled to take part in the entire process by which ministers are ordained to their office.

Leading the debate on the other side was Dr. Charles Hodge of Princeton Theological Seminary. Dr. Hodge believed that elders could not be properly identified with the presbyters of the New Testament, and since elders of Hodge's day were not true elders in the New Testament sense, they had no right to participate in the laying on of hands in the ordination of a minister.[22] The 1844 General Assembly supported the position of Hodge and others by reaffirming its action of the previous year declaring that elders could not participate in the laying on of hands in the ordination of ministers. The General Assembly saw the ordination ceremony as "simply a declaratory ministerial act."[23] As a part of this declaratory ministerial act, the laying on of hands then belonged only to those ordained as ministers.

The polity debates of the 1830s and 1840s were not simply North-South differences. Dr. Thomas Smyth of Charleston, South Carolina, was a leader, along with Hodge, of the more traditional point of view. The Thornwell-Hodge debate, joined in by others with a deep interest in polity, gave the Presbyterian Church in the United States of America some of its most profound thinking about church government. Although not sectional in origin, the debate did lead to some significant, long-standing differences between the churches of the North and of the South. The position of Thornwell, Breckinridge, and others was made constitutional in the South when the PCUS adopted its new *Book of Church Order* in 1879. The 1879 Constitution took several steps to advance the standing of elders in the church's life. The wording of the first two paragraphs of the chapter in the 1879 Form of Government titled "Of the Ruling Elder" is instructive:

> As there were in the Church, under the law, Elders of the people for the government thereof, so, in the Gospel Church, Christ has furnished others besides the Ministers of the Word, with gifts and commission to govern when called thereunto, which officers are entitled Ruling Elders.

> These Ruling Elders do not labor in the Word and doctrine, but possess the same authority in the courts of the Church as the Ministers of the Word. [IV.3.1, 2]

The section of the 1879 PCUS Form of Government on the presbytery specified that a quorum of presbytery required three ministers belonging to the presbytery and at least one elder. Although this ratio is a long way from parity, it is a step in that direction because of the requirement that one ruling elder must be present in order for presbytery to meet [V.4.3]. The quorum of a synod required the presence of any seven ministers within the synod and at least three elders. There was a further provision that no more than three of the ministers could belong to one presbytery [V.5.2]. For a meeting of the General Assembly, each presbytery was entitled to send ministers and ruling elders in pairs. That is, if the presbytery could send only one minister, then it also could send one ruling elder. However, a quorum for a meeting of a General Assembly was eighteen commissioners, one half of whom had to be ministers, and at least five of whom had to be elders [V.6.2, 4]. In other words, the requirement for a quorum suggested that the presence of ministers was more important than the presence of elders.

The chapter of the 1879 Constitution titled "Of Church Orders" contains a provision that all church officers are to be ordained by the laying on of hands:

Those who have been lawfully called are to be inducted into their respective offices by the ordination of a court.

Ordination is the authoritative admission of one duly called to an office in the Church of God, accompanied with prayer and the imposition of hands, to which it is proper to add the giving of the right hand of fellowship. [VI.2.1, 2]

Although the Presbyterian Church in the United States of America (PCUSA) was much slower in changing its Constitution to give additional authority to elders, many voices throughout that denomination joined in advocating for strengthening the office of elder. Samuel Miller, who spoke so powerfully from his base in Princeton in the 1830s, had many followers in the PCUSA. In the 1870s the question around which the debate was carried on was whether elders could serve as moderators of judicatories. Once it was determined that elders could serve, then other questions arose.

One fascinating document from the last decade of the nineteenth century is a pamphlet titled *A Sermon or Address on the Elder Moderator and the Ruling Elder*. This sermon was delivered before the Presbytery of Westchester of the Synod of New York at its meeting in Stamford, Connecticut, in 1894. Ralph E. Prime began by recounting his experience as the first elder to moderate his presbytery. One of the first questions that arose was whether he would preach the sermon. Six months later, when he retired, he most assuredly preached the sermon, even though he titled it "A Sermon or Address." The sermon was a learned lecture on the history of Presbyterian polity and of the Presbyterian Church. Prime told story after story of elders serving as moderators of various judicatories in various places. About one third of the way through his sermon Prime concluded that in matters related to polity it is, indeed, right to make changes! Having reached that conclusion, he turned to the text from Romans 11:13: "I magnify mine office." And indeed Prime did! He called on elders to exercise their office according to the highest standards of faithfulness.[24]

Parity in Governance

It was not until the latter half of this century that the complete equality of elders with ministers in exercising governance was established in all branches of what has become the Presbyterian Church (U.S.A.). The Joint Committee on Presbyterian Reunion maintained equal numbers of ministers and elders in the membership of governing bodies but, in the case of certain committees, went a step beyond what Presbyterians had understood as parity, establishing a new formula of representation. Many committees of governing bodies are now to be composed of one third ministers, one third laywomen, and one third laymen [G-9.0801a, G-13.0111a, G-13.0202d]. In an article titled "We Can Be More Than We Are" included in the Joint Committee's resource packet, James E. Andrews made the following comment: "There are times when true parity cannot be achieved by continuing to require half ministers and half elders."[25] The limitation of ministers to one third of the membership of certain committees is an attempt to further empower the church's elders, deacons, and nonofficer members. It is interesting to note that the *Book of Order* speaks in terms of "laywomen and laymen" rather than of elders who are women and elders who are men. While the term "laywomen and laymen" in this context is clearly meant to include elders, service on certain presbytery, synod, and General Assembly committees is not limited to those who have been ordained to church office. Nonordained members are also eligible to serve.

The journey to achieve parity between elders and ministers and to grant to the office of elder the proper authority and responsibility has been a long one in Presbyterianism. Many Reformed churches in the world today still do not find it necessary to set apart elders and deacons by ordination with the laying on of hands. It has been a significant contribution of Presbyterianism in the United States to emphasize that the office of elder must be accorded the same dignity and respect that is given to the office of minister of the Word and Sacrament. Future chapters of this book will consider the responsibilities of today's elders, functioning both individually and as members of sessions and more inclusive governing bodies. This chapter's glimpses into the past have established the importance of the office of elder within the Reformed tradition.

Chapter Five

THE OFFICE
OF
DEACON

Nancy Jones attended a conference on the church's mission sponsored by her presbytery. In a small-group discussion Betty Pierce, a member of a church in a nearby town, spoke enthusiastically about the activities of her church's deacons, who reach out in a wide variety of ways to persons in need in the community. Nancy was amazed. Her church had not had any deacons in years and, as far as Nancy knew, her church was doing very little to help the poor or others in need. When Nancy shared her surprise with the group, Bill Green, from the presbytery's largest church, pointed out that the deacons in his church are in charge of promoting stewardship, taking up the offering during worship and counting it after the service, and, of course, ushering. Since these tasks are very demanding ones in his large church, the deacons have almost no time or energy for service in the community. Bill too gained new ideas from what Betty had shared. But by now, everyone in the group had become somewhat confused about just what deacons are supposed to do.

The *Book of Order* [G-6.0402] states the function of deacons succinctly:

It is the duty of deacons, first of all, to minister to those who are in need, to the sick, to the friendless, and to any who may be in distress both within and beyond the community of faith. They shall assume such other duties as may be delegated to them from time to time by the session, such as leading the people in worship through prayers of intercession, reading the Scriptures, presenting the gifts of the people, and assisting with the Lord's Supper. (See W-3.3616.)

The Constitution is clear. The primary duty assigned to all deacons is that of ministering to persons in need or in distress. This function is broadly stated to encompass service to any person in need anywhere. No limits of location or of categories of need exist. The sick and the friendless are specifically mentioned, but the deacons' service is not limited to these two groups. Deacons are to minister to any who may be in distress.

Second, deacons are to assume any other duties that the session chooses to delegate to them. A 1998 amendment adds the specific suggestion of leading in portions of the worship service. Many churches have long traditions of the deacons' fulfilling particular functions. The Constitutions of the two predecessor denominations listed additional duties to those now specified in the Presbyterian Church (U.S.A.) *Book of Order,* and what the Constitutions did not add, tradition did.

In order to understand some of the current confusion and diversity surrounding the role of the deacon—and whether there should even be a separate office of deacon—it is necessary to look at the ways in which the office of deacon developed and changed within the Reformed tradition, especially in the United States.

The Office of Deacon in the Reformed Tradition

When in the mid-sixteenth century John Calvin developed a polity for governing the church in Geneva, one of the offices for which he found a scriptural basis was the office of deacon. Calvin turned to the story of the appointing of the seven in the sixth chapter of Acts and saw there deacons who cared for poor and distributed alms to them. According to Acts, when the apostles heard that some church members felt that the relief of the poor was not being handled fairly, they asked that this part of their work be entrusted to a separate group of seven persons who would not have the responsibility of preaching and so could focus their attention on the work of serving tables. Calvin concluded: "Here, then, is the kind of deacons the apostolic church had, and which we, after their example, should have."[1]

Following Calvin, Presbyterians of Scotland provided for the office of deacon in the *First Book of Discipline* of 1560. There was one important difference between Calvin and the Scots, however. Scottish polity permitted deacons to be members of church courts—what we today know as governing bodies. However, by the time the *Second Book of Discipline* was legally enacted by the Acts of Parliament in 1592 Calvin's view predominated in Scotland, and it was specified that deacons were not to be members of any church court.[2]

The 1788 Constitution

The first Constitution of the Presbyterian Church in the United States of America, adopted by the Synod of New York and Philadelphia in 1788, contained a very brief chapter titled "Of Deacons." As was the custom throughout this first Form of Government, Scripture passages were cited (and some even quoted) to support the constitutional text. These Scripture passages are helpful references for persons today interested in the office of deacon. The texts cited are Philippians 1:1; 1 Timothy 3:8–15; Acts 6:1–2 (quoted); and Acts 6:3, 5–6 (quoted). Take time to read these passages with care.

The language of the 1788 Form of Government is itself very helpful for understanding the developing role of the deacon:

Of Deacons

The scriptures clearly point out deacons as distinct officers in the church, whose business it is to take care of the poor, and to distribute among them the collections which may be raised for their use. To them also may be properly committed the management of their temporal affairs in the church. [V]

Other sections of this Form of Government provided for the election and ordination of deacons. As with elders, there was no mention of the laying on of hands in ordination, only the provision that the deacon "shall be set apart, by prayer, to the office . . . and the minister shall give him, and the congregation, an exhortation suited to the occasion" [XII].

A careful reading of these early constitutional provisions makes clear that care of the poor is the primary function of the deacon. To care for the poor involves the distribution of the money collected for their benefit, and this aspect of the deacon's task is specifically mentioned.

In addition to caring for the poor, a second function is mentioned—the management of the church's temporal affairs. It should be noted that this management "may be properly committed" to the deacons. It is not essential to the office as is the care of the poor.

Encouraging Churches to Institute the Office

Although the earliest American Presbyterian Constitution recognized deacons as "a distinct office in the church," many congregations did not make use of the office. With the renewed interest in polity that developed in the 1830s, efforts were made to strengthen the office of deacon. The Old School General Assembly on at least three occasions in the 1840s and 1850s urged congregations to appoint deacons. In 1841 the Old School Assembly noted that, in response to the urging of the 1840 Assembly that presbyteries urge their churches to appoint deacons, there was some indication that "to a considerable extent the Presbyteries had taken order on the subject."[3]

Also, throughout the mid-nineteenth century numerous spokespersons published pamphlets and articles in periodicals urging the church to recognize the importance of the office by electing deacons and then admonishing deacons themselves to fulfill their ministry of service. Although the language is clearly that of an earlier day, the reasoning that was used has an amazingly contemporary ring to it.

Of major concern was the intent of the biblical texts concerning the office of deacon. Were deacons appointed only for a particular time and place, or should the New Testament references to deacons be understood as important for the church's life in all times and places? Opinions differed: Some viewed the office as perpetual, while others reasoned that only those churches with many poor people among their membership needed to continue the office of deacon.

A forceful advocate for the permanency of the office was the Reverend James B. Ramsey. In an essay read before the Synod of Virginia in 1858 and later published in pamphlet form, Dr. Ramsey, while acknowledging that the deacon is generally viewed as unimportant in the Presbyterian Church, proceeds to develop a number of compelling arguments for the importance of the office in the ongoing life of the church.

According to Ramsey, the church's obligation to care for the poor rests on more than a general duty of compassion to those who suffer. It rests "on the far stronger grounds of the union of all believers with Christ and with each other."[4] Ramsey uses the language of 1 Corinthians 12: We are all "one body in Christ, and every one members one of another." "And whether one member suffer, all the members suffer with it. . . ." Ramsey concludes, "The care of the poor, relieving their wants and soothing their sorrows, and encouraging their crushed spirits, is, therefore, a duty entwined in the very nature of the Christian life—springing naturally and necessarily out of the believer's union with Christ."[5]

Ramsey also emphasizes the importance of the church's corporate, ordered response to the service of the poor. It was not enough to trust this crucial task

to take its chances among individual sympathies. From the very first it was recognized as a church duty, a matter of public arrangement by the whole body. Just as their abundant and spontaneous offerings for such as were in need were the natural expression of the feeling that they were all members one of another, so this official attention to it by the Church, in her organized capacity, was a necessary result of the principle then so deeply and vividly felt, of her unity in Christ.[6]

The care of the poor is a distinct function of the church, and one that demands a corporate, not an individual, response. It is for these reasons that Ramsey advocates understanding the office as perpetual and universal. Ramsey has several answers for those who believe that whenever the care of the poor "can be attended to by the session without interfering with other duties, it is perfectly right to do so, and to dispense with this office until the same exigency arises as in the primitive church." He cites the Acts story and reasons that the apostolic church could have very easily increased the number of elders to care for those in need rather than creating a separate office. The work of receiving and disbursing the church's charities "was of such a nature that it was better to be entirely separated from all other duties, and committed to a distinct body of officers—distinct not only from the Apostles themselves, but also from those to whom they had committed the government and teaching."[7]

An additional argument advanced by Ramsey has much relevance for the church of our day. Ramsey recognized that the duties already assigned to the pastor and the elders were so extensive as to make it very difficult for these officers to perform the duties of deacons as well. "The fact is, that where there are no deacons, and their duties are left to the Session, they are in almost all cases, scarcely performed at all. This whole function of the Church lies paralyzed."[8] As a corollary Ramsey added:

> But it may be asked, of what use are deacons to take care of the poor in churches where there are no poor, or but two or three? *That, indeed, is a sadly defective state of the Church where there are no poor; there must be something very deficient in its zeal and aggressiveness, if amidst the multitudes of poor around us, and mingling with us, there are none in the church itself. . . .*
>
> But, even supposing that within the bounds of some particular congregation there are no poor that need the church's aid; still, are there not multitudes of God's poor elsewhere that need aid? And is not such a favored church especially bound to extend her help to the less favored? And outside of the Church—among the ignorant multitudes in our own land, and the impoverished nations of our world, has God not chosen ones to be looked after, sought out and gathered in? And are not such churches especially called upon to go forth on errands of mercy to these—errands like that of Jesus Himself to our poor world—personally to those within their reach, and by their messengers to others?[9]

Changes in Understanding of the Office

While Ramsey and others were exhorting churches to institute the office of deacon to be the agent of the church's ministry of compassion, an evolution in the understanding of the office was also under way. Functions that were at first simply logical extensions of the primary work of the deacon became more and more prominent aspects of the deacon's task. It is easy to see how the emphasis on the deacon as the manager of the church's money and as the keeper of church property could evolve from the earliest constitutional provisions, especially when one keeps in mind the biblical tradition on which the office of deacon is based. From distribution of the money to the poor it is a short step to the distribution and collection of all the church's funds. And the management of the temporal affairs of the church, which could be "properly committed" to the deacons, could become such a large responsibility as to be viewed as the primary task of the deacons. Unfortunately, over a period of time, that is exactly what happened in many congregations that did use the office of deacon.

Developments in the Presbyterian Church U.S.

The first constitutional changes surrounding the office of deacon occurred in the *Book of Church Order* adopted by the PCUS in 1879. The description of the duties of deacons may not seem to be significantly altered, and yet the beginning of a direction of change can be seen. The primary emphasis was still on the care of the poor. However, where the language had been "to distribute among them [the poor] the collections which may be raised for their use," the duty now became "the collection and distribution of the offerings of the people for pious uses, under the direction of the Session" [IV.4.2]. The provision from the 1788 Form of Government then followed: "To the deacons, also, may be properly committed the management of the temporal affairs of the church." The management of all of the church's financial affairs could thus be assigned to the deacons—both the collection of benevolent money and of money for the church's "temporal affairs" and, in addition, the distribution of all such funds.

Writings of PCUS leaders over the next several decades show how these constitutional provisions were perceived and used. An 1895 tract prepared by one synod for distribution to the deacons of all its churches pointed out that "the work of the Deacon in the modern church has been greatly enlarged" and "it is evident that the success and efficiency of the church must rest very largely upon the Deacons." After encouraging deacons to adopt the "Envelope System," the tract continued: "Success in business is attention to detail. This will be true of this work."[10] A pamphlet published by the Committee of Publication of the PCUS in 1897, while emphasizing that the deacon's financial function was subordinate to the chief function of caring for the poor, still spoke of the deacon as "the authorized financial officer of Christ's Kingdom" and admitted that the emphasis on the deacon as "financial officer" or "revenue officer" was the more widely acknowledged and practiced role of the deacon.[11]

The Executive Committee of Christian Education and Ministerial Relief of the PCUS published in 1917 or 1918 a pamphlet titled *The Deacon's First Responsibility*. The purpose of this pamphlet was to improve ministers' salaries. Apparently the failure of congregations to increase significantly pastors' salaries in a time when the cost of living had doubled in four years had created a substantial hardship for many ministers and their families. Still, the fact that a publication of an official General Assembly committee would state by its title and very directly in the opening paragraph that the provision of a fair living for the pastor is the "first responsibility" of the deacon represents a significant shift in the understanding of the office.[12]

In 1922 the PCUS revised the section on the deacon once again. The new constitutional provision began with the language of service to the poor. In fact, that language was expanded somewhat. The emphasis on the deacon's role in relating to stewardship and the care of church property expanded even more. The weight of words placed the emphasis away from caring for persons with special needs. Because the constitutional provisions of 1922 still influence the tradition of a significant portion of the church, there is value in quoting the section on the responsibilities of the office:

> It is the duty of the Deacons to minister to those who are in need, to the sick, to the friendless, and to any who may be in distress. It is their duty also to develop the grace of liberality in the members of the church, to devise effective methods of collecting the gifts of the people, and to distribute these gifts among the objects to which they are contributed. They shall have the care of the property of the congregation, both real and personal, and shall keep in proper repair the church edifice and other buildings belonging to the congregation. In matters of special importance affecting the property of the church, they cannot take final action without the consent of the congregation. In the discharge of their duties the Deacons are under the supervision and authority of the session. In a church in which it is impossible for any reason to secure Deacons, the duties of the office shall devolve upon the Ruling Elders. [47-II]

The Presbyterian Committee of Publication produced a pamphlet by the Reverend Edward Mack interpreting the new constitutional provisions. Mack saw the constitutional revision as "in reality the ratification of a conception and usage long existent in many of our best organized and most active churches, and found by them to be the best means for conducting the temporal and benevolent activities of the church."[13] Mack also emphasized the point that both the office of elder and that of deacon are "concerned with spiritual service, but service differing in detail, in which each has its own peculiar fitness and its own call and commission from Christ."[14] Mack rejected the view that the deacon is a secular office. He saw the church's separation between its secular affairs and its spiritual affairs as an artificial distinction. The deacon is not simply young material to be developed for the eldership. Rather, the deacon's spiritual life and service represent and challenge the consecration of the Christian's life and possessions to Jesus Christ.[15]

Mack saw the constitutional revision of 1922 as lifting the office of deacon "from disparagement and partial disuse into special honor and large opportunity."[16] Apparently the office did become widely used throughout the PCUS, but it is not as certain that the problems surrounding the church's understanding and utilization of the office were solved. Because of the overlapping responsibilities of the diaconate and the session the opportunity existed for tension and confusion. In spite of the interpretation of the denomination's Assembly committees, the view of the deacons as "junior elders" flourished in many congregations.

In the 1961 revision of the PCUS *Book of Church Order,* the section on the deacon was rewritten once again. The movement this time was in the direction of condensing the whole section. The fact that the deacons carry out their work under the authority of the session was further clarified, including the fact that the church's regular budget must be approved by the session. This chapter, with two important amendments, remained in effect until the time of reunion. One change was to make the language throughout the chapter inclusive of women (1978). The other was to specify that "a congregation by a majority vote may elect not to use the office of deacon. In such a case, or in a case where deacons cannot be secured, the function of the office shall always be preserved and shall devolve upon the Ruling Elders and the Session" [12–5, adopted in 1971].

Trends in the Presbyterian Church U.S.A.

What view of the office of deacon developed in the Presbyterian Church U.S.A. from the latter part of the nineteenth century until it united with the United Presbyterian Church of North America (UPNA) to form The United Presbyterian Church in the United States of America? The PCUSA part of the Presbyterian family maintained the identical language of the 1788 Form of Government until it united with the UPNA Church in 1958. The continuity of constitutional provisions does not mean, however, that there was uniformity in understanding or use of the office. The 1871 General Assembly urged congregations to use the office of deacon. Pamphlets were written and circulated to reinforce the Assembly's message and also to educate congregations to understand the office as one of service to the poor. Congregations were urged to assume their rightful responsibility in caring for the poor, first among their own members and then extending out into the community. Churches were told that they had left too much of this responsibility to others. The clear message was that "God regards the poor, intends that his people shall care for them, and has appointed the deaconship as a proper agency to carry this intention into effect."[17]

In the PCUSA, as in the PCUS, care was taken to point out the problems inherent in assigning the functions of deacons to the ruling elders. "Experience proves that when the duties of various callings are heaped upon one person, they are seldom all well performed.... Were the deaconship filled and its duties faithfully performed, there would still remain enough to do to employ the time and energies of our ruling elders."[18]

In 1897 the Presbyterian Board of Publication first published *A Manual for Ruling Elders and Church Sessions*, which contained information about the office of deacon. It placed on sessions the responsibility for bringing about the election of deacons, as soon as possible, in churches that did not have them.[19] This manual specified that deacons must be organized as a board and must act corporately. "The deacons no more than the elders can act on their individual responsibility. They should meet and organize as a board with a chairman, secretary, and treasurer."[20] In 1915 a new chapter, "Of the Board of Deacons," was added to the PCUSA *Book of Order*. It contained provisions for the organization and accountability of a board of deacons. Although it added no new specific responsibilities for deacons, it did suggest that the board of deacons "may perform such other administrative, charitable and community duties, the disbursement of charitable funds included, as may be determined upon, after consultation with and action by the session" (XXV,4).

The Presbyterian Church U.S.A. never moved as far in the direction of emphasizing the deacons' role in financial affairs as the PCUS did. Instead the PCUSA used more and more the pattern, which began even before the writing of the 1788 Form of Government, of committing much of a church's financial business to trustees. Trustees were not mentioned in early constitutions. They were not ecclesiastical officers, but civil officers, that is, persons assigned certain responsibilities in relation to state governments. The movement in the direction of entrusting matters to trustees was controversial for a significant period of time. Practice varied from church to church as to how much of the church's "temporal affairs" was committed to trustees and how much to deacons.

In 1892 thirty-two presbyteries overtured the General Assembly of the Presbyterian Church U.S.A., asking for an inquiry into "prevalent methods of managing church temporalities by means of Boards of Trustees."[21] The report of the Special Committee on Church Temporalities in 1896 shows something of the complexity and difference of opinion surrounding the relationship of deacons and trustees. The special committee attempted to ease tensions and clarify responsibilities by proposing an amendment to the Form of Government chapter "Of Deacons," which would have favored deacons over trustees as managers of the church's temporal affairs. The amendment was not approved! The variety of practice from church to church remained.

Deacons in the United Presbyterian Church of North America

The United Presbyterian Church of North America brought to its 1958 union with the Presbyterian Church U.S.A. a constitutional understanding of the deacon that emphasized service to the poor and also the collection and distribution of the congregation's benevolent offerings. A unique emphasis was placed on visitation, both of the sick and of the people in their homes, and on the deacons as "helpers to the pastor and the elders." It is helpful to see the exact language of the UPNA *Book of Government and Worship:*

> Deacons are helpers to the pastor and the elders of a congregation in the work of the Lord as visitors to the sick, ministers to the poor, suc-corers to those in trial, and messengers of the gospel in the homes of the people.[22]

Under qualifications for the office, it is mentioned that deacons "should be persons of such liberality of spirit in honoring the Lord with their sub-stance that they may be leaders of the people in the right use of the talents which the Lord has placed in their hands."[23] In addition to "the collection and distribution of the offerings of the people for charitable and mission-ary purposes, under the advice and direction of the session," the board of deacons may also have properly committed to it the management of the congregation's temporal affairs.

The UPNA stream of the Presbyterian family thus brought a concept of deacon very similar to that of other parts of the church, but with special emphasis on the deacon as helper to the pastor and elders, as visitor in the homes of the people (understood as meaning house-to-house evangelism), and as an example to the congregation by their own practice of good stew-ardship.

It appears that the United Presbyterian Church of North America also shared the problems that other Presbyterian denominations had sur-rounding the use of the office of deacon. A 1938 pamphlet published by the United Presbyterian Board of Publication and Bible School Work be-moaned the fact that the majority of churches did not have deacons and that "in some churches where there is such a board it is as inactive as the lowest note on the piano."[24]

The United Presbyterian Church in the U.S.A.

The new Constitution of The United Presbyterian Church in the United States of America, adopted on that church's formation in 1958, contained a chapter on the office of deacon which was an expansion beyond the pro-visions that either of the two predecessor churches had made constitu-tional. The organizational structure of the board of deacons was included within the chapter on the office of deacons. Of more importance were the sections that described the purpose and duties of the office.

The office of deacon was defined as "one of sympathy and service, after the example of the Lord Jesus" [X-1]. The duties or responsibilities of the board were as follows:

The board of deacons shall minister to those in need, to the sick, to the friendless, and to any who may be in distress, in accordance with the Scriptural duties of the office. There may be delegated to the board of deacons, under the direction of the session, certain specifically designated responsibilities relating to the development of the grace of liberality in the members of the church, to the devising of effective methods of collecting the gifts of the people, to the finances and properties of the church, and to its evangelistic, missionary and educational programs. The board of deacons shall assume such duties, not limited to the foregoing, as may be delegated to it by the session. [X-5]

Congregations could choose whether or not to elect deacons. In those congregations that did choose to use the office there was a great deal of leeway as to what duties, in addition to ministering to persons in need, could be delegated by the session to the board of deacons. Stewardship, finances, and church property are specifically mentioned, but so are evangelism, missionary work, and Christian education. Other duties not specifically mentioned could be delegated to the board of deacons by the session. A very diverse pattern of activity could, and did, develop. If a congregation chose not to elect deacons, then the *Book of Order* specifically provided that all the duties and powers of the deacons (those in X-5 quoted above) could be delegated to trustees—in addition to those duties that trustees regularly assumed.

The constitutional provisions concerning the office of deacon remained unchanged during the years of the UPCUSA's life, with one significant addition. The language throughout was made inclusive of women, and one sentence was added as follows: "The office of deacon shall be open to all members regardless of race, ethnic origin, disability, sex, marital status, or age" [40.02].

Recovering the Essence of the Office of Deacon

The reunion of 1983 brought together a variety of traditions surrounding the office of deacon. Some congregations of the UPCUSA had no tradition of a diaconate, with all the functions of such a group assumed by the session or by the trustees. Some congregations of the PCUS had in recent years exercised their constitutional option of electing "not to use the office of Deacon" [12-5], with all the responsibilities of a board of deacons falling on the session. Many congregations from both streams of the church had active boards of deacons. But those of the former PCUS came from a tradition where the secondary functions assigned to the diaconate (after the primary function of service to those in need) were all related to stewardship education, financial planning and management, and property management. Diaconates of congregations from the UPCUSA stream had the greatest variety of patterns, since the functions suggested as appropriate for their work extended beyond the areas of stewardship education and financial and property management to more general program responsibility—specifically evangelistic, missionary, and educational programs. These last-mentioned areas of responsibility were more closely related to the primary task of service. Where the management of the church's "temporalities" was delegated to trustees, the church's board of deacons had been free to develop a ministry of service, both directly (that is, performed by the deacons themselves) and by service-related program responsibility in the overall life of the congregation.

The framers of the *Book of Order* of the Presbyterian Church (U.S.A.) were faced with patterns of church life that lacked a clear understanding of the function of the deacon. How might the essence of the office be emphasized, first in the Constitution of the reunited church, and then in its life? The *Book of Order* recovered the distinctiveness that has long eluded the office of deacon by stating the nature of the office in the simplest possible terms. Churches are free to continue in whatever pattern of effectively using the office has been meaningful to them in the past, since sessions may delegate whatever responsibilities they like to the deacons. And churches are also free to discover a new significance in an office that perhaps they have combined with the office of elder (choosing not to have a separate board of deacons) or which they perhaps have used but in a way that has lacked vitality and creativity.

The constitutional statement of the Presbyterian Church (U.S.A.) makes it very clear why Presbyterians ordain deacons. Deacons are ordained (set into an ordered pattern of church life) for the purpose of "minister[ing] to those who are in need, to the sick, to the friendless, and to any who may be in distress" [G-6.0402]. Any other functions deacons serve may be extremely valuable, but they are secondary to the function of service. Deacons are ordained to serve, and not just to serve the church in some administrative function. Deacons are ordained to serve those who are in need, in a very direct and personal way.

The form of service emphasized by deacons will differ according to place and situation. Some churches may focus a large portion of their service on meeting special needs of persons with a particular disability. The deacons of one church may concentrate on enabling the elderly of their community to experience fuller days, utilizing and sharing their special gifts. Another church's deacons may choose to operate a night shelter for the homeless of a community. The deacons of several churches in a city could join forces in a larger effort to meet specific community needs. The ways of fulfilling the specific responsibility of deacons seem endless.

In 1998 amendments were added to Form of Government G-6.0402 and G-6.0403 that greatly enhance the office of deacon in the Presbyterian Church (U.S.A.). G-6.0402 adds that the persons who are to be served by deacons are "both within and beyond the community of faith." The same passage also suggests that a secondary function be added to the responsibility of deacons, that of leadership in worship.

Reformed churches have placed less emphasis upon a liturgical function for deacons than many of our partner churches within the ecumenical church. A major study of ordination presented to the 1992 General Assembly suggests adding a liturgical dimension to the functions of the deacon. Deacons should lead in the portions of the liturgy that most relate to their responsibility for ministries of service to the powerless and others in need, namely reading the gospel lesson, gathering and presenting the gifts of the people, and preparing and assisting in serving the Lord's Supper.[25] It is the 1992 ordination report that, after significant study in the church, led to the 1998 amendment adding new responsibility to the office of deacon.

The same ordination study also calls for the other far-reaching 1998 amendment to the office of deacon, the provision for deacons to be individually commissioned by the session and not organized into a board of deacons. According to the study, the core functions of the office of deacon all involve following the self-emptying pattern of Christ in service to others either on a one-to-one basis or to particular groups in the church or community. These functions do not require that deacons be organized as a board. Time spent in organizing, planning, and attending meetings can reduce the amount of time and energy for person-to-person service. Also, a limited term of active service, while important in an office focusing upon decision-making and governance, is not an issue when the office focuses upon setting an example and persuading others to join together in reaching out to persons in need. There is room for flexibility in the way the office of deacon functions in the life of the church.[26]

The door is now open for a congregation to elect one or more persons to the office of deacon who would be trained, examined, and ordained by the session and who would then be commissioned by the session to particular tasks of diaconal ministry. The tasks may be accomplished through the deacon's professional work in such fields as medicine, education, or social work or through, volunteer service in a particular ministry. The commissioned deacons may together be involved in a particular project on behalf of the congregation. Ordinarily the session will review the work of the commissioned deacon each year and may renew, alter, or terminate the commission [G-6.0403b].

Congregations are free to choose to use both patterns of organization for deacons at the same time or to use either of the patterns alone. Churches that have chosen not to use the office of deacon but rather to have all of the responsibilities of deacons assumed by the session may find this to be a good time to reassess their mission and consider the possibilities of each pattern of diaconal service for expanding the church's ministry.

It is the responsibility of the session to oversee and lead in all aspects of the church's life. Not so the deacons. They have the advantage of a limited responsibility, with the freedom to concentrate on one task. A church can choose to give to its deacons no duty other than relieving human need. A church can turn the deacons loose to learn, to act, to try and try again, as it searches for the most effective ways of fulfilling its ministry of compassion.

Electing and ordaining persons to the office of deacon is the way the church seeks to assure in the ordering of its corporate life that the ministry of compassion is never overlooked.

Chapter Six

A FIRST LOOK
AT
THE SESSION

The session of Little Chapel Presbyterian Church is struggling with a question that is troubling the members. A new family has been visiting regularly for several months. The two enthusiastic teenagers have invigorated the high school church school class. Their mother has added a much-needed alto voice to the choir. The pastor has visited the family twice, urging them to join the church. They have indicated their interest in doing so. However, the father, an articulate, well-educated person, has made it clear to the pastor and another session member that although a member of the Presbyterian Church for all his adult life, he is not now able to affirm faith in Jesus Christ as Lord and Savior. He would like to transfer his membership to Little Chapel Church with the rest of the family, as long as the session will not ask him any questions. It is the policy of the Little Chapel session to ask every person seeking membership in the congregation to reaffirm the questions asked of those making a profession of faith. The session believes it should continue its policy, but it fears losing a new family, especially this one.

The session of Green Valley Presbyterian Church was taking a look at its membership rolls in order to assure their accuracy. When they came to the name Jane Wilkes, the whole group seemed to be in agreement that she should be placed on the inactive roll. "We haven't seen her in worship or in any of the church's programs for a year or two," remarked one elder. "She has become totally inactive," commented another. Then the pastor asked, "Have we done anything to reach out to her and encourage her to resume active involvement here? Frankly, I forgot about Jane. I called her perhaps two years ago, but I haven't done anything since. Have any of you?"

The session of every Presbyterian church is responsible for the mission and government of that church. The Form of Government lists many of the responsibilities and powers of the session in G-10.0000, the main chapter on that particular governing body. However, additional responsibilities are assigned to the session in other parts of the Form of Government, Directory for Worship, and Rules of Discipline. The purpose of this chapter is twofold: first, to bring together in outline form all the responsibilities of the session, in order to provide an overview of the total leadership task assigned to the governing body of every congregation and, second, to discuss certain of these responsibilities in detail.

An Overview of Responsibilities and Powers

An outline of the responsibilities of the session might enable elders to grasp the scope of their duties and to think creatively about their own life and the ministry to which they have been called, elected, and ordained. It is suggested that readers who serve on sessions work through the outline with care. For your convenience, the chapters of this book dealing in more detail with the various responsibilities are cited at the right.

Responsibilities and Powers of the Session for the
Mission and Government of the Particular Church

I. Equipping the church's members to be evangelists (chapter 9)
and providing opportunities for them to share
their faith

II. Receiving members in various categories (chapter 6)
of membership
A. Three ways of receiving members
B. Four categories of membership
C. Preparation for membership
D. Accurate membership rolls

III. Leadership of the congregation in reaching out (chapter 9)
A. In participation in mission of the whole church
in the world
B. In ministries of personal and social healing and
reconciliation within the particular community
C. In discovering God's activity in the world
and in planning for change, renewal, and
reformation under God's Word

IV. Ordering the life of the particular church
A. Providing for the worship of God's people (chapter 14)
See detailed chart on pages 186–187
B. Developing and supervising the edu- (chapters 6 and 8)
cational program

C. Challenging the people with the privilege   (chapter 11)
   of responsible stewardship of money, time,
   and talents

D. Establishing the annual budget and deter-   (chapter 11)
   mining the distribution of benevolences

E. Instructing, examining, ordaining,   (chapters 2 and 3)
   installing, and welcoming elders
   and deacons

F. Delegating and supervising the work   (chapters 6 and 11)
   of deacons, trustees, and all other
   church organizations

G. Providing for the administration of the   (chapter 8)
   church's program including employment (with
   concern for EEO) and compensation of staff

H. Providing for the management   (chapter 11)
   of the church's property

V.   A continuing responsibility for members   (chapter 6)
      and their growth and equipment for ministry

      A. Personal and pastoral care

      B. Educational programs including the Service
         for the Lord's Day and the church school

      C. Sharing in fellowship

      D. Sharing in mutual support

      E. Nurturing members through life's transitions

      F. Opportunities for witness and service in the world

      G. Correcting patterns of discrimination on the
         basis of race, sex, age, and disability

      H. Supporting inquirers and candidates
         for ministry of the Word and Sacrament
         and other professional service

      I. Reviewing with members their   (See also chapter 2)
         fulfillment of membership responsibilities

      J. Encouraging members who have moved
         away from the area to establish
         membership elsewhere

      K. Moving persons to the inactive roll

      L. Deleting persons from all rolls

VI.   A continuing responsibility for church officers   (chapter 6)

      A. Inquiring into the faithfulness of elders
         and deacons in fulfilling their responsibilities

      B. Engaging in a process for education and
         mutual growth of session members

VII.   Beyond the congregation—relationships with
other governing bodies, the community, and
the ecumenical church
     A. Electing or nominating persons to serve   (chapter 10)
       as members of presbytery, synod, and General
       Assembly in such a way as to implement
       principles of inclusiveness
     B. Observing and carrying out any   (chapter 10)
       constitutional instructions from higher
       governing bodies
     C. Welcoming representatives of presbytery   (chapter 10)
     D. Proposing overtures through presbytery   (chapter 10)
       to the synod or General Assembly
     E. Establishing and maintaining local   (chapter 9)
       ecumenical relationships necessary for
       the church's life and mission

VIII.   Serving in judicial matters in accordance   (chapter 13)
with the Rules of Discipline

IX.   Calling meetings of the congregation   (chapter 12)

In 1995 the Form of Government was amended to emphasize the session's responsibility for evangelism. The church through the amendment process chose to place a special emphasis upon the importance of a wholistic approach to evangelism by making the following provision the first in the long list of responsibilities and powers of the session [G-10.0102a]:

> to provide opportunities for evangelism to be learned and practiced in and by the church, that members may be better equipped to articulate their faith, to witness in word and deed to the saving grace of Jesus Christ, and to invite persons into a new life in Christ, in accordance with G-3.0300.

It is important to note the emphasis upon evangelism education in this provision. The session's responsibility is to equip church members to be evangelists and then to create opportunities for persons to practice what they learn and to encourage them to do so.

Gathering the Community of Faith

The second responsibility assigned to the session is to receive members into the church [G-10.0102b]. (This responsibility is assigned to presbytery when a church is being organized, but as soon as the church is constituted by presbytery and a session duly elected and installed, the responsibility becomes that of the session.)

The session receives persons into active church membership in three ways: "upon profession of faith, upon reaffirmation of faith in Jesus Christ, or upon satisfactory certification of transfer of church membership" [G-10.0102b]. This concise statement concerning the reception of members is augmented significantly in the earlier chapter of the *Book of Order* on "The Church and Its Members" [G-5.0000]. Here the understanding of church membership is based on God's incarnation in the life, death, and resurrection of Jesus Christ. "One becomes an active member of the church through faith in Jesus Christ as Savior and acceptance of his Lordship in all of life. Baptism and a public profession of faith in Jesus as Lord are the visible signs of entrance into the active membership of the church" [G-5.0101a].

This book's chapter "Calling to Office in the Church" (chapter 2) discusses the call of Christ to church membership and the responsibilities assumed by church members. Here our purpose is to look at those things sessions must understand in order to fulfill their role in building up the church through the reception of church members.

It is important for elders to understand that there are four categories of membership in the Presbyterian Church (U.S.A.). Thus far we have been talking about *active* members, those persons who present themselves for membership through profession of faith, reaffirmation of faith, or transfer of their membership from another congregation. An active member, by presenting herself or himself to the session to become a member of that particular church, voluntarily submits to the government of the Presbyterian Church (U.S.A.) and agrees to participate actively in the church's work and worship.

> An active member is entitled to all the rights and privileges of the church, including the right to participate in the Sacrament of the Lord's Supper, to present children for baptism, to take part in meetings of the congregation, and to vote and hold office. [G-5.0202]

The session, after careful study and discussion with the congregation, may set other conditions of active membership, but any such conditions must meet the needs of the particular church and must be consistent with the order and confessions of the Presbyterian Church (U.S.A.) [G-5.0202]. Perhaps a distinction should be made between *entering* and *maintaining* membership in a congregation. In G-5.0103 and G-10.0102b it is made clear that the reason for denying membership to any person must have to do with the profession of faith (or lack of such a profession). Membership is never to be denied to any person "because of race, economic or social circumstances, or any other reason not related to profession of faith" [G-10.0102b].

Those who do not maintain their active membership by responsible participation in the life of the church may be placed on the *inactive* roll by the session but only after the session has tried without success to help the member reestablish active involvement in the church's worship and ministry. By definition, "An inactive member of a particular church is one who does not participate in the church's work and worship. An inactive member is entitled to all the rights and privileges of an active member except the right to speak in the meetings of the congregation and to vote and hold office" [G-5.0203].

A third category of membership is the *affiliate* member. This person is an active member of another congregation of the Presbyterian Church (U.S.A.) or another denomination who is *temporarily* located away from the church of active membership and who desires to be affiliated with a church where active involvement is possible while maintaining membership in the home church. The session receives persons as affiliate members when they present a certificate of good standing from the session of a Presbyterian church or from the appropriate governing body of a church of another denomination. This membership must be renewed every two years [G-10.0302a(4)]. "An affiliate member is entitled to all the rights and privileges of an active member except the right to vote and hold office" [G-5.0204]. These rights would include the right to speak in meetings of the congregation.

The remaining category of membership is that of the baptized member:

> A baptized member of a particular church is a person who has received the Sacrament of Baptism and who has been enrolled as a baptized member by the session but who has not made a profession of faith in Jesus Christ as Lord and Savior. Such baptized members are entitled to the pastoral care and instruction of the church, and to participation in the Sacrament of the Lord's Supper. [G-5.0201]

Baptized members enter the church's membership as infants or children, brought by their believing parents or others "rightly exercising parental responsibility" who, reaffirming their own faith, claim the covenant promises of God on behalf of the child and promise "to provide nurture and guidance within the community of faith" [W-2.3014]. Baptized members become active members at the time that they make a profession of faith in Jesus Christ as Lord and Savior, thereby claiming for themselves the faith in which they were baptized. Those who do not make a profession of faith as adolescents or young adults remain baptized members of the church until such time as they do claim the faith of their baptism. (Baptized members may remain in that category of church membership throughout an entire lifetime. Baptized members are not placed on the inactive roll by the session. By definition, inactive members are those who were once active members and have ceased participating in the life of the church. Baptized members may be deleted from the roll by the session under certain circumstances that will be discussed later in this chapter.)

The session has the extremely important responsibility of preparing persons for entering the community of faith, that is, for becoming church members. This responsibility begins with preparation for baptism [W-6.2001]. If the person being baptized is an infant or young child, then the preparation should be done with the parent(s) or other responsible person(s) presenting the child for baptism. In addition to encouraging parents to present their children for baptism "without undue haste, but without undue delay" [W-2.3012a], sessions should remind parents of the meaning of baptism and its significance and counsel the parents or persons "rightly exercising parental responsibility" on their role in nurturing the child in the Christian life [W-2.3012b]. As the child grows, the session becomes responsible for nurturing the child "in understanding the meaning of Baptism, of the Lord's Supper, and of their interrelation" [W-2.3012e]. The session's responsibility becomes an ongoing one as the child develops and grows. The session particularly is charged with exercising the whole congregation's responsibility "to nurture those who are baptized to respond to the invitation to the Lord's Supper. . . . When the child begins to express a desire to receive this Sacrament, the session should take note of this and provide an occasion for recognition and welcome" [W-4.2002].

Especially emphasized in the Form of Government chapter on membership is the session's preparation of the children of the congregation to make their public profession of faith in Jesus Christ. "Instruction shall be given in the meaning of this profession, the responsibilities of membership, and the faith and order of the Presbyterian Church (U.S.A.)" [G-5.0402a]. As they prepare for active membership, the children of the church are preparing to participate in the worship, mission, governing, and decision-making life of the congregation. Those children who are not baptized in earlier years are also to be instructed in the meaning of the sacrament of baptism.

Instruction similar to that given to the children of the church when they make their profession of faith is also to be given to all persons who profess their faith and enter active membership. The Form of Government states that it is up to the session to determine whether the person should receive instruction before or after the public profession of faith [G-5.0402b].

The Form of Government also states that appropriate instruction is to be offered to those who join a particular congregation by reaffirming their faith or by transfer of certificate of membership [G-5.0403]. The implication is that sessions should seek ways to make the preparation for membership appropriate for the particular persons who come to unite with the church. A person long inactive in the church but now reaffirming faith in Jesus Christ and picking up once again the responsibilities of membership might well need to receive fairly extensive preparation—perhaps as much as the person professing faith for the first time. A person long an active church member but new to the Presbyterian family might be interested in some special learning opportunities about the Reformed tradition. A person who has been very active as an officer and member of a presbytery council in another part of the country might need to learn only about the mission emphasis of the new congregation and new presbytery.

When taken seriously, the overall responsibility of the session in the gathering of the community of faith is one that requires significant time and effort. The session is responsible for seeking out potential members, extending the invitation to membership to visitors and newcomers, encouraging parents to present their children for baptism, nurturing baptized members as they move toward professing their own faith, instructing those who come to faith and wish to profess it publicly for the first time, and providing a meaningful opportunity for them to make their profession before the congregation. The session is further responsible for preparing and counseling those who reaffirm their faith and those who come by transfer of their certificate of membership, giving an opportunity to both for renewing their commitment to Jesus Christ in a service of worship. Sessions are specifically charged with the responsibility of maintaining accurate rolls of the four categories of church members [G-10.0102r and G-10.0302a,b]. Only the session, through its clerk, has the right to place new names on the membership rolls or to remove, or delete, names from the rolls. The care that a session gives to its roll-keeping responsibilities shows that session's respect for the individual church members and its valuing of the call to church membership.

A Continuing Responsibility for Members

The session of every Presbyterian church has an ongoing responsibility for the church's members. The session is to extend personal and pastoral care [G-10.0102e]. At the least this would include becoming acquainted with the church's members (a task that has to be carefully organized in very large churches, recruiting other members, perhaps elders not actively serving on the session, to assist). In small and medium-sized congregations session members can visit church members in their homes, perhaps accompanying the pastor, but also extending the ministry of visitation beyond that which the pastor can do. An individual session member can assume special responsibility for becoming better acquainted with selected families, greeting them at church occasions and seeking a variety of opportunities to reach out in friendship, so that the elder can then be present in times of crisis and special need. Pastoral care can indeed be extended by persons in the church other than pastors—and to say this in no way diminishes the important role of the pastor for pastoral care of the congregation.

Christian Education. The "educational programs including the church school" are specifically mentioned as one of the ways that the session fulfills its responsibilities for the growth of the church's members and their equipment for ministry [G-10.0102e]. The session needs to be certain that the educational program is designed to enable the growth and equipment for ministry of all the church's members. The session must think about the various age groups that make up the church. It must not forget those persons who have disabilities, both mental and physical. The session should seek to provide educational opportunities for the growing number of single persons of all ages who are a part of the church family. Some churches focus attention on educational programs for families, a much-needed emphasis, but design the learning experiences in such a way that single persons or single-parent families feel excluded. Sessions that find that their church has very few persons in one particular age group need to look closely at the intergenerational learning materials that are now available. The fact that a church has only one or two elementary-school-age children does not relieve the session of the responsibility to provide some type of educational experience for the one or two.

The Directory for Worship highlights Christian nurture as a mutual ministry of church members to one another [W-6.1002–.1003]. Emphasis is placed on the nurture of members "through all of life and life's transitions." Specifically mentioned as occasions important for nurturing are the times of "entering the community of faith," "assuming responsibility in the world," "living out Christian vocation in public, active life," and continuing discipleship "in circumstances offering new limitations and new freedoms" [W-6.2001–.2004].

The Directory for Worship identifies the Service for the Lord's Day, "when the Word is proclaimed and the Sacraments are celebrated," as "the central occasion for nurture in the church" [W-6.2006]. The importance of this statement cannot be overemphasized. The old Directory for the Service of God (which was replaced by the Directory for Worship in 1988) states, "The church institutions created for nurture are primarily the church school and other classes and seminars for education."[1] It is an extremely important development for the *Book of Order* to move from an emphasis on the church school to the Service for the Lord's Day as being central to the educational or nurturing task of the church. Speaking of the Service for the Lord's Day, the Directory for Worship continues [W-6.2006]:

> All members of the community, from oldest to youngest, are encouraged to be present and to participate. Educational activities should not be scheduled which prevent regular participation in this service (W-3.1004).

The Directory for Worship does identify other occasions for nurture provided by the church. The "classes of the church school" and "other groups and fellowships organized for education and nurture" are among the occasions listed [W-6.2006a,b].

Fellowship and Service. The session is also charged with caring for members through "sharing in fellowship and mutual support, and opportunities for witness and service in the world" [G-10.0102e]. Yes, this responsibility, along with personal and pastoral care and the church's educational programs, can be seen in programmatic or organizational terms. Sessions can ask the questions: Is our church properly organized? Are there any weak links in our program? What program pieces do we need to add to have a better-balanced church life? The *Book of Order* pushes sessions to ask the questions from the point of view of helping members to grow and to be equipped for service. Without opportunities to be a part of a caring community and to give and receive support, church members do not develop as whole persons. Nor do they do so without finding opportunities for witness and service in the world beyond the caring community of the congregation. One ongoing focus of the life of every session should be thoughtful, prayerful concern for the wholeness of the individuals committed to the session's care. Sessions must pause in the midst of their task-oriented meetings and activities to raise questions about their care of persons.

Inclusiveness. Closely related to the concern for personal growth of members is the responsibility placed on the session, as on all other governing bodies, to fulfill the church's commitment to diversity and inclusiveness. As the session cares for the church's members it must constantly ask who has been excluded from "full participation and access to representation in the decision making of the church" [G-4.0403].

We have discussed the question of inclusiveness relationship to the election of church officers. What about other areas of the church's life? How accessible are the church buildings? Can a person in a wheelchair participate fully in the church's worship and program? Can persons who have difficulty walking move to all parts of the building? Is there the barrier of a flight of steps making access to worship difficult? Are persons with disabilities asked to serve on session committees and to teach in the educational program? Look over the membership lists of session committees. Are they inclusive of a wide variety of ages? Are the young people in the church asked to assume some responsibilities that contribute to the life of the whole church? Does the church find ways to use the tremendous gifts of time and talent that its retired members have to offer? Are persons of races other than the majority one really included in the life of the congregation? Do they have the opportunity to share the gifts they bring from their racial ethnic heritage? And are the gifts of the women in the congregation utilized to the fullest? Sessions need to ask these hard questions regularly, and to develop strategies for continuing progress in making the church more inclusive in its total life.

Candidates for Professional Service. Another responsibility of the session toward the church's members is that of supporting those who explore the possibility of becoming inquirers (and later candidates) for the ministry of the Word and Sacrament or for other professional service in the church. The main responsibility for inquirers and candidates is lodged in the presbytery. However, persons seeking to enter into a covenant relationship with presbytery as inquirers for the ministry of the Word and Sacrament "shall indicate to the session . . . a desire to explore the personal implications of becoming a minister" [G-14.0303a]. If, after consulting with the session, the person wishes to proceed, the session must then make a recommendation to presbytery concerning the applicant [G-14.0303d]. (The participation of the session is mentioned in the Form of Government only in relationship to candidates for the ministry of the Word and Sacrament. The entire inquiry and candidacy process for those preparing to serve as ministers is spelled out in some detail in G-14.0300 and G-14.0400. In G-11.0103q the presbytery is "to receive under its care persons preparing for professional service in the church, and to commission them when appropriate [G-14.0102]." It is reasonable to assume that the session should be involved in a way comparable to that prescribed when the person is preparing for ordination to the ministry of the Word and Sacrament, although this assumption is not explicitly stated.)

After the inquiry phase has been completed and the presbytery has determined that the inquirer should become a candidate, presbytery may provide that the actual service of reception into candidacy take place in the presence of the candidate's congregation, if presbytery is requested to do so by the inquirer and the session [G-14.0305h]. To conduct the service of reception within the candidate's church is another way of emphasizing the responsibility of the session and the congregation of membership to support the candidate through the time of preparation. The *Book of Order* [G-14.0306a(2)] makes clear the distinction between the roles of the session and the presbytery:

> During the phases of inquiry and candidacy the individual continues to be an active member of his or her particular church and subject to the concern and discipline of the session. In matters relating to preparation for the ministry, the individual is under the oversight of the presbytery, through the committee on preparation for ministry.

The session has the same responsibilities toward an inquirer or a candidate as toward any other church member. In addition, the session's "concern" includes providing support—both emotional and financial, if needed—for the person's preparation for ministry. The session is required to appoint an elder to serve as a liaison person with the inquirer or candidate and with the responsible committee of presbytery. The presbytery

must send to the sponsoring session a copy of the written report of the annual consultation [G-14.0309]. This procedure should ensure that the session remains informed about the candidate's progress.

Members Reviewing Their Membership Responsibilities. An additional responsibility entrusted to sessions is that of encouraging members regularly to review their fulfillment of the responsibilities of membership. Sessions need
to ask themselves how they will go about giving the required encouragement to members, so that members will themselves "regularly review and
evaluate the integrity with which they are involved in the ministry of the
church and consider ways in which their participation in the worship and
service of the church may be increased and made more meaningful" [G-
5.0501]. Perhaps at the same time that members are evaluating for themselves their fulfillment of the responsibilities entrusted to them as members,
the session might review how well it has fulfilled its responsibilities for the
growth and equipment for ministry of the church's members!

Inactive Members. The remaining responsibilities of sessions concerning
members have to do with those who either move away from the church's
community and must seek another church of membership or neglect the
responsibilities of membership. A part of maintaining the integrity of the
church's membership is to deal responsibly with persons who are no
longer active, for whatever reasons.

With regard to members who have moved so far away as to be unable to
participate actively in the work and worship of the church, the session's ongoing pastoral responsibility to these persons requires that it encourage them
to take up membership in another community of God's people. Persons who
have had an extremely meaningful relationship with a particular church
may wish to postpone the leave-taking and may feel that moving their membership promptly somehow suggests disloyalty to the church that has meant
so much. The session of the church from which one is moving can be a
tremendous help by pointing out in a caring way that establishing an active
involvement in a new congregation as quickly as possible is a way of witnessing to the centrality of the old congregation in a person's life experience.
The *Book of Order* requires the session to assist the member in the process of
finding a new church, not only by reminding a person of the importance of
seeking the new connection, but also by notifying a church in the new community and requesting it "to provide pastoral care with a view to membership." As a further step to assure that the member is contacted, the session is
required to notify the presbytery office and/or the stated clerk of the presbytery encompassing the person's new community [G-10.0302a(2)(c)].

With regard to those members who have become inactive without moving beyond the geographical area, the session is responsible for seeking them

out and for counseling with them about their neglected responsibilities [G-5.0502]. Of course, such counseling should seek to ascertain the reasons for a member's inactivity. Perhaps the session needs to hear of areas of the church's life that should be strengthened, of concern that should be extended, of criticisms that should be taken seriously. Only after the session "shall have made diligent effort to discover the cause of the member's non-participation and to restore the member to activity in the church's work and worship" may the session transfer a member to the inactive roll—and then only after "that member shall have failed intentionally to participate in the work and worship of the church for a period of one year." [G-10.0302a(3)(a)]. After the session has transferred the member to the inactive roll, the session is still responsible for providing pastoral care to that person. If a two-year period of extending pastoral care does not succeed in restoring the person to active membership, then the session may delete the person's name from the inactive roll without giving the person any further notice [G-10.0302b(7)].

Deleting Names from Rolls. There are other situations in which the session shall or may delete the names of persons from the various rolls of the church. When a member requests that her or his membership be transferred to another church, that person's name is deleted from the roll by the session, but not until notice is received that the member has actually been received into membership in the other church [G-10.0302b(1)]. Such precautions are taken to assure that the person's membership is not "lost," that the person is always a member of the church of Jesus Christ—unless that person really intends to give up church membership. The process of receiving members by transfer from one church to another is frequently simplified if the receiving church accepts someone into membership pending receipt of the certificate of transfer. Then the person has already been received when the transferring session receives notice of the request for transfer, and it can delete the person's name immediately. Whenever a session issues a certificate of transfer for parents of young children, the certificate shall include the names of the children and shall specify whether they have received the sacrament of baptism. When certificates are issued for elders and deacons they shall include the record of ordination [G-10.0102r].

Other situations that call for the deletion of members from the rolls of the church include the member's request that membership be terminated (which is granted only after the session makes a "diligent effort to persuade the member to retain membership"), the member's joining of another church without requesting transfer of membership, and the member's renouncing of the jurisdiction of the church [G-10.0302b(3) and (4)]. Also, when a nonresident member has been encouraged to join a church in the new community and has been placed on the inactive roll for at least a year, then that person's name may be deleted from the roll without further notice [G-10.0302b(5)]. When a member moves and the session is unable "after due and diligent search" to find out where the member has gone, the session may, after a one-year period, remove the person from membership [G-10.0302b(6)]. After the death of a member the date of death is recorded and the name deleted [G-10.0302b(8)]. Also, when a member is ordained as a minister of the Word and Sacrament and proper notice is received from the ordaining presbytery, the person's name shall be deleted from the roll after the ordination is recorded, along with the fact that the person has been transferred to the roll of a specific presbytery [G-14.0406].

Some readers may be puzzled by all this complexity surrounding transferring membership and deleting persons' names from various rolls. Remember that Presbyterians have a very high view of church membership. That valuing of membership leads us to be very careful as we transfer and terminate membership in particular churches. The Constitution also provides for what happens to members when a church is dissolved by presbytery. In that situation the presbytery assumes jurisdiction over the church's members until it grants them certificates of transfer to other churches [G-10.0302b(2)]. The person's membership is not "lost," but preserved in the presbytery. When presbytery dismisses a church to another denomination, presbytery may also assume jurisdiction over members desiring to remain members of the Presbyterian Church (U.S.A.) until they choose a congregation with which to unite.

A Continuing Responsibility for Church Officers

Along with the session's responsibility and power to "instruct, examine, ordain, install, and welcome into common ministry elders and deacons on their election by the congregation" is the power and responsibility to hold them accountable for fulfilling their obligations [G-10.0102l]. Elders and deacons, along with ministers of the Word and Sacrament, promise at the time of ordination (and again whenever installed for a new term of service) to fulfill their office in obedience to Jesus Christ and to "seek to serve the people with energy, intelligence, imagination, and love" [G-14.0207d and h]. When persons are not taking these commitments seriously, the session should "inquire into their faithfulness" [G-10.0102l]. Actually such inquiry is not limited to those who are being obviously negligent, for the session should encourage all elders and deacons to be more faithful in fulfilling their offices.

The session is also responsible for engaging in an educational process, presumably ongoing, so that the elders may grow both individually and corporately and so that the church may be better served [G-10.0102k]. The session is responsible for its own growth! There is a sense in which it can be claimed that if this responsibility is neglected, then many of the others assigned to the session will suffer. A stagnant session cannot lead a vital congregation.

The session is given the overall responsibility for the mission and government of the particular church. A major portion of this responsibility involves the gathering of the Christian community and the continuing growth and equipment for ministry of the church's members and officers. However, the session's responsibility does not stop here. The session is to lead the congregation in reaching out in ministry to the community and to the world. The responsibility for mission will not long be fulfilled if the responsibility for those who are the church is overlooked. The body of Christ must itself be nourished in order to serve.

Chapter Seven

MINISTERS SERVING CONGREGATIONS

A growing suburban church was exploring the possibility of calling its first associate pastor to assume a portion of the increasing responsibilities facing the pastor. Then the church suddenly found itself in a different situation. The pastor who had served so faithfully for the past eight years accepted a call to a church in another part of the country. During an initial meeting of the session with representatives of presbytery's committee on ministry, a member of the committee commented casually that the church's present needs might best be met by a clergy couple serving as co-pastors. The session members looked puzzled. Then the presbytery representative explained that the church now, in effect, had two vacancies at once. One option was the traditional one of calling first a pastor and then an associate. The other was the newer one of calling co-pastors with equal responsibility. At the congregational meeting to elect a pastor nominating committee, the task of the committee could be stated in such a way as to leave the committee free to seek the best pastoral leadership. The session members left that meeting with many new ideas.

The congregation of Dry Canyon Church had recently requested presbytery to dissolve the relationship between the congregation and its pastor of only two and one-half years. The pastor at first did not concur in the request, but after meeting with presbytery's committee on ministry, finally decided that the pastoral relationship was irreparably broken. Presbytery did dissolve the relationship. Several session members began talking immediately about electing a nominating committee to seek another pastor. After meeting with the committee on ministry, however, the majority of the members saw the wisdom in following presbytery's advice. Presbytery had suggested that it name a stated supply for the church, to serve for at least six months and probably a year before the church even thought about seeking a pastor. Perhaps Dry Canyon Church even then should not think about calling another pastor fulltime. Other possibilities should be considered. For now one thing was clear:

Members of Dry Canyon Church needed some more time to re-think the church's mission and to heal the wounds caused by their difficult experience with their previous pastor. All agreed that the church would benefit from the leadership of a stated supply.

Why do churches call pastors? A church, led by its session, can be a healthy Christian community without a pastor. And yet the *Book of Order* clearly states: "Every church should have the pastoral services of a minister of the Word and Sacrament" [G-14.0501a]. Presbyterians have long emphasized the importance of highly educated ministers. Certain responsibilities in the life of the congregation are assigned to the pastor alone. Others are the responsibility of the session, of which the pastor is a member and the moderator. Still others are assigned to the pastor in conjunction with the board of deacons, of which the pastor is an advisory member. It is extremely important to consider the role of the pastor in the overall life of the particular church, but first it is necessary to take a closer look at the office of minister of the Word and Sacrament as set forth in the *Book of Order*.

The Office of Minister of the Word and Sacrament

As the Lord has set aside through calling and training certain members to perform a special ministry of the Word and Sacrament and has committed to them a variety of work to do, the church through the presbytery calls them to the responsibility and office of ministers of the Word and Sacrament. Such ministers shall be members of presbytery which shall designate them to such work as may be helpful to the church in mission, in the performance of which they shall be accountable to the presbytery. They shall be responsible for participation in the larger ministry of the church in addition to the duties to which they are called and designated by the presbytery. [G-6.0201]

This section emphasizes the role of presbytery as the governing body that has jurisdiction over ministers. "The church through the presbytery" calls persons to this special form of ministry and "designates" or approves their involvement in any specific work. The work appropriate for ministers is to be work that is "helpful to the church in mission." Serving in a pastoral relationship to a particular church is only one of many specific tasks ministers perform that advance the church's witness and mission. Other forms of service mentioned in the *Book of Order* are the responsibilities of "educators, chaplains, pastoral counselors, campus ministers, missionaries, partners in mission, evangelists, administrators, social workers, [and] consultants" [G-6.0203]. Presbyteries, by approving any particular work, may add to the list of appropriate tasks for the involvement of ministers of the Word and Sacrament.

All ministers hold membership in a presbytery, never in a congregation. All ministers are accountable to their presbytery. They may also be accountable to a variety of other persons or groups, both within the church and beyond the church. For example, a hospital chaplain is accountable to the hospital for which he or she works, as well as to the presbytery. A General Assembly Council staff member is accountable to the GAC, the General Assembly, and the presbytery of membership.

In addition to the specific work to which they are called, all ministers of the Word and Sacrament have some responsibility for participating in the larger ministry of the church. For ministers serving congregations this responsibility involves them in the overall work and mission of presbytery and, at certain times, in the ministry of synod and General Assembly. Ecumenical involvement is also included [G-6.0202a]. Sessions and congregations need to understand that the pastor has this responsibility to wider governing bodies and to the ecumenical church and to encourage the pastor to be active in this work. Of course it is possible for a pastor to become overinvolved in the work and mission of presbytery, synod, General Assembly, and ecumenical associations to the neglect of the congregation to which the pastor has primary responsibility. Pastor and session together should discuss the appropriate amount of time and energy that the pastor will expend in service to the larger church. For ministers serving presbytery, synod, or the General Assembly, and those in other specialized ministries, participation in the larger ministry of the church includes involvement not only in the work of other governing bodies but also in the life of a particular congregation. Many of these ministers assume significant responsibility in the congregation in which their family holds membership.

Continuing Members of Presbytery

All ministers are continuing members of a presbytery, but their category of membership in that presbytery may differ. They may be active members, members-at-large, or inactive members [G-11.0406]. In order to be an active member of a presbytery a minister must be involved in a work that meets "written criteria developed by the presbytery for validation of ministers within its bounds" [G-11.0403 as amended in 1998]. Standards to be used by presbyteries in developing their particular criteria include G-6.0100, G-6.0200, and the following five criteria from G-11.0403:

a. The ministry of continuing members shall be in demonstrable conformity with the mission of God's people in the world as set forth in Holy Scripture, *The Book of Confessions,* and the *Book of Order* of this church.

b. The ministry shall be one that serves others, aids others, and enables the ministries of others.

    c.   The ministry shall give evidence of theologically informed fidelity to God's Word. This will normally require the Master of Divinity degree or its equivalent and the completion of the requirements for ordination set forth in G-14.0402.

    d.   The ministry shall be carried on in accountability for its character and conduct to the presbytery and to organizations, agencies, and institutions.

    e.   The ministry shall include responsible participation in the deliberations and work of the presbytery and in the worship and service of a congregation.

Ministries that fulfill the criteria established by the presbytery are known as "validated" ministries. Validated ministries may be in any of four different settings: (1) within congregations of this church, (2) in other service of this church, (3) in service beyond the jurisdiction of this church, or (4) honorably retired [G-11.0408]. Because of its scope and purpose, this book will focus its attention upon those validated ministries that are "within congregations of this church."

Active members of a presbytery have the right to take part in its meetings and to speak, vote, and hold office [G-11.0406a]. These same rights are also extended to members-at-large. A *member-at-large* is defined as "a minister of the Word and Sacrament who has previously been admitted to the presbytery or another presbytery as an active member, and who now, without intentional abandonment of the exercise of ministry, is no longer engaged in a ministry that complies with all the criteria in G-11.0403" [G-11.0406b]. The important phrase here is "without intentional abandonment of the exercise of ministry." The intent of this provision is to allow those ministers who, for a wide variety of reasons, are between calls to a specific service to maintain their involvement in presbytery. The fulfillment of family responsibilities is specifically cited as one reason for member-at-large status. Even though they are not engaged in a work that meets all the criteria for a validated ministry, members-at-large retain all the rights of active members within the presbytery. Many members-at-large have even more time for service on presbytery committees and in presbytery mission endeavors than those who are active members. By applying to presbytery and then renewing that request annually, a minister without a call may continue to contribute a great deal to the life of the presbytery. The member-at-large is instructed to comply with as many of the five criteria for validated ministries as possible and is encouraged to become a parish associate in a congregation.

An *inactive member* of presbytery is one who "is now voluntarily engaged in an occupation that does not comply with all of the criteria in G-11.0403." A minister who is no longer actively seeking a ministry that does meet the criteria may be placed in the inactive category through the initiative of the minister or of the presbytery. Inactive members do not have the right to take part in presbytery meetings or to speak, vote, hold office, or serve on committees, except that the inactive member may speak when presbytery is considering a matter concerning him or her [G-11.0406c].

Pastoral Relations with Congregations

A minister of the Word and Sacrament can serve a congregation in a variety of pastoral relations. The permanent pastoral relations are pastor, co-pastor, and associate pastor [G-14.0501]. There is now a category of designated pastoral relationships that includes pastor and co-pastor [G-14.0501]. The temporary pastoral relations are interim pastor, interim co-pastor, interim associate pastor, stated supply, temporary supply, and organizing pastor [G-14.0513]. Ministers who are honorably retired, who are members-at-large of presbytery, or serving in a specialized ministry outside of a congregation may serve a particular church as a "parish associate" on a limited basis.

Permanent Pastoral Relationships

Pastors, co-pastors, and associate pastors are elected by the vote of the congregation with the presbytery actually establishing the relationship between the minister and the congregation [G-14.0501]. The process of calling the pastor by the congregation and the presbytery's role in examining the minister (if the minister comes from another presbytery), approving the call, and installing the minister are discussed in chapters 2 and 3 of this book. The installed pastor of a church is expected to fulfill all the functions of a pastor to that congregation unless there is an associate pastor or a parish associate who assumes certain of the pastoral responsibilities.

"Co-pastors are ministers who are called and installed with equal responsibility for pastoral ministry" [G-14.0501c]. Each is considered a pastor of the church. The way they share their responsibilities within the church must be agreed on with the session and must be approved by the presbytery. Co-pastors alternate in moderating the session, assuming both are present. If one is absent, then the other presides. As the session ordinarily shall not meet without the pastor present, by implication the *Book of Order* suggests that the session is not to meet without at least one of the co-pastors present [G-10.0103a]. Ordinarily the session is not permitted deliberately to exclude any co-pastor from its meeting. When two pastors serve together as co-pastors and one of them leaves the position, the other remains as pastor of the church [G-14.0501c].

The call to an associate pastor must specify the particular function which that minister is to fulfill [G-14.0501f]. The associate pastor is to be directed in the assigned functions by the pastor in consultation with the church's session. Significant changes in the functions of an associate pastor become changes in the terms of call and must be approved by the presbytery. The changes must also be approved by the congregation, a participant in the calling process.

Dissolving Permanent Pastoral Relationships

Since presbytery actually establishes the relationship between any installed pastor and the congregation, presbytery must dissolve that relationship [G-14.0601]. The initiative for dissolving the pastoral relationship may come from the minister or from the congregation. If the minister initiates the request, then the congregation is asked to concur. When a congregation initiates the request, then concurrence is sought from the minister. When minister and congregation concur in requesting that the relationship be dissolved, then the presbytery itself may dissolve the relationship or may delegate that responsibility to the committee on ministry or to presbytery's council. When the minister and congregation are not in concurrence, the presbytery shall hear the nonconcurring party. After that hearing, presbytery must make its decision, taking into account the total situation. When a presbytery finds that "the church's mission under the Word imperatively demands it," the presbytery may take the initiative to dissolve the pastoral relationship [G-11.0103o]. This may be done through the committee on ministry as provided in G-11.0502j or by an administrative commission when presbytery has given it the specific power of dissolving the pastoral relationship [G-9.0503a(3)].

Designated Pastoral Relationships

Designated pastoral relationships are an in-between category of relationships between a minister of the Word and Sacrament and a congregation. They are not permanent ones in that they are for a limited term of between two and four years. However, designated relationships are technically not temporary ones, since by definition a temporary pastoral relationship involves neither a formal call issued by a congregation nor a formal installation [G-14.0513]. It is helpful to quote a portion of the constitutional provision [G-14.0501g]:

> A designated pastor or co-pastor(s) is a minister of the Word and Sacrament approved by the committee on ministry to be elected for a term of not less than two nor more than four years by the vote of the congregation. The relationship shall be established by the presbytery. The only designated pastoral relationships are pastor and co-pastor. Such a pastor or co-pastor(s) shall be nominated by the congregation's pastor nominating committee only from among those designated by the committee on ministry of the presbytery. The con-

gregation and the minister both must volunteer to be considered for a designated term relationship. Such a call may be established only with the prior concurrence of the committee on ministry of the presbytery. The terms of the call shall be approved by the presbytery. The minister shall be installed by the presbytery. When the minister is pastor, he or she shall be moderator of the session. The sections on calling and installing a pastor shall apply. (G-14.0502–.0507) (See G-14.0501a.)

Since the relationship of designated pastor became constitutional in 1988, some congregations and presbyteries have found it helpful as a method of providing pastoral service to congregations without the delay of a sometimes lengthy search process to secure a permanent pastor. Also, use of the designated pastor relationship has freed up congregations to "try out" a pastoral relationship for a significant period of time to see if it is a "fit." A designated pastor may be called as the permanent pastor of the church, just as a stated supply may be. In fact, a frequent hope in establishing the relationship of designated pastor is that the relationship will work out so well that the congregation will want to make it permanent.

Temporary Pastoral Relationships

When a church finds itself without a pastor, it is the responsibility of the session and the presbytery to secure pastoral leadership for the congregation. If the congregation that loses its pastor has an associate pastor, the associate may be asked to assume some or all of the responsibilities of the pastor. Another option is for the associate pastor to continue in his or her assigned functions and to ask an interim pastor to assume the functions that were being fulfilled by the pastor until the church is ready to call a new pastor. When a temporary pastoral relationship is established, no formal call is issued, and there is no formal installation [G-14.0513].

By definition an *interim pastor* is "a minister invited by the session of a church without an installed pastor to preach the Word, administer the Sacraments, and fulfill pastoral duties for a specified period not to exceed twelve months at a time, while the church is seeking a pastor" [G-14.0513b]. Before securing an interim pastor the session must obtain the concurrence of the presbytery through the committee on ministry. A minister serving as interim pastor for a congregation that is seeking to fill the position on a permanent basis is not permitted to receive the permanent call as the next installed pastor. The reason for this prohibition is to protect the congregation's freedom to choose its own officers, specifically its pastors. Without such a provision, any congregation that was extremely pleased with the ministry of an interim pastor could place the pastor nominating committee under considerable pressure to call that person to the permanent position. It is the view of the PC (USA) that preserving the pastor nominating committee's right to conduct a thorough and open search outweighs the benefits of permitting an interim pastor to become pastor.

In 1988 a new section was added to the Form of Government creating the temporary pastoral relationship of *interim associate pastor* [G-14.0513c], and in 1994 the *interim co-pastor* was added [G-14.0513b]. The provisions for both relationships closely parallel those for an interim pastor. The invitation to serve is extended by the session after it receives the concurrence of presbytery through its committee on ministry. The service is for a specified period, which may not exceed twelve months, unless extended by the session (in consultation with the presbytery). An interim co-pastor or interim associate pastor may not be called to be the next installed pastor, co-pastor, or associate pastor of a church that he or she has served as interim associate pastor.

If the church is not seeking a pastor, then the church may be served by a *stated supply*. This temporary relationship is described in G-14.0513a:

> A stated supply is a minister appointed by the presbytery, after consultation with the session, to perform the functions of a pastor in a church which is not seeking an installed pastor. The relation shall be established only by the presbytery and shall extend for a period not to exceed twelve months at a time. A stated supply shall not be reappointed until the presbytery, through its committee on ministry, has reviewed her or his effectiveness. A stated supply who is a member of the presbytery may, with presbytery's approval, serve as moderator of the session.

Some churches are served by the same stated supply for many years. It becomes very difficult to see any difference between the stated supply and an installed pastor. In many small churches stated supplies serve parttime, some only leading worship and conducting weddings and funerals as needed. The difference in amount of time spent used to be the noticeable distinction between installed pastors and stated supplies. In recent years, however, more and more small churches have installed pastors who serve on a parttime basis. The real difference is the way the minister enters into the relationship with the church. The installed pastor is called by the congregation through a pastor nominating committee. The stated supply is appointed by the presbytery. After reviewing the stated supply's performance over the preceding year, presbytery may choose not to reappoint him or her. Presbytery can appoint the minister to serve for only one year at a time, because only the congregation has the power to elect its own officers for an extended period of time.

The *Book of Order* does not place any restriction on a stated supply's becoming the elected permanent pastor of a church. Working closely with presbytery, a congregation that has had a good experience under the leadership of a stated supply pastor could decide that it was now possible to call a permanent pastor, perhaps on a very limited and parttime basis. The congregation could elect a pastor nominating committee with the clear expectation that the person serving as stated supply would be one person considered by the committee. It would be extremely important that the committee be open to consider other persons who might be interested in the position, in order that the PC(USA)'s commitment to inclusiveness in employment might be fulfilled [G-13.0201b].

Another temporary pastoral relationship is that of *temporary supply*. It is described in G-14.0513d:

> A temporary supply may be a minister, a candidate, a commissioned lay pastor, or an elder secured by the session to conduct services when there is no pastor or the pastor is unable to perform pastoral duties. The session shall seek the counsel of presbytery through its committee on ministry before securing a temporary supply.

Before securing a person for any pastoral services more extensive than preaching one or two Sundays, the session must be in conversation with its presbytery. Section G-14.0513e suggests that, with the approval of presbytery's committee on ministry, the session may secure the services of an inquirer or candidate as a temporary supply. To serve in this way may enable the inquirer or candidate to gain much-needed experience in pastoral ministry. However, it may be necessary to involve two presbyteries in the decision-making process. The presbytery in which the church is located must give assurance that the inquirer or candidate will receive "appropriate guidance and supervision." The presbytery responsible for the inquirer or candidate must give its approval of the temporary supply relationship [G-14.0513e].

It is important to note that a temporary supply may be called as pastor or associate pastor of a church served as temporary supply, but not "unless six months have elapsed since the end of the temporary supply relationship" [G-14.0513d].

Other Patterns of Leadership

The *Book of Order* includes provisions for additional ways that pastoral leadership may be provided in congregations. A new temporary relationship was added in 1992 that enables a new church development to be served by an *organizing pastor* [G-14.0513f]. This relationship is established by presbytery appointment. An organizing pastor is to be called according to the procedural principles set forth in G-9.0702 and G-9.0704 and the foundational principle of diversity and inclusiveness of G-4.0403. The organizing pastor may be designated as a member of presbytery's administrative staff. When the new church is formally organized by presbytery, the congregation has the option, with the approval of the committee on ministry and the presbytery, of calling the organizing pastor to be its installed pastor without electing a pastoral nominating committee and conducting a search. The congregation's other option is to go through the entire process of searching for a pastor. Thus, the congregation's freedom to choose its own pastor is preserved.

Another way for a minister of the Word and Sacrament to serve a congregation is as a *parish associate*. This option is available under certain carefully described circumstances. A partial description is as follows:

> A parish associate is a minister who serves in some validated ministry other than the local parish, or is a member-at-large, or is retired, but who wishes to maintain a relationship with a particular church or churches in keeping with ordination to the ministry of the Word and Sacrament. [G-14.0515]

The key to understanding the parish associate is the recognition that this minister must be honorably retired, must have been designated by presbytery as a member-at-large, or must already be serving in a validated ministry, one that does not involve a pastoral relationship with any congregation. The relationship of parish associate provides a way for retired or specialized ministers or ministers currently unable to serve in a validated ministry to enrich the life and mission of a congregation by using their pastoral skills. The pastor nominates the prospective parish associate to the session and the presbytery, both of which must approve the relationship. A formal call is not issued. The parish associate may serve with or without remuneration. The parish associate is responsible to the pastor. The designation as a parish associate is reviewed annually by presbytery's committee on ministry (1) to assure that the parish associate is not expending so much time and energy in that relationship as to interfere with the effective fulfillment of the specialized ministry that is the minister's main responsibility, (2) to assure that the work of the parish associate does not interfere with the effective functioning of the installed pastoral staff of the church, and (3) to ascertain that the specialized ministry of the parish associate continues to meet the criteria of a validated ministry (unless the parish associate is a member-at-large). "Ordinarily no more than one parish associate will be related to a particular church" [G-14.0515]. A 1997 *Book of Order* amendment provides that a parish associate may not be called to serve as pastor or associate pastor of the church until at least six months after the parish associate relationship has ended [G-14.0515a].

The remaining pattern of pastoral leadership for congregations is a new one that assigns functions previously reserved to ministers of the Word and

Sacrament to elders commissioned by the presbytery. Prior to 1996 some congregations were served by commissioned lay preachers who led worship and preached on a regular basis. Presbytery could authorize the commissioned lay preacher to administer the Lord's Supper. In 1996 the name of this relationship was changed to *commissioned lay pastor*, acknowledging that some of these persons were performing broader pastoral duties. In 1997 the door was opened for commissioned lay pastors to assume significant additional responsibilities [G-14.0801c]. Presbyteries may authorize a commissioned lay pastor to administer the Sacrament of Baptism and to moderate the session when the moderator appointed by the presbytery invites the lay pastor to do so and provides supervision. The lay pastor may be authorized to perform a marriage service when invited by the session and permitted by state law. Presbytery may give the commissioned lay pastor voice in presbytery or go a step further and grant both voice and vote. When a vote is given, it is counted in the elder commissioner category for the purposes of determining parity between elders and ministers.

The commissioned lay pastor works under presbytery's supervision through the committee on ministry or through the moderator of the session of the church being served. A minister of Word and Sacrament is to be assigned as a mentor and supervisor to each commissioned lay pastor [G-14.0801d]. Presbytery may grant the commission to a lay pastor for up to three years and may renew or terminate it at any time [G-14.0801b]. Presbytery is required to review the lay pastor's work annually.

Lay pastors receive training approved by the presbytery in the areas of Bible, Reformed theology and the Sacraments, polity, preaching and worship, pastoral care, and teaching. They then are examined by the appropriate presbytery committee in these areas and as to their personal faith and motives for seeking the commission. When presbytery is satisfied with the applicant's qualifications, he or she is asked questions patterned after the questions asked of church officers. A final question concerns acceptance of the responsibilities of the lay pastor. Presbytery then commissions the lay pastor with prayer and a declaration of the new relationship.

The definitional statement of the commissioned lay pastor relationship becomes a good summary of its significance and potential [G-14.0801a]:

> The commissioned lay pastor is an elder of the Presbyterian Church (U.S.A.), who is granted a local commission by the presbytery to lead worship and preach the gospel, watch over the people, and provide for their nurture and service. The commission is valid only in one or more congregations designated by the presbytery.

Through this wide variety of pastoral relationships between a minister of the Word and Sacrament and a congregation and, in some cases between an inquirer, a candidate, an elder, or a commissioned lay pastor and a congregation, the Presbyterian Church (U.S.A.) seeks to assure that every church has leadership with at least some degree of training to preach the Word, lead worship, and give pastoral care.

The Distinctive Role of the Pastor

There are certain responsibilities that are so much a part of the work of the pastor as to be essential for all ministers of the Word and Sacrament who serve congregations, unless another minister is also serving the same congregation and assuming some of these functions in their entirety. When we speak of the pastor in this section, we will not be distinguishing between the types of pastoral relationships. The word "pastor" is used to refer to the entire pastoral role—those functions that Presbyterian polity assigns to ministers of the Word and Sacrament who serve particular congregations in any pastoral capacity, temporary, designated, or permanent.

The foundational passage of the Form of Government referring to the pastoral role is G-6.0202a, a critically important passage in the *Book of Order*. It describes the pastoral task as follows:

> [S]he or he is to be responsible for a quality of life and relationships that commend the gospel to all persons and that communicate its joy and its justice. The pastor is responsible for studying, teaching, and preaching the Word, for administering Baptism and the Lord's Supper, for praying with and for the congregation.

The passage continues to describe other responsibilities of the pastor within the congregation, but they are responsibilities that the pastor *shares* with the elders or deacons. Only those responsibilities quoted above are singled out as the particular responsibility of pastors.

According to G-6.0202a, the pastor's task of communicating the gospel cannot be separated from living it. The daily life of the pastor matters. The quality of the pastor's life and the interpersonal relationships that the pastor develops must themselves witness to the gospel and its power to bring joy and establish justice. The relationships that the pastor establishes with members of the church are foundational for any long-term, significant communication. When the pastor lives the gospel and establishes significant relationships, then the pastor's preaching and teaching can be heard.

The pastor is the primary person responsible for studying, preaching, and teaching the Word within the congregation. It is to this task that the minister is ordained and from which the office receives its name. Ministers of the Word and Sacrament are not the only persons within the church who can and should study, preach, and teach the Word, but they are uniquely equipped through years of theological education. Congregational expectations should allow the pastor adequate time for preparation for preaching and teaching. The pastor who brings fresh insights into preaching and teaching must engage in disciplined study.

All church officers should have a basic understanding of the Reformed doctrine of Baptism and the Lord's Supper. One source in our Constitution is the Directory for Worship. The *Book of Confessions* is a much more thorough theological and historical resource. When newly elected elders and deacons are examined by the session after a period of study, they are asked about their knowledge of Presbyterian doctrine. The sacraments should surely be one of the subjects studied and examined. Ministers of the Word and Sacrament study the doctrine of the sacraments in their seminary courses and must pass a written examination for ordination on worship and the sacraments in order to be ordained [G-14.0310d(4)].

Normally only ministers of the Word and Sacrament administer the sacraments. However, the *Book of Order* enables presbyteries to authorize certain elders to administer the Lord's Supper when a minister is not available [see G-11.0103k,z]. In addition, commissioned lay pastors may be granted the authority to administer baptism as well as the Lord's Supper [G-14.0801c(1) and (2)].

The final pastoral task mentioned in that foundational section on pastors [G-6.0202a] is that of "praying with and for the congregation." The Directory for Worship includes "the prayers offered on behalf of the people and those prepared for the use of the people in worship" among the pastor's responsibilities that are not subject to the authority of the session [W-1.4005a(3)].

The above-quoted passage describes the pastor's praying *with* the congregation in public worship. However, it should be emphasized that G-6.0202a also places on the pastor the responsibility of praying *for* the congregation. It can be a source of great strength to a congregation and to individual members to know that their pastor regularly prays for them. The congregation and the session need to recognize the importance of the minister's setting aside time for the ongoing development of his or her own spiritual life.

Ministers of the Word and Sacrament are officers of the church set aside through calling and training to perform special functions in the life of the church. These functions center around proclaiming the Word through preaching and the sacraments. Ministers are members of presbytery, designated by the presbytery to a particular work. Ministers serve congregations in a variety of pastoral relationships, some permanent and some temporary. However, all of these pastoral relationships have a great deal in common, for the essential tasks of the pastor should be fulfilled in every congregation. The pastor, by the quality of his or her life and by the relationships formed with the congregation, is to communicate the gospel, its joy and its justice, through studying, teaching, and preaching the Word, through administering the sacraments, and through praying with and for the people.

Chapter Eight

OFFICERS
AND STAFF
WORKING TOGETHER

A new pastor had been at Flat Prairie Presbyterian Church for a few months when members of the session began hearing complaints from some of the church members that the pastor frequently used translations of the Bible different from the pew Bible. Previous pastors had never used any other version. The elders discussed the situation among themselves. One pointed out that the session had no right to instruct the pastor in such matters. The pastor spent three years in seminary studying the Bible, even learning both Hebrew and Greek. The pastor was clearly the best qualified person to determine which translation of a given Scripture passage was most helpful for use in the congregation's worship. Another elder suggested that the elders should inform the pastor of the dissatisfaction that was beginning to develop. Then the pastor could seek the best ways to alleviate the situation, perhaps conferring with the session.

The secretary of Winding Creek Presbyterian Church was visiting a friend. They were discussing problems related to their jobs. The church secretary, not a member of the Presbyterian Church, commented, "If I only understood what things other staff members were responsible for it would make my job so much easier. And it would help to know when certain things have to be completed. I do pretty well keeping up with my work, but sometimes I don't understand the big picture. I feel that we have two pastors, a director of education, and a music director all running around frantically doing a variety of things, but I can't figure out who does what, and I'm not sure they know!"

How can church officers best work together for the well-being of the church they serve? How can the officers work with any staff that the session may have employed in addition to the pastor? The roles of the different officers are distinct and yet interlocking. How can the church's officers best work together, and with all employed staff, for the building up of the church?

Pastors and Elders Working Together

The Form of Government, after outlining the special functions of the pastor, continues [G-6.0202a]:

> With the elders, the pastor is to encourage the people in the worship and service of God; to equip and enable them for their tasks within the church and their mission in the world; to exercise pastoral care, devoting special attention to the poor, the sick, the troubled, and the dying; to participate in governing responsibilities, including leadership of the congregation in implementing the principles of participation and inclusiveness in the decision making of the church, and its task of reaching out in concern and service to the life of the human community as a whole.

The list of responsibilities the pastor shares with the elders is longer than the list that is assigned to the pastor alone. Before we discuss these shared responsibilities, it is helpful to compare the basic statement in G-6.0304 on the responsibilities of the office of elder:

> It is the duty of elders, individually and jointly, to strengthen and nurture the faith and life of the congregation committed to their charge. Together with the pastor, they should encourage the people in the worship and service of God, equip and renew them for their task within the church and for their mission in the world, visit and comfort and care for the people, with special attention to the poor, the sick, the lonely, and those who are oppressed. They should inform the pastor and session of those persons and structures which may need special attention. They should assist in worship. . . . They should cultivate their ability to teach the Bible and may be authorized to supply places which are without the regular ministry of the Word and Sacrament. . . . Those duties which all Christians are bound to perform by the law of love are especially incumbent upon elders because of their calling to office and are to be fulfilled by them as official responsibilities.

A reading of the two passages quoted above can lead to only one conclusion: It is the intent of Presbyterian polity that pastors and elders work *together*. When communication breaks down between elders and pastor and when they do not support and supplement each other in their work of ministry, then something is seriously wrong within the life of the congregation. Open communication and mutual respect are the keys to effective service. Pastors and elders must be able to share not only ideas but also feelings with one another, both in one-to-one conversations and in meetings of the session. The statement that elders "should inform the pastor and session of those persons and structures which may need special attention" is a clear call to open communication between pastor and elders.

Both passages quoted above charge pastors and elders together with encouraging the people in the worship and service of God. "Encourage" is a very positive verb. It contains the ideas of motivating, lifting up, challenging, inspiring. The word "encourage" suggests much more than simply telling people to do something or admonishing them for not doing it. To encourage is to enable the people to "lift [their] drooping hands and strengthen [their] weak knees" (Heb. 12:12) so that they may indeed worship and serve their God.

Joint Responsibilities for Worship

Pastor and session working together have very specific responsibilities in the area of worship, according to both the Form of Government and the Directory for Worship. The session is assigned the responsibility and the power in G-10.0102d: "To provide for the worship of the people of God, including the preaching of the Word and the sharing of the Sacraments, and for the music program, in keeping with the principles in the Directory for Worship." The overall responsibility of making certain that a well-ordered opportunity for worship is available to the congregation lies with the whole session, including, of course, the pastor, who is a member of that session. If there is no pastor, then the session must make provision for a regular worship opportunity, including Word and Sacrament, working closely with the presbytery to assure the best leadership possible. A 1998 addition to the basic passage on the elder lifts up the responsibility of elders to assist in the worship service itself and cites several sections of the Directory for Worship that specifically mention the participation of elders in various aspects of the congregation's worship, including the Sacraments of Baptism and the Lord's Supper and the service of ordination.

The pastor has the particular responsibility for the selection of Scripture, the sermon topic, the prayers, the selection of music, the use of art forms, and the administration of the sacraments. However, arranging for the congregation's worship life is too important a responsibility to be left to any one individual. It is a corporate responsibility of the church's session. The specific worship-related responsibilities of the session according to the Directory for Worship include general oversight and approval of public worship; determining occasions, times, and places of worship; supervising the music program; authorizing the baptism of children; instructing those believers being baptized as to the significance of the sacrament and of their profession of faith; determining when the sacrament of the Lord's Supper will be celebrated; deciding when to receive offerings for special purposes; and designating times in addition to Sunday for corporate worship.

Joint Responsibilities for Congregational Care

Returning to G-6.0202a and G-6.0304, we are reminded that the pastor, with the elders, is assigned the responsibility "to exercise pastoral care, devoting special attention to the poor, the sick, the troubled, and the dying." Elders, together with the pastor, are to "visit and comfort and care for the people, with special attention to the poor, the sick, the lonely, and those who are oppressed." The responsibility of the session for the continuing care for the congregation is discussed at length in chapter 5 of this book. Here the important point to emphasize is the *corporate nature* of caring for God's people. The responsibility is assigned to elders as well as to pastors. Elders are to perform individual acts of caring for the people of the congregation, giving special attention to those with special needs. It is the joining together of many individual acts of care that emphasizes the church as the body of Christ. The pastor has received special training that should enable him or her to be of particular help in many difficult situations, but this expertise in no way takes the place of the ongoing care provided by the church's elders, deacons, and other members.

Joint Responsibilities for Governance

One of the basic responsibilities of ministers serving as pastors is to participate in governing responsibilities, along with the elders [G-6.0202a]. The Constitutions of both predecessor denominations made the same point, using the terminology "to exercise the joint power of government" with the elders. The current *Book of Order*, however, adds a very important phrase to the original idea. The responsibility of the pastor becomes "with the elders . . . to participate in governing responsibilities, including leadership of the congregation in implementing the principles of participation and inclusiveness in the decision making of the church." The PC(USA) *Book of Order* places on all its pastors the responsibility of assuming a leadership role in helping their congregations act on the principles of participation and inclusiveness, so basic to this *Book of Order*. Pastors can no longer claim that they should not be involved in this aspect of the church's life. Pastors and elders together are to take the initiative in helping congregations to understand the commitment of the Presbyterian Church (U.S.A.) to include all groups of its members in the church's decision-making processes. This new responsibility includes the breaking down of many types of barriers: the idea that women should not be ordained to office; the overlooking of some age groups, especially youth and older adults; the racism that prevents the church from utilizing the talents of its racial ethnic members; and the failure to recognize the gifts of persons with disabilities. Pastors are called on to lead their people to new understandings, new recognitions of the worth of all God's people, and new actions of inclusiveness.

Pastors, Deacons, and Elders Working Together

"With the deacons the pastor is to share in the ministries of sympathy, witness, and service" [G-6.0202a]. When the deacons are organized into a board, the pastor is an advisory member of that board (as are co-pastors and associate pastors). The board of deacons elects its own moderator and secretary. Pastors are to use their theological and pastoral expertise in advising the board about its particular responsibilities for ministering to persons in need or distress. They are also to become directly involved in the ministries of compassion, sharing with the deacons in meeting human need.

As pastors are assigned responsibility for working with the board of deacons, so is the rest of the session. The board of deacons, like all other organizations within the church, operates under the jurisdiction of the session. The board of deacons is not a governing body. Like other church organizations, the board of deacons submits its records to the session, which can void or amend any of the board's actions or direct it to reconsider any decision. However, the session should focus its attention on encouraging the board of deacons. The session is especially assigned the responsibility of support, as well as review and control [G-10.0102m]. The board of deacons and the session are instructed by the *Book of Order* to hold joint meetings at least annually to consider common concerns [G-6.0405].

In addition to its fundamental responsibility of engaging in a ministry of compassion, the board of deacons is to assume whatever duties may be delegated to it by the session. If the session delegates additional duties to a board of deacons, which carries out these duties for and in place of the session, then good communication between the session and the board of deacons becomes even more critical. Many churches have chosen not to use a separate office of deacon but to have the elders acting individually and the session acting corporately fulfill the functions of the office of deacon. Some congregations that have made this decision have done so because the two bodies of officers had difficulty working together. In order for each body of officers to support and enrich the other, good communication and a mutual respect for the God-given gifts and functions of each body must be present. Pastors can do much to foster communication and respect between these two groups of officers.

A 1998 amendment to the Form of Government opens up a new pattern of diaconal service. No longer is there a requirement that a church's deacons be organized into a board. A congregation may elect one or more deacons who, when ordained, are commissioned by the session to "particular tasks with the responsibilities of their office" [G-6.0403b]. After a review of the commissioned deacon's service, ordinarily conducted annually, the session may renew, alter, or terminate the commission.

Staff Relationships Within the Church

In addition to the church's officers—pastors, elders, and deacons—many churches hire staff persons to carry out vital functions in the life of the church. It is extremely important that the contributions of staff members be affirmed, that communication be open between the session, the deacons, and the church's employed staff, and that staff and officers understand the interrelatedness of their tasks. In many cases sessions work more closely with staff members than do deacons. There can, however, be significant exceptions to this generalization. A session could hire a staff person to work fulltime with the deacons in a special ministry to persons in need in the community. Then the quality of the relationship between that staff member and the deacons would be of primary importance.

For the purposes of this discussion, it is helpful to think of all ministers of the Word and Sacrament who serve a congregation in any official pastoral relationship as members of the staff. This would include parish associates, who may serve with or without remuneration. As pointed out previously, ministers are not employed by the session or the congregation. The presbytery is a necessary partner in establishing any pastoral relationship. Ministers are members of the church staff, however. (Pastors, co-pastors, and associate pastors are included among the church's officers. But for the remainder of this chapter it is helpful to think in terms of the relationships between elders and deacons as officers on the one hand, and staff members on the other.)

The *Book of Order* says very little about the relationships among the various members of the church staff. It does specify that when the staff includes co-pastors they have equal responsibility for pastoral ministry. However, the way they share the pastoral duties within the congregation is to be agreed on by the session and approved by the presbytery [G-14.0501c]. The division of responsibility is not to be a private understanding shared only by the two (or more) co-pastors. When the staff includes associate pastors, their calls are to specify the particular functions that they are responsible for fulfilling. Associate pastors are directed in their work by the pastor in consultation with the session [G-14.0501f]. Parish associates are "responsible to the pastor, as head of staff" [G-14.0515a].

To say more about the relationships among particular staff members quickly takes us beyond the *Book of Order*. The *Book of Order* does specify that the session has significant personnel responsibilities in the employment of staff. It is clear that in exercising its overall supervisory role for the governance and mission of the church, the session is responsible for seeing that the staff team works well together. A poorly functioning staff that lacks mutual respect, open and frequent communication, and a clear understanding of their various responsibilities does much to hamper the church's mission and program. Sessions should encourage pastors to hold frequent staff meetings, some including the entire employed staff and others including only those members who share particular responsibilities and concerns. The session cannot assume that staff concerns are the responsibility of the pastor alone. If problems develop within the staff of the church, the session should insist that the pastor, and perhaps other staff members, receive some continuing education in the area of personnel relationships. A consultant could be brought in to work with the pastor, the session (or representatives of the session), and the entire staff to clarify relationships and develop better patterns of communication.

The Session's Personnel Responsibilities

G-10.0102n assigns to the session the following responsibility:

> to provide for the administration of the program of the church, including employment of nonordained staff, with concern for equal employment opportunity, fair employment practices, personnel policies, and the annual review of the adequacy of compensation for all staff, including all employees.

Following the principle of leaving as many organizational decisions as possible to the governing body involved, the *Book of Order* does not specify how the personnel function is to be fulfilled; it only assigns the function to the proper group. Many sessions choose to fulfill this responsibility through a session personnel committee. Help is available through the General Assembly Council to enable such a committee to proceed with its work. Particularly valuable is the book *Guidelines for a Session Personnel Committee*, revised in 1997 by Churchwide Personnel Services in the National Ministries Division of the General Assembly Council.[1]

The *Book of Order* does lift up several aspects of the personnel function for special attention. One of these is concern for equal employment opportunity. Once again the Constitution stresses the principles of inclusiveness and diversity. The employment aspect of the church's increased concern for inclusiveness is emphasized at several points. G-9.0104a requires that all governing bodies work "to become more open and inclusive" and to "pursue affirmative action hiring procedures aimed at correcting patterns of discrimination. . . ." G-13.0201b assigns to the General Assembly Council the responsibility to "institute and coordinate a churchwide plan for equal employment opportunity and affirmative action for members of racial ethnic groups, for women, for various age groups, for persons regardless of marital condition (married, single, widowed, or divorced), and for persons with disabilities." The 197th General Assembly (1985) endorsed the Churchwide Equal Employment Opportunity Plan developed by the General Assembly Council. The section of the plan concerning congregations is extremely important in any consideration of the session's personnel function:

> The witness of congregations is the basis for all other expressions of the church's life. Each congregation is urged to implement its procedures of calling, recruiting, hiring, and promoting for all job classifications without regard to racial ethnic group, sex, age, disability, or marital status. Each congregation is urged in all phases of employment, for all job classifications, to follow the equal employment opportunity program of its presbytery. These commitments to equality should include but not be limited to compensation, benefits, leaves of absence, performance evaluations, reduction in force and return to service, continuing education opportunities, and termination.[2]

To extend equal employment opportunity to persons of all racial ethnic groups, both sexes, various ages, and different marital conditions and to persons with disabilities is one way the church lives its faith and bears witness to the community.

Another personnel concern highlighted for the session's special attention in G-10.0102n is "the annual review of the adequacy of compensation for all staff." The subject of compensation for church staff is an extremely complex one. Since 1980 the church has conducted several major studies of compensation, and the General Assembly has adopted reports on various aspects of the compensation issue. Overall, little progress has been made toward standardizing compensation within the Presbyterian Church (U.S.A.).

A 1988 Assembly-adopted report titled *Churchwide Compensation Policy Guidelines* includes basic principles that should undergird all church compensation plans, theological background material, and information to assist in establishing salary ranges. The *Churchwide Compensation Policy Guidelines* (available from the Human Resources Office in Louisville) gives helpful guidance to sessions and congregations as they consider the adequacy of compensation for pastors and all other members of the church staff.[3]

The Important Role of the Educator

One other member of the church staff has received much attention in recent years as the Presbyterian Church has struggled with questions of justice and accountability. From the early part of this century, churches have greatly benefited from the abilities and efforts of professionally trained church educators (or directors of Christian education), who feel called to and responsible for a special ministry of education in the life of the congregation. The Presbyterian Church's overall emphasis on the importance of education, not only for its leaders but also for its members, led the church to seek staff members who are specialists in Christian education.

Some church educators are also ministers of the Word and Sacrament (serving as pastors or associate pastors), but other educators do not feel the added calling to ministry of the Word and Sacrament.

Church educators perform a wide variety of functions in the educational ministry of a particular church. In many churches the session assigns the educator broad responsibility for planning and administering the church's educational program. Specific tasks include recommending curriculum for the church school, training those who assume the responsibility of teaching and leading, making available resources to enrich the curriculum, advising on possible teaching methods, working with the session committee responsible for Christian education, evaluating the comprehensiveness of the program to see that all groups within the congregation are served, and, of course, actually doing some teaching himself or herself. Some churches seek educators with special interests and skills in working with one particular age group within the church, such as children or youth. A session might ask an educator to supervise the overall educational program but to give special attention to designing and administering adult education experiences. It is extremely important that the pastor and session work closely with the educator, so that the education program of the church is an integral part of the total life and ministry of the congregation.

Many persons who serve as educators in local churches have received a master's degree in Christian education from a Presbyterian theological school. High educational standards for those serving in the church's educational ministry have been encouraged by a process of certification. In 1962 the Presbyterian Church U.S. established standards for the certification of Christian educators. The United Presbyterian Church adopted similar standards in 1982. However, many educators, even though certified, experienced inadequate accountability and support in their work.

Ordination to a separate office is a solution that has been advocated by many supporters of the church's educators. Amendments to create a new office of educator were approved by the 1982 General Assembly of the PCUS and sent to the presbyteries, where they received the approval of the necessary majority. The amendments were then enacted by the 123rd and final General Assembly of the PCUS. By the time of their enactment, however, they had no practical effect because that same General Assembly also gave final approval to Presbyterian reunion. The *Plan for Reunion* did not include ordination or certification of educators.

Two years after reunion the 1985 General Assembly approved a group of amendments that would create the office of educator. The amendments did not receive a majority vote of the presbyteries. In 1987 a compromise was proposed when new constitutional provisions for the certification of Christian educators were brought to the Assembly. These provisions did receive the required majority vote of the presbyteries and became constitutional in mid-1988. They were expanded when additional provisions were added in 1991. The *Book of Order* defines certification as the "means whereby the church recognizes the gifts, preparation, and effective service of those persons called to and employed in the ministry of education in the church" [G-14.0702].

The General Assembly, through its National Ministries Division, provides the certification process that evaluates both the educator's academic preparation and work experience and also examines competency in the areas of biblical interpretation, Reformed theology, human development, religious education theory and practice, polity, and the program and mission of the Presbyterian Church (U.S.A.) [G-14.0703]. This certification process is administered by the Educator Certification Council, which establishes standards; designates, in consultation with presbyteries, advisors to work with those seeking certification; evaluates examinations; and grants certificates on behalf of the General Assembly Council [G-14.0704].

Presbyteries are assigned the responsibility of supporting the certification process by encouraging their educators to seek certification, providing guidance through the appointed advisor, and advocating with sessions for continuing education funds and time for educators seeking certification [G-14.0705a].

Once an educator receives the highest level of certification (i.e., becomes a Certified Christian Educator), the presbytery must provide a service of recognition for the newly certified educator, guidelines for compensation and benefits for certified educators within the presbytery, access to the committee on ministry for support, and the privilege of the floor with voice at all presbytery meetings [G-14.0705b and c].

The image of the church as Christ's body reminds us that each part of the church must fulfill its special function in order for the body to be healthy and whole. Elders and deacons must perform those particular tasks committed to them. Pastors must fulfill their special calling in the life of the church.

Other members of the church staff have their particular responsibilities to carry out. These different parts must work together, supporting and upholding each other so that the church can indeed be Christ's body in the world.

Chapter Nine

LEADING THE CHURCH IN MISSION

Sam Washington was asked to serve on his church's evangelism committee, but he confessed to the elder who called him that he had very little enthusiasm for this area of the church's work. "The word 'evangelism' brings to mind people preaching on street corners or making door-to-door calls. Those kinds of things make me uncomfortable."

The pastor of Dunscomb Presbyterian Church reported to the session that a paper on economic justice had been sent out by the General Assembly for study in the churches, and he asked their advice as to how the study might best be carried out. After some discussion, one elder said, "I don't see why we should be studying economics at all. That seems pretty secular to me. Why can't we leave that kind of thing to the experts and get on with our own business?"

Jane Perry and Dan Moore were riding home together after a meeting of their church's mission committee. "I am getting discouraged," said Jane. "We spend most of our time in these meetings dealing with the concerns of our own congregation, and I think mission means more than that. I know there must be needs in our community that the church should be meeting, but we can't seem to find out what they are."

The Nature of Mission

If you were to say the word "mission" to a group of church members and ask what word came to mind in response, many of them would probably say, "international" or "foreign." Many of us grew up associating mission primarily with efforts to carry the gospel to other lands. Missionaries were seen as saintly souls who packed up family and belongings and went to India or China. Even the term "home mission" usually referred to efforts in places far removed from where we were. For many people, being involved in mission meant giving to the yearly offering to support the church's work overseas.

A careful reading of the Bible, however, gives a very different understanding of mission in the church. Over and over again the Scriptures point out that God's people are chosen, not simply for their own benefit, but that they might be instruments of blessing to the world. God promised Abraham that "by you all the families of the earth shall bless themselves" (Gen. 12:3). In Isaiah 49:6 the Lord says:

> "It is too light a thing that you should be my servant
> to raise up the tribes of Jacob
> and to restore the preserved of Israel;
> I will give you as a light to the nations,
> that my salvation may reach to the end of the earth."

First Peter 2:9 states: "You are a chosen race, a royal priesthood, a holy nation, God's own people." Why? So "that you may declare the wonderful deeds of him who called you out of darkness into his marvelous light." The Apostle Paul says that not only has Christ reconciled us to God but also he has given us "the ministry of reconciliation" (2 Cor. 5:18). Shortly before he died, Jesus prayed for his chosen ones and said, "As thou didst send me into the world, so I have sent them into the world" (John 17:18). According to Matthew's Gospel, his last words before ascending into heaven were "Go therefore and make disciples of all nations" (Matt. 28:19). As the *Book of Order* [G-4.0201] puts it:

> The Church is a fellowship of believers which seeks the enlargement of the circle of faith to include all people and is never content to enjoy the benefits of Christian community for itself alone.

Mission is not a facet of the church's work or an appendage of the church. It is not a function to be carried out by special individuals alone or supported only by certain auxiliary groups. Neither is mission primarily something that takes place in distant lands. Instead, the church's mission is carried out when, as a body and as individuals, it seeks to know and do the will of God in its own community as well as throughout the world. This is why the church exists.

The Bible clearly teaches that from the beginning, God has been working to bring about the salvation of all creation. This work of God is the pattern for the church's mission. The *Book of Order* [G-3.0101–.0103] gives us a concise review of this "salvation history":

> Even when the human race broke community with its Maker and with one another, God did not forsake it, but out of grace chose one family for the sake of all, to be pilgrims of promise, God's own Israel.

God liberated the people of Israel from oppression; God covenanted with Israel to be their God and they to be God's people, that they might do justice, love mercy, and walk humbly with the Lord. . . .

God was incarnate in Jesus Christ, who announced good news to the poor, proclaimed release for prisoners and recovery of sight for the blind, let the broken victims go free, and proclaimed the year of the Lord's favor. Jesus came to seek and to save the lost; in his life and death for others God's redeeming love for all people was made visible; and in the resurrection of Jesus Christ there is the assurance of God's victory over sin and death. . . .

God's redeeming and reconciling activity in the world continues through the presence and power of the Holy Spirit, who confronts individuals and societies with Christ's Lordship of life and calls them to repentance and to obedience to the will of God.

It is in imitating Jesus by seeking and obeying God's will that the church finds its identity. It could be said that the church is most truly itself when it is engaged in mission. This is not to deny the importance of other aspects of a congregation's life, such as worship or fellowship. Rather, a church that is busy reaching out to the world will generally find its worship enhanced and its fellowship strengthened. An introverted, self-centered congregation falls short of Christ's intention for the church and cannot long prosper. Mission is the "salt" that keeps faith from becoming rancid.

Facets of the Church's Mission

What does mission look like? The answers to that question are as numerous as the shades of color in a rainbow. Each individual Christian and each congregation should be involved in mission in ways that are appropriate to their particular situation. Yet, in spite of this variety of forms, it is possible to group most of the ways we carry out our mission under one of the following three categories.

Evangelism. Evangelism has acquired a bad reputation among many Presbyterians. Perhaps the main reason for this is that we often confuse evangelism itself with certain methods of doing evangelism that make us uncomfortable. In the first example at the beginning of the chapter, Sam Washington's negative reaction to the word "evangelism" illustrates this problem.

Evangelism could be defined simply as sharing the good news. Objectively, this means telling the story of Jesus Christ and inviting those who do not know him as Savior and Lord into relationship with him. Subjectively, it means the personal witness of an individual or congregation to what God through Jesus Christ has done for them. Evangelism is so central to the mission of the church that the *Book of Order* was revised in 1995 to list providing "opportunities for evangelism to be learned and practiced in and by the church" first among the responsibilities and powers of the session [G-10.0102a].

To do evangelism does not necessarily mean that we must preach on street corners. Rather, whenever and however we share this good news with those who do not have a personal relationship with Christ we are involved in evangelism. This may take the form of teaching our children the truths of the faith and leading them to trust and love God. It may take the form of witnessing to those outside the faith about what the relationship with Jesus Christ has meant to us and inviting them to accept him into their lives. It may take the form of leading those who are Christian in name only (even though they may be church members) to examine their assumptions about the faith and come into a living relationship with Jesus. Evangelism may also be facilitated as new congregations are established and constituted within the church.

Sharing the good news is the unique mission of the church. Secular organizations may engage in activities that resemble some other facets of the church's mission, but evangelism is the responsibility of the church alone. We are the ones who have firsthand experience of what it means to know Christ as Lord and Savior; it is our duty and our privilege to share our faith with others. Sharing the good news is the ultimate goal of all the church's work. The particular programs churches develop in this area will differ, shaped by the circumstances and needs of the people around them. However, we should be careful in devising programs and training persons in evangelism that the methods we use to share the gospel are consistent with the good news itself. Sessions should regularly evaluate the means by which this part of the church's mission is being carried out to make sure that they are appropriate and effective and that they have biblical and theological integrity.

In evaluating a plan or approach to evangelism, a session should satisfy itself that the plan does the following:

1. *It takes sin seriously.* Human need is a great motivating factor for sharing the good news. There are people everywhere in extreme distress of spirit. We believe that the root cause of much of this distress is alienation from God, our Creator. Self-help, psychological adjustment, or a better economic condition will not ultimately satisfy the deepest of human needs and are not the final aim of evangelism. Rather, this outreach begins with the assumption that human beings are "without hope except in God's sovereign mercy,"[1] and it seeks to restore the loving, mutual relationship with God that brings true peace and fulfillment.

2. *It focuses on Jesus Christ and God's grace.* Christian evangelism seeks to introduce people to God as revealed in Jesus Christ. For us, to know God fully means to know Jesus, and to know Jesus is to know a God of grace

and love. This is the good news: "God so loved the world that he gave his only Son, that whoever believes in him should not perish but have eternal life" (John 3:16). The object of evangelism is to introduce people to a risen, living Christ who brings healing, forgiveness, and hope into their lives. Intellectual assent to the truths of the gospel are involved in this process, but the true goal is a personal relationship of trust and commitment.

3. *It offers a new quality of life.* To be in relationship with Christ is to be a new person. The gospel promises that as we seek to follow Christ, those things that have twisted our lives and separated us from God and other people will die away. We will not be enslaved by them any longer. This process takes a lifetime, and it is only possible as we live daily with Christ and claim the power of the Holy Spirit. We find support and companionship for this new life in the church. It is appropriate, as persons consider a commitment to Christ, to make them aware that this includes a call to involvement in mission. Christians join together in "proclaiming the good news" and in "working in the world for peace, justice, freedom, and human fulfillment" [G-5.0102a, i]. Evangelism that has integrity will seek to integrate new converts into a community of believers and to challenge them to live out their faith in the world.

4. *It respects the right to choose.* The saving relationship with God through Jesus Christ is one of freedom, love, and trust. It is not a relationship that can be created by means of fear or guilt. All approaches to evangelism should respect the integrity of others, especially their right to accept or reject the gospel freely. The development of faith may be a very slow process. A person may say "no" to God many times before finally saying "yes."

While presenting the gospel clearly and offering persons the opportunity to choose Christ, evangelists must be careful not to rush people into decisions they are not ready to make. Emotional coercion or manipulation works against the Holy Spirit, who is trying to enable persons to make the choice for God of their own free will. This free choice, enabled by the grace of God, is at the heart of the kind of relationship God wants to have with human beings.

Proclaiming the gospel is at the very heart of all the church's work. We are called to make the good news visible in the world by our love and care for others and to make it audible through our testimony about and proclamation of God's mighty works of grace.

Service. Jesus used the image of the suffering servant from the book of Isaiah to describe his work in the world. The Gospels are full of stories reflecting Jesus' willingness to be involved in the lives of people in need. He healed the sick, cast out demons, fed the hungry, saved those threatened by storms, and raised the dead. These stories tell us that Jesus cared deeply about people, and they call us to imitate him in giving of ourselves to others.

It is a significant part of the church's mission to participate in God's activity in the world by

(a)   healing and reconciling and binding up wounds;

(b)   ministering to the needs of the poor, the sick, the lonely, and the powerless;

(c)   engaging in the struggle to free people from sin, fear, oppression, hunger, and injustice;

(d)   giving itself and its substance to the service of those who suffer;

(e)   sharing with Christ in the establishing of his just, peaceable, and loving rule in the world. [G-3.0300c(3)]

As the quotation above indicates, ministries of service should be grounded not only in compassion but also in a godly concern for justice. The biblical call to justice leads us toward the goal of "meeting the basic needs of all for food, shelter, clothing, work, health and education, in our nation and beyond. It includes justice in the context of governmental and political life, justice amidst competing economic systems and widely disparate economic conditions, and justice in racial relationships" ("The Life and Mission Statement of the Presbyterian Church (U.S.A.)," 1985, par. 27.446). This concern for justice should not be satisfied with simply meeting the needs of the moment, but should drive us to grapple with the injustices that caused the needs. (See the next category of mission in this chapter, "Prophetic Witness.")

No church can claim to be carrying out the mission to which Christ calls it unless it is involved in ministering to people outside its fellowship. These ministries will take different forms, depending on the opportunities and resources available. One church, for instance, might begin a support group for recently bereaved people in the community. Another congregation might serve a hot meal to people who otherwise would have nothing to eat. A church with a number of health care professionals among its members might start a clinic. Another might sponsor a day-care center with scholarships for children whose parents cannot pay full tuition. A small congregation might begin a program of visitation to home-bound persons in its community. A large church could begin a school for emotionally disturbed children. The possibilities are as varied as the needs of people.

Ministries of compassion flow from our experience of being ministered to by a loving God. They are empowered by the Spirit of Christ dwelling in us. The first step toward a ministry of service is to be aware of what is going on in the community around the church. What are the needs of people? Helpful guidance and advice in this area can come from welfare agencies, school principals, public health officials, visiting nurses, community leaders, mental health workers, and others in the helping professions. Is there some need that no secular agency or other church is meeting?

Often the impetus to begin such a ministry will come from an individual who has had personal contact with someone in need. A news story might spur concern and lead church members to respond. Sometimes people come to the church asking for help. At other times social agencies may refer clients to the church for assistance with their problems. Every community has people who need help in some way. It is the church's task to seek them out and minister to them in the name of Christ.

The *Book of Order* [G-6.0402] indicates that the session may delegate the administration of programs of service to the deacons. This is particularly appropriate because

> it is the duty of deacons, first of all, to minister to those who are in need, to the sick, to the friendless, and to any who may be in distress.

Churches that have retained the office of deacon should evaluate this office in light of its potential for ministries of "sympathy, witness, and service" [G-6.0401]. (See chapter 5 of this book.)

It has been said that we live today in a global village.[2] The truth of this statement is borne out by the frequency with which we have the needs of people very far away from us brought into our homes by the media. As residents of this global village, we cannot claim to have fulfilled our mission of service until we have reached out beyond our local community. It is the responsibility of the session "to lead the congregation in participation in the mission of the whole Church in the world" [G-10.0102c]. Church members should be encouraged to participate in the mission of worldwide service through giving to general mission budgets and special offerings. It is the responsibility of the session to inform the congregation of the need for these funds and to find creative ways to motivate it to give.

Just giving money is not enough, however. Christians should be encouraged to give of themselves to people in need outside their own community. Our denomination provides opportunities for this kind of service as well. Congregations should also be urged to remember our denomination's mission coworkers in their prayers, not forgetting to pray for our partner churches in mission all over the world. The *Mission Yearbook for Prayer and Study*, produced annually by our denomination, is a good resource here.

Our church also provides opportunities for persons to give of themselves through travel-study tours and through temporary work in various mission settings. Participation in this kind of service is often a life-changing experience. Sessions should be alert to these opportunities and make sure that they are publicized to the congregation. The vocation of long-term mission coworkers should also be held before the congregation in ways that would encourage openness to God's call.

Prophetic Witness. As the prophets of old sought to speak the word of God to the issues of their day, so must we speak God's word to the issues and evils that confront us. A third facet of our mission as disciples of Christ is to bring the judgment and gospel of God to bear on the structures, values, and culture of our time.

As Christians become involved in ministries of service, it is natural that they should also become concerned about the causes of the problems they are seeking to remedy. Feeding hungry people may lead a congregation to grapple with the problem of unemployment, and then with deeper economic issues. A ministry with refugees might raise interest in matters of the United States government's foreign policy.

Yet this movement from the particular to the general frequently raises questions about the church's right to speak on so-called secular matters. These things are often controversial and may spark conflict in the church when members have differing opinions. In spite of all this, we cannot claim to be faithful in our mission if we are not faithful in the public arena. The Lordship of Christ extends not only to individuals but also to societies, which are called "to repentance and to obedience to the will of God" [G-3.0103]. The very fact that "the Word became flesh and dwelt among us" (John 1:14) compels us to question the division of our concerns into separate categories of sacred and secular.

The mission of prophetic witness is carried out in at least two ways. One, we are to be involved in the reformation of the world. The gospel has a forward thrust, and it carries the whole world toward the final coming of God's reign. If Christ is Lord of all the earth, and not just of the church, then it is appropriate that we share with him in the "establishing of his just, peaceable, and loving rule in the world" [G-3.0300c(3)(e)]. This task immediately brings us into contact with social and political structures. It involves working for change in these structures and speaking out against what we believe to be wrong in them.

It is for this reason that church governing bodies make pronouncements and write study papers on issues such as economic justice. Our pronouncements are verbal witnesses to God's claim on society. They seek to proclaim Christian values and bring these values to bear on particular questions. They are guides to church members in the ethical decisions of life. They are announcements to those outside the church of what we believe God's word to be on a certain issue.

The task of reformation also includes working to change things from the way they are into the way we believe God wants them to be. This may involve political action—for example, working for the adoption of fair housing laws in a city or for the improvement of the prison system in a state. It may involve economic action, such as boycotts of products made by companies that indulge in unethical practices. Changing structures, whether on the local, national, or world level, is a difficult task. It is usually accomplished most effectively as congregations, governing bodies, and ecumenical groups join in common witness, prayer, and action.

One particular area of prophetic witness that has come to the fore in recent years is that of peacemaking. We believe that Christians are called to seek the good of all people, not just our own good. "The world is torn and divided by hostility, suspicion and the oppressive use of power and resources. Peace can only be achieved on the basis of just and sustaining relationships among all people" ("The Life and Mission Statement of the Presbyterian Church (U.S.A.)," 1985, par. 27.448). The future of our world may depend on how faithful Christians are in this area of our witness. "We continue to seek peace not in fear but with hope, through Christ who breaks through every barrier of division and hostility to be our peace and the world's" ("Life and Mission Statement," 1985, par. 27.448). It is the duty of all Christians to do what they can as individuals to make a difference for good in the world. The great problems of our day—hunger, war, racism, poverty, and the threat of terrorism, among others—may seem insurmountable. Yet apathy and discouragement indicate lack of faith in the God for whom all things are possible.

The reformation of the world and its values to bring them more into line with the intentions of God is not a task we undertake or expect to accomplish by human effort alone. Yet, "without utopian illusion that the Kingdom of God is a human creation, the people of God press themselves and the world in the direction of the Kingdom of God that is coming. Here success is measured more by faithfulness than by achievement."[3]

A second area of prophetic witness is the reformation of the church itself. The *Book of Order* reminds us that "the Church of Jesus Christ is the provisional demonstration of what God intends for all of humanity." As such, "the Church is called to be a sign in and for the world of the new reality which God has made available to people in Jesus Christ" [G-3.0200a]. In the Christian community we are to live out the promises of God so that those outside the church can see a picture of what God is doing in the world.

This does not mean that the church is perfect; in fact, most sins found in the world can be found in the church. Rather we are to be engaged in a continual process of self-examination, confession, and renewal. The motto "always being reformed" is a Presbyterian witness to God's grace and power, as well as a confession of human imperfection. We should never be content to tolerate in the church the sins that we deplore in the world—pride, injustice, and prejudice, in particular. Rather we are always to be working to make the whole life of the church into a witness for God,

> demonstrating by the love of its members for one another and by the quality of its common life the new reality in Christ; sharing in worship, fellowship, and nurture, practicing a deepened life of prayer and service under the guidance of the Holy Spirit. [G-3.0300c(2)]

It is the responsibility of the session in the particular church to lead the church in self-examination on a regular basis and to plan for "change, renewal, and reformation under the Word of God" [G-10.0102j]. The session itself should always be alert to opportunities for the church to be more Christlike. Every area of the church's life, including employment practices, salary policies, and the processes for nomination and election of officers, should reflect the goodness and justice of God. In order for this mission of the reformation of the church to be carried out, the *Book of Order* [G-3.0401] states that four kinds of openness are necessary:

> . . . to the presence of God in the Church and in the world, to more fundamental obedience, and to a more joyous celebration in worship and work;

> . . . to its own membership, by affirming itself as a community of diversity, becoming in fact as well as in faith a community of women and men of all ages, races, and conditions, and by providing for inclusiveness as a visible sign of the new humanity;

> . . . to the possibilities and perils of its institutional forms in order to ensure the faithfulness and usefulness of these forms to God's activity in the world;

> . . . to God's continuing reformation of the Church ecumenical, that it might be a more effective instrument of mission in the world.

By keeping itself alert and open to the movement of the Holy Spirit, the church can allow God to reform it until it is more nearly the image of Christ in the world. Then the very life of the church itself will be a witness to the good news.

Beyond Polity

Much of the work of the session is involved in leading the church in mission. It is a complex and often difficult responsibility. Effective programs of mission seldom simply happen. They require careful planning, administration, and evaluation. G-9.0400 offers a brief treatment of the relationship between the mission of the church and its administrative structures. The focus of this book is polity, and the actual process by which a session plans and carries out mission is beyond its scope. However, session members who are concerned with leading this area of the church's life should make a careful study of the ways in which a church can set goals for mission and create structures to achieve them.

An Ecumenical Note

The mission that Jesus Christ entrusted to his church is greater than any one denomination or religious body. It calls all Christians to put their differences aside in order to find common ministries in the world. "The unity of the

Church is a gift of its Lord and finds expression in its faithfulness to the mission to which Christ calls it" [G-4.0201]. This century has seen a growth in tolerance and unity among believers of different communions. In working together in common ministries, we have found that we indeed have "one Lord, one faith, one baptism, one God and Father of us all" (Eph. 4:5–6). While questions of doctrine and practice may still separate us, we sense the reality of each other's faith when we serve soup together at a night shelter or work together to sponsor refugee families. Cooperation across ecumenical lines allows the combining of resources and talents to accomplish together more than one church could accomplish alone. This is particularly true in the area of meeting human needs.

Christian unity is also an important tool for witness and evangelism. Jesus himself prayed that his followers might be united "so that the world may know that thou hast sent me and hast loved them even as thou hast loved me" (John 17:23). When the church of Jesus Christ speaks with a unified voice, the world is more likely to listen. Also our unity is a sign to the world of the peace and power of God.

On the subject of ecumenical relations and mission, the *Book of Order* [G-15.0101–.0103] states:

> The Presbyterian Church (U.S.A.) seeks to manifest more visibly the unity of the church of Jesus Christ and will be open to opportunities for conversation, cooperation, and action with other ecclesiastical bodies and secular groups.
>
> The Presbyterian Church (U.S.A.) will seek to initiate, maintain, and strengthen its relations to, and to engage in mission with, other Presbyterian and Reformed bodies and with other Christian churches. . . .
>
> All governing bodies of the church, in consultation with the next higher governing body, shall be authorized to work with other Christian denominations in . . . common mission.

Sessions, presbyteries, and higher governing bodies should always be alert to ways they can join in mission with other churches. They are charged to establish and maintain such relationships as will enlarge and make more effective the life and mission of the church in their particular locality [G-10.0102q, G-11.0103u, G-12.0102p, G-13.0103p, G-15.0302d].

Mission is the heartbeat of the church. We are called to be faithful disciples of our Lord, who spent his life sharing the good news, serving others, and witnessing to God's love and purpose for the world. This task may not always be easy or comfortable. However, in spite of the difficulties "the Church is called to undertake this mission even at the risk of losing its life, trusting in God alone as the author and giver of life, sharing the gospel, and doing those deeds in the world that point beyond themselves to the new reality in Christ" [G-3.0400].

Chapter Ten

PRESBYTERY, SYNOD, AND THE GENERAL ASSEMBLY

Paul Allan and his pastor were on their way to attend a meeting of presbytery. Paul noticed a large book titled "Minutes" on the back seat of the car and asked what it was. His pastor explained that these were the minutes of the meetings of their session during the past year and that he was taking them to the presbytery meeting to be reviewed. "Do they think we are doing something wrong?" asked Paul. "Why does presbytery want to review our minutes?"

Sally Coe was attending a new-member class, and the subject for the evening was the way that presbytery, synod, and the General Assembly function. After the pastor's presentation, Sally commented, "I think I know something about what presbyteries do because I served on my presbytery's youth council when I was a teenager. And I believe I understand the basics about the General Assembly and its work. But I don't understand how synods fit into the picture at all."

The session of Highdale Presbyterian Church was studying the sacraments together as part of their annual continuing education retreat. The topic of children receiving Communion arose, and one elder questioned whether it was really necessary for children to be baptized before participating in the sacrament. "In spite of what the *Book of Order* says, it doesn't seem right to me that children should be denied the Lord's Supper because their parents have not had them baptized. I wish I knew how to try to get this rule changed."

More Inclusive Governing Bodies

Individual ministers and elders have no power of governance in the Presbyterian system of polity. Their authority is always exercised in groups of presbyters constituted as governing bodies. These governing bodies represent the unity of the church beyond the level of the particular congregation.

At some time in their careers, many elders will have the opportunity to serve as commissioners to a governing body beyond the session. Indeed, it is the duty of both elders and ministers to serve not only their particular congregation but also the church at large [G-6.0302]. When elected to serve as members of presbytery, synod, or the General Assembly, "elders participate and vote with the same authority as ministers of the Word and Sacrament, and they are eligible for any office" [G-6.0302]. The *Book of Order* takes great pains to specify that higher governing bodies are made up as much as possible of equal numbers of ministers of the Word and Sacrament and elders. This helps to ensure that a true parity will exist between the two kinds of presbyters and that the members who are ministers of the Word and Sacrament will not consistently outnumber those who are elders.

The governing bodies above the level of the session now in use in the Presbyterian Church (U.S.A.) are presbytery, synod, and the General Assembly. They are constituted in ascending order, that is, presbytery exercises governance over a number of sessions, synod over a number of presbyteries, and the General Assembly over the whole church. In regard to the relationships between governing bodies, the *Book of Order* [G-9.0103] states:

> All governing bodies of the church are united by the nature of the church and share with one another responsibilities, rights, and powers as provided in this Constitution. The governing bodies are separate and independent, but have such mutual relations that the act of one of them is the act of the whole church performed by it through the appropriate governing body. The jurisdiction of each governing body is limited by the express provisions of the Constitution, with powers not mentioned being reserved to the presbyteries, and with the acts of each subject to review by the next more inclusive governing body.

One application of the above principles is that each more inclusive governing body reviews the minutes of meetings of the bodies it oversees. In answer to the question raised in the first example at the beginning of the chapter, presbytery's request to see the minutes of a session is generally not due to any suspicion of wrongdoing. This is a regular, yearly procedure required by the Constitution [G-10.0301]. Reviewing minutes is one way that a governing body exercises its responsibility to review the actions of the governing bodies for which it is responsible. If the reviewing body does happen to find significant error in the proceedings, it can require that the error be corrected [D-3.0400].

As stated above, governing bodies have only those powers specifically granted to them by the Constitution. This principle, along with that of the relationships among governing bodies, is important in understanding how presbytery, synod, and the General Assembly work together. These aspects of our polity can be reviewed in chapter 1 of this book. Rules relating to the meetings of governing bodies are discussed in chapter 12.

Responsibilities in Common. All governing bodies of the church (including the session) have certain responsibilities in common. In general, "they may frame symbols of faith, bear testimony against error in doctrine and immorality in life, resolve questions of doctrine and of discipline, give counsel in matters of conscience, and decide issues properly brought before them under the provisions of the *Book of Order*" [G-9.0102b]. They also authorize the serving of the Lord's Supper, and in general, "do those things necessary to the peace, purity, unity, and progress of the church under the will of Christ" [G-9.0102]. Any and all powers exercised by governing bodies are strictly within the bounds of the church and have no force of civil law.

In reading through the specific responsibilities and powers of the more-inclusive governing bodies [presbytery, G-11.0000; synod, G-12.0000; the General Assembly, G-13.0000] in the *Book of Order*, it will be noticed that all three carry out certain comparable functions in relation to the particular part of the church that is under their care. The following is a brief review of the responsibilities common to presbytery, synod, and the General Assembly.

1. *Mission.* The first duty specified for each of these governing bodies is that of leading the church in mission. Presbytery does this with and through its particular churches; synod, with and through its presbyteries; and the General Assembly, with and on behalf of the whole church. These governing bodies are also charged not only to participate in mission through their constituent groups but also with planning and doing mission themselves. Further, they are to develop broad mission strategies that coordinate the efforts of the groups under their care and eliminate unnecessary duplication of effort and inefficient use of resources. Each governing body should have a mission statement with specific objectives in written form and should make this statement available to its constituent groups.

2. *Inclusiveness.* Every presbytery and synod and the General Assembly are responsible to put into practice the principles of participation and inclusiveness outlined in G-4.0400 and G-9.0104. This mandate relates to many of the functions of the governing body, such as hiring staff, electing commissioners to other governing bodies, and establishing the membership of its "committees, councils, boards, and other policy-making and policy-recommending bodies" [G-11.0103d]. The functions of a body relating to inclusiveness are carried out in order "to assure fair representation in its decision making" [G-12.0102d]. Presbyteries in particular are charged to counsel with churches that do not have the diversity of the congregation represented in the membership of the session [G-11.0103e].

3. *Judicial functions.* Presbytery, synod, and the General Assembly are each given the responsibility to "serve in judicial matters in accordance with the Rules of Discipline" [G-11.0103r, G-12.0102l, G-13.0103o]. These responsibilities are generally carried out through permanent judicial commissions and are discussed more fully in chapter 13 of this book.

4. *Review and control.* As discussed above, each governing body is to review each year the activities of the governing bodies over which it has jurisdiction to make sure that they are in accord with the Constitution of the church. This is generally done by reviewing the minutes of meetings. This function of review and control is discussed more fully in chapter 1 of this book.

5. *Ecumenical relations.* At its own level each presbytery and synod and the General Assembly are to "establish and maintain those ecumenical relationships which will enlarge the life and mission of the Church" [G-11.0103u, G-12.0102p, G-13.0103s]. This ordinarily means that each governing body relates to some comparable governing body of another Christian church or participates in councils of churches in its area of jurisdiction. Synod is also specifically charged with joining in mission efforts with other denominations and agencies in its area [G-12.0102i].

6. *Administration.* Each more inclusive governing body is given the power to set up any councils, committees, commissions, etc., required to help it do its work better. These groups are discussed at the end of this chapter.

7. *Warning against error.* The *Book of Order* states that synod and the General Assembly have the power "to warn or bear witness against error in doctrine or immorality in practice," synod in its area of jurisdiction [G-12.0102m], and the General Assembly either in or outside the church [G-13.0103p]. This power relates to the church's mission of prophetic witness and the ministry of discipline and pastoral care. This power is not specifically listed in the responsibilities and powers of the presbytery in G-11.0103; however, it is implied by the responsibility of the presbytery to "develop strategy for the mission of the Church in its area," which we have shown in chapter 9 of this book to include the mission of prophetic witness [G-11.0103a].

The remainder of this chapter will give a brief survey of the duties and powers peculiar to each of the three more-inclusive governing bodies and then of the administrative structures that all more-inclusive governing bodies may use to carry out their duties. It is not intended as an exhaustive explanation of all the duties of presbytery, synod, and the General Assembly. Anyone who is elected a commissioner to one of these governing bodies should make a careful study of the appropriate sections of the *Book of Order* and of the manual of the governing body on which he or she will serve.

Presbytery

The linchpin of the presbyterian system of church government, the presbytery, originated in Scotland in the sixteenth century. It was devised in order to bind local congregations scattered across the nation into one denomination while protecting the freedom of those congregations to elect their own officers. Without resorting to the use of the unpalatable (to Presbyterians) office of bishop, presbyteries provided the administrative machinery necessary for "efficient central and local organization on a national scale."[1] In fact, it can be argued that the presbytery serves basically the same function in presbyterian polity that the bishop serves in episcopal polity.

Presbytery is the governing body next above the session, and it has jurisdiction over the sessions of all Presbyterian Church (U.S.A.) congregations within its geographical bounds. A presbytery is composed of "all the churches and ministers of the Word and Sacrament within a certain district" [G-11.0101]. When the presbytery meets for business, its members include

> all ministers who have been received into the presbytery,
> all elders properly commissioned by their sessions to represent the congregations at that meeting,
> any elders from churches selected by presbytery to redress any imbalance between the numbers of ministers and elders,
> any elder elected moderator of the presbytery, whether or not appointed as a commissioner by his or her session.

The presbytery may also elect to membership for their term of office "an officer (other than moderator), a chairperson of a standing committee, a member of the council of presbytery, or an elder elected by the presbytery as executive presbyter, associate executive presbyter, or other exempt staff." [G-11.0101c]

The Responsibilities of Presbytery. The work that is peculiar to the presbytery falls into three general categories: that relating to congregations, that relating to ministers of the Word and Sacrament, inquirers, and candidates, and that relating to synod and the General Assembly.

1. *Relating to congregations.* Presbytery is responsible for a wide range of duties in relation to its congregations. In addition to those mentioned above in the discussion of common duties, the presbytery is assigned

> to provide encouragement, guidance, and resources to its member churches in the areas of leadership development, church officer training, worship, nurture, witness, service, stewardship, equitable compensation, personnel policies, and fair employment practices;
>
> to provide pastoral care for the churches and . . . [to visit] sessions . . . on a regular basis (G-11.0502c). [G-11.0103f,g]

Presbytery has the power to organize new congregations, to merge or to divide congregations, and to dismiss a church to another denomination or dissolve the church, all this being done in consultation with the members of the congregation [G-11.0103h,i]. It is presbytery that decides where a new church will be located or where an existing congregation may move. This is in order to prevent the competition and waste of resources that occur when churches of the same denomination are established too close to each other. Presbytery also considers and acts upon "requests from congregations to take the actions regarding real property as described in G-8.0000" [G-11.0103y]. These actions include, among others, selling real property, and taking on a mortgage.

As noted above, presbytery shall arrange for sessions to be visited on a regular basis. These visits provide an opportunity for the presbytery to "consult through appropriate representatives with governing bodies below . . . it concerning mission priorities, program, budgeting, the establishment of administrative staff positions, equitable compensation, personnel policies, and fair employment practices" [G-9.0404b]. Concerns of the session can also be voiced to the representatives of presbytery at this time, making for improved communication between the governing bodies.

When a church is without a pastor, presbytery takes special oversight of that church, appointing a moderator for the session, providing for the pulpit to be supplied, and doing other things necessary in the absence of an installed pastor. Presbytery also hears and acts on requests from congregations for exemptions relating to inclusiveness of the session [G-14.0202a].

2. *Relating to ministers of the Word and Sacrament, inquirers, and candidates.* A great deal of the space allotted to the work of presbytery in the *Book of Order* deals with matters relating to ministers. Ordinarily each minister is a member of the presbytery where he or she works. The minister members of presbytery are called "continuing members" [G-11.0403]. Presbytery is to function as the pastor of its continuing members, providing pastoral care and visiting all of them on a regular basis [G-11.0103g]. This pastoral function is an important one and should be taken seriously, particularly in light of the fact that many ministers have no other source of pastoral care and concern. It is frequently carried out by the committee on ministry or by a presbytery staff person under the supervision of that group.

Presbytery has the power to "ordain, receive, dismiss, install, remove, and discipline ministers" [G-11.0103n]. It is the prerogative of presbytery both to establish the relationship between a congregation and a particular minister and to dissolve that relationship when necessary. This means that congregations do not have absolute power over the hiring and firing of ministers. In the case of a church calling a minister, the committee on ministry makes recommendations to presbytery about the suitability or unsuitability of the call as specified in G-11.0502d. A church has no power to dissolve the pastoral relationship on its own. Instead, it makes a request to presbytery that this be done, and if the request is in order and in the best interest of the church, presbytery may grant the request [G-14.0600].

Not all ministers are pastors of particular churches. Presbytery also has responsibility for oversight of those continuing members who work in other areas of ministry. Therefore it has the power to "designate ministers to work as teachers, evangelists, administrators, chaplains, and in other forms of ministry recognized as appropriate by the presbytery" [G-11.0103p]. These ministers have the same rights in and responsibilities toward presbytery as continuing members who are pastors.

In addition to its relationships with its continuing members, presbytery is also responsible to care for inquirers and candidates for the ministry and for other fulltime Christian service. The presbytery through its committee on preparation for ministry is responsible to see that such inquirers and candidates receive full and adequate preparation for their future ministry. In this area the *Book of Order* specifies that "presbyteries shall enter into covenant relationship with those preparing to become ministers of the Word and Sacrament" [G-14.0301]. This responsibility also involves electing elders and ministers to serve on the Assembly-wide committee that grades the written ordination examinations of candidates for the ministry of the Word and Sacrament when requested to do so [G-11.0103m].

3. *Relating to synod and the General Assembly.* Another major function of presbytery is relating to the two more inclusive governing bodies. This is a very important function in that crucial communications between the more inclusive governing bodies and sessions of local churches are often funneled through the presbytery. Presbytery participates in the deliberations of synod and of the General Assembly by electing commissioners to serve as members of these governing bodies at a particular meeting or meetings. It also hears and receives reports from the commissioners when they return from the meetings. Further, the *Book of Order* specifies that the presbytery is responsible for ensuring that the orders of the more inclusive governing bodies are carried out within the presbytery [G-11.0103t(2)].

Presbytery has the privilege and the duty to propose to the synod or the General Assembly "such measures as may be of common concern to the mission of the whole church" [G-11.0103t(3)]. This is an avenue of progress and change in the church. For instance, in the example at the beginning of the chapter, the elder concerned about unbaptized children could have used this avenue to get his concern before the wider church. He could have written what is called an "overture," expressing his thoughts on the matter and suggesting a particular remedy. This overture could be presented to his session and, if adopted, could be sent to the presbytery for its adoption. The overture would be discussed at a meeting of presbytery, and, if adopted by presbytery, it would be sent to the General Assembly for action. Presbytery can also originate overtures itself when necessary, and overtures relating to regional concerns may be sent to synod for action. For example, a presbytery might originate an overture to synod asking that a nursing home be built within the bounds of the synod and supported by synod funds.

A particularly important function in this area is that of amending the Constitution of the church. This is a matter in which the presbyteries and the General Assembly work together. When an amendment to the *Book of Confessions* is proposed (often through overtures from presbyteries) and approved by one General Assembly, it goes to all the presbyteries of the church for their affirmative or negative vote. Affirmative votes by two thirds of the presbyteries are required to amend the *Book of Confessions*. If the amendment is then approved again by the next General Assembly, it is enacted. A simple majority of presbyteries voting yes is required to amend the *Book of Order*. If the necessary votes by the presbyteries are not achieved, the suggested amendment fails. If the affirmative votes are sufficient, the amendment is enacted. These processes for amendment are detailed in G-18.0000.

About the Delegation of Certain Responsibilities. Amendments to the *Book of Order* approved by the 197th General Assembly (1985) gave presbyteries discretionary powers to delegate certain responsibilities to its council or to the committee on ministry. Under these provisions, presbytery may delegate to its council "responsibility for action between meetings of presbytery on such specific areas of its responsibilities as it shall deem appropriate . . . with the provision that all such actions be reported to the next stated meeting of the presbytery" [G-11.0103v]. It may also delegate to the committee on ministry broad powers relating to the establishment and dissolution of the pastoral relationship. Details relating to the delegating of these powers are found in G-11.0502h and G-14.0507c.

For quick reference, here is an outline of the responsibilities and powers of presbytery:

I. Mission [G-11.0103a,b,c]
   A. Develop strategy for its area
   B. Coordinate the efforts of churches
   C. Start programs to carry out the ministry of the larger church in its area
   D. Engage in ecumenical relationships that will enlarge the Church's mission

II. Inclusiveness [G-11.0103d,e]
   A. Show inclusiveness in its structures and affirmative action in its employment practices
   B. Help churches to be inclusive

III. Duties to congregations [G-11.0103f,g]
  A. Provide help, guidance, and resources
  B. Provide pastoral care and regular visits

IV. Powers in regard to congregations [G-11.0103h,i,j,k,x,y]
  A. Organize churches
  B. Divide, dismiss, and dissolve churches
  C. Control location of churches
  D. Oversee pastorless churches
  E. Review minutes and records of sessions
  F. Act on requests for exemptions regarding real property
  G. Authorize lay administration of the Lord's Supper when needed

V. Inquirers and candidates [G-11.0103l,m,q]
  A. Care for candidates for ministry and inquirers
  B. Elect readers of ordination examinations
  C. Care for candidates for professional service other than ministry of the Word and Sacrament and commission them for ministry

VI. Powers in regard to ministers [G-11.0103n,o,p]
  A. Ordain, receive, dismiss, install, remove, and discipline ministers
  B. Establish and dissolve pastoral relationships
  C. Designate other than pastoral ministries
  D. Set minimum compensation standards for ministers and certified Christian educators

VII. Judicial [G-11.0103r,s]
  A. Serve as a court of the church
  B. Exercise original jurisdiction

VIII. Administration [G-11.0103v,w]
  A. Establish a nominating committee
  B. Establish and oversee the work of its agencies, committees, and commissions

IX. Relating to more inclusive governing bodies [G-11.0103t; G-18.0201, .0301]
  A. Elect commissioners
  B. See that orders are carried out
  C. Propose matters of common concern
  D. Vote on amendments to Constitution

Synod

The governing body next above the presbytery is synod. Over seventy years before the first meeting of a Presbyterian General Assembly in this country, the first synod was already in operation. It was organized as the Synod of Philadelphia in 1717, with four member presbyteries.

Synods are regional in nature, providing a broader base for mission than is usually available to individual presbyteries. Depending on a number of factors, including density of population and the number of churches in a given region, the geographical bounds of synods will vary. However, each synod must be composed of not fewer than three presbyteries [G-12.0101]. When the synod meets for business, its members are those commissioners (both elders and ministers) elected by the constituent presbyteries.

The Responsibilities of Synod. The work of synod is focused in two main directions: in relating to its member presbyteries and in relating to the General Assembly.

1. *Relating to presbyteries.* In addition to the duties of synod toward presbyteries discussed under the heading "Responsibilities in Common," the *Book of Order* cites a number of others. One of the most important functions of synod is described in G-12.0102j: "To provide services and programs for presbyteries, sessions, congregations, and members within its area that can be performed more effectively from a broad regional base."

It is more efficient and better stewardship for synod to do or provide certain things for all its presbyteries than for each presbytery to duplicate the effort. In some cases, synod enables ministries that would be difficult or impossible for a single presbytery to support. For example, church-related colleges are often supported by a synod or synods. This enables several presbyteries to share the burden of support and the benefit of having the institution in their area. Children's homes, facilities for ministry to the elderly, conference centers, camps, and church-related secondary schools are examples of institutions that may be supported in this way by synods.

Synods are also charged to "develop and provide resources as needed to facilitate the mission of its presbyteries" [G-12.0102e]. These resources might include a synod-wide media center with a library of films, books, tapes, and other education media. Synod may provide funds and advice for new church development among its presbyteries. Often programs of leadership training will be offered on a synod-wide level. While there may be only a handful of people in a single presbytery interested in the problems of drug and alcohol abuse, for example, synod could provide training and planning opportunities in this area for all its presbyteries. In this way synod helps to broaden the quality of programs and the scope of mission of its member presbyteries.

Synod's further responsibility is to work with its presbyteries as they establish general mission budgets and hire administrative staff for the presbytery. In these areas, synod is to hold before the presbyteries their responsibility for participation in the mission of the wider church and for implementing inclusive employment practices [G-12.0102f]. Synod is also to work with the presbyteries' committees on ministry and to help them "in matters related to the calling, ordaining, and placement of ministers" [G-12.0102g]. The permanent judicial commissions of synod are an important part of the judicial system of our church.

Synod is an important link of communication among the presbyteries and between the presbyteries and the General Assembly [G-12.0102h]. Depending on the structure of the synod, this function may be carried out in part through synod's council. This council is composed of representatives elected or appointed by each of the member presbyteries and meets between meetings of the synod itself. Publishing regular newsletters or magazines is another means of furthering communication. Synods should try to find effective, creative ways to carry out this function, shaping the means to the needs of their particular situation.

The *Book of Order* also lists several powers that synods have in relation to presbyteries. Along with those common powers discussed earlier, synod shapes the boundaries of presbyteries within its area. Included is the power to "organize new presbyteries and to divide, unite, or otherwise combine presbyteries or portions of presbyteries previously existing" [G-12.0102k]. In the years following the reunion of the United Presbyterian Church in the United States of America and the Presbyterian Church in the United States, there was much activity of this kind as presbyteries of the former churches that shared geographical boundaries had those boundaries rearranged. Synod exercises this power subject to the approval of the General Assembly.

2. *Relating to the General Assembly.* The responsibilities of synod in relationship to the General Assembly are more limited than those of presbyteries. Synods do not, for example, elect commissioners to the General Assembly; this right is reserved for presbyteries. Synods are charged, however, with seeing that the orders of the General Assembly are communicated and carried out within the synod.

Synods, like presbyteries, are also responsible for proposing to the General Assembly "such measures as may be of common concern to the mission of the whole Church" [G-12.0102o]. This responsibility reflects the other side of communication between the presbyteries and the General Assembly. Not only does synod tell the presbyteries what the General Assembly has decided, but it also communicates to the General Assembly the concerns of the presbyteries.

An outline of the powers and responsibilities of synods:

I. Mission [G-12.0102a,b,c,e]
   A. Develop strategy for its area
   B. Start programs that carry out the mission of the larger church
   C. Develop and implement plans for mission with its presbyteries
   D. Resource presbyteries for mission

II. Duties to presbyteries [G-12.0102f,g,h,j]
   A. Consult about budgets and staff
   B. Assist in placement of ministers
   C. Stimulate communication among governing bodies
   D. Provide services and programs

III. Organize, divide, unite, or otherwise combine presbyteries [G-12.0102k]

IV. Administrative and judicial duties [G-12.0102l,n,o,q,r,s]
   A. Serve in judicial matters
   B. Review records of presbyteries
   C. Relate to the General Assembly
   D. Develop administrative services necessary to carry out goals
   E. Establish and oversee the work of agencies, task forces, and councils
   F. Establish a nominating committee

V. Ecumenical [G-12.0102i,p]
   A. Facilitate ecumenical mission work
   B. Establish and maintain ecumenical relationships

The General Assembly

The first meeting of a Presbyterian General Assembly in the United States was held in 1789 in Philadelphia, Pennsylvania. It reflected the practice of the Scottish Church in gathering commissioners from all the presbyteries to meet together and conduct business on a denomination-wide basis. The unity of the separate parts of the church—congregations, sessions, presbyteries, and synods—is represented by the General Assembly. When it meets for business, its members are the commissioners (elders and ministers in equal numbers) elected by the presbyteries.

The Responsibilities of the General Assembly. The powers and duties of the General Assembly are many and wide-ranging. A number of these have already been discussed in the section on common responsibilities. Here we will focus on duties and powers in two main areas, those relating specifically to synods and those relating to the whole church.

1. *Relating to synods.* As the next more inclusive governing body, the General Assembly has particular responsibilities toward the synods of the church. The General Assembly is to supervise the work of synods and to help them take an active, effective role in the mission of the whole church [G-13.0103k]. This involves providing resources and leadership training for mission on the synod level. The General Assembly also exercises governance over the synods, reviewing their minutes and seeing that they act in accord with the Constitution of the church. One facet of governance is that of setting the boundaries of synods. The General Assembly can "organize new synods and . . . divide, unite, or otherwise combine synods or portions of synods previously existing" [G-13.0103m]. As mentioned above, when synods desire to change the boundaries of presbyteries or organize new presbyteries, the General Assembly must approve their proposals.

2. *Relating to the whole church.* The General Assembly "constitutes the bond of union, community, and mission among its congregations and governing bodies" [G-13.0103]. For this reason, many of the responsibilities of the General Assembly are carried out in relation to or on behalf of the whole church.

The first duties listed in the *Book of Order* are those involved with mission and program. The General Assembly sets priorities, develops objectives and strategies, and provides resources to carry out the mission of the entire denomination. This includes programs and ministries of evangelism, service, and prophetic witness. The character of these programs should be such as will foster diversity and balance within the mission of the whole church. The General Assembly is also authorized to set up the administrative systems needed to carry out this mission [G-13.0103a,b,c,d,e].

The sphere of mission for the General Assembly is the whole world. While other governing bodies may engage in specific mission projects elsewhere in this country or overseas, the Assembly coordinates the overall national and international mission program of the church. The General Assembly commissions mission coworkers for their ministries. It also maintains relationships with our partner denominations in other countries and coordinates our work with them.

Another duty is "to provide services for the whole Church that can be performed more effectively from a national base" [G-13.0103f]. These services may include a denominational curriculum for the education program of the congregation, a denominational press that publishes books of particular interest to Presbyterians, and systems for coordinating the movement of ministers within the church. In order to fulfill its responsibility to provide for communication within the church, the General Assembly may support a denominational magazine and/or newspaper. The General Assembly also provides resources and direction for the evangelism, justice, and service ministries of less inclusive governing bodies. As with presbyteries and synods, the General Assembly is allowed to form and oversee any agencies or other groups necessary to carry out this work. These agencies include a General Assembly Council, whose duties are discussed in G-13.0200.

On behalf of the whole church, the General Assembly maintains relationships with bodies of other faiths and denominations. Representatives of these groups are often invited to meetings of the General Assembly as ecumenical participants. The Constitution also gives the General Assembly certain powers relating to receiving or uniting with other ecclesiastical bodies under the provisions of G-15.0300. One such exercise in ecumenical relating is the "Formula of Agreement" between our church, the Evangelical Lutheran Church in America, the Reformed Church in America, and the United Church of Christ. The formula was voted by the 1997 General Assembly and approved by the presbyteries, going into effect in June of 1998. It is included in the 1998–1999 *Book of Order*. This agreement between the four denominations required no new structures or changes in our ordination practices. However, it did have the effect of bringing us into full communion with these other three denominations. Full communion means that there is mutual recognition among the churches that each is a true church of Jesus Christ and also that each will recognize ordinations to ministry by the other churches as valid. Celebrating the Lord's Supper together is also part of full communion.

As the highest governing body in the church, the General Assembly is given the power "to decide controversies brought before it and to give advice and instruction in cases submitted to it, in conformity with the Constitution" [G-13.0103q]. In cases of judicial process, the General Assembly exercises this function through its Permanent Judicial Commission. The rulings of this Permanent Judicial Commission in appeals from the decisions of lower governing bodies are final. Often issues of concern to the wider church will be brought before the General Assembly in the form of overtures from lower governing bodies or of resolutions from commissioners to the General Assembly. The decisions and advice of the General Assembly on these matters are printed in its minutes. From time to time in carrying out this duty the General Assembly will also authorize statements or study papers on current issues to be written and distributed to the churches.

The following is an outline of the responsibilities and powers of the General Assembly:

I. Mission and program [G-13.0103a–f]
   A. Set priorities for the whole church
   B. Develop objectives and strategy
   C. Provide necessary program functions

D. Carry on national and worldwide ministries
E. Provide its own administrative services
F. Provide appropriate services for the whole church

II. Administrative [G-13.0103g,h,j,x]
A. Maintain an office of the General Assembly
B. Oversee its agencies and Council
C. Provide for communications in the church
D. Review the work of the office of the General Assembly

III. Powers in relation to synods [G-13.0103k,l,m,n]
A. Oversee and resource the synods
B. Review records of all synods
C. Organize, unite, or divide synods
D. Approve the organization or division of presbyteries by synods

IV. Discipline and advice [G-13.0103o,p,q,r]
A. To serve as the highest court of the church in judicial matters
B. To warn against error or immorality
C. To decide controversies and give advice
D. To interpret the *Book of Order*

V. Ecumenical [G-13.0103s,t,u,v,w]
A. Maintain ecumenical relationships on behalf of the whole church
B. Correspond with other churches
C. Receive other churches into our denomination
D. Authorize synods to receive appropriate ecclesiastical bodies
E. To unite with other churches as allowed by the Constitution

Committees, Commissions, Agencies, and Councils

The *Book of Order* states that a governing body "may delegate particular aspects of its task to councils, boards, agencies, commissions, and committees, but always on the basis of accountability to the governing body" [G-9.0403]. This means that the work of the body is carried out by these groups between its meetings, yet they are all responsible to the governing body for their actions. While governing bodies are required to have certain specific committees, in general the *Book of Order* gives a great deal of flexibility in making decisions about the structure of a particular governing body.

A commission is a group given the authority to "consider and conclude matters referred to it by a governing body" [G-9.0502]. Disposition by a commission is final disposition. When such actions are reported to the governing body and recorded in its minutes, they become the actions of the body itself. In the case of judicial commissions, the decision of the commission becomes a final judgment when a copy of the written decision is signed by the clerk or moderator of the commission [D-7.0402(c)].

There are two types of commissions, administrative and judicial. Among the functions of administrative commissions are organizing and merging churches, ordaining and installing ministers, and visiting churches involved in conflict [G-9.0503a(3)]. Judicial commissions consider and decide cases of process. Every presbytery and synod and the General Assembly must have a permanent judicial commission to serve as outlined in the Rules of Discipline. A committee has a narrower field of responsibility than a commission, serving only to "recommend appropriate action or to carry out directions or decisions already made by a governing body" [G-9.0501a]. The actions of committees must be reported to their governing body for action. Much of the work of the church is carried out by committees. The *Book of Order* [G-9.0902] requires that each presbytery have a council, a Committee on Representation, a Committee on Ministry, a Committee on Preparation for Ministry, a Nominating Committee, and a Permanent Judicial Commission. Synods must have a Council, a Committee on Representation, a Nominating Committee, and a Permanent Judicial Commission. The General Assembly must have a Committee on Representation, an Advisory Committee on the Constitution, a Nominating Committee, a Permanent Judicial Commission, and a council [G-13.0108, .0111, .0112].

The work these bodies do is crucial to the effective functioning of the church. Nominating committees nominate persons to serve on all elected bodies of the church [G-9.0801, 13.0111]. The nominating committees of presbytery, synod, and the General Assembly are composed of one-third laymen, one-third laywomen, and one-third ministers. At the presbytery level, the Committee on Ministry "pastors" the ministers in the presbytery, counsels with ministers and churches in difficulty or conflict, and encourages communication among congregations, ministers, and the presbytery [G-11.0501a]. The Committee on Preparation for Ministry is responsible to supervise and care for those received by the presbytery as inquirers and candidates for ministry of the Word and Sacrament [G-14.0300]. At the General Assembly level, the Advisory Committee on the Constitution counsels the General Assembly on all questions relating to the interpretation of the *Book of Order*, including proposed changes. In preparation for meetings of the General Assembly, all new business that relates to the Constitution is referred to this committee for consideration and recommendation.

A feature of our reunited church's *Book of Order* is the Committee on Representation. Each presbytery and synod and the General Assembly are required to have such a committee, the major duty of which shall be to advise the governing bodies with respect to their membership and that of their committees, boards, agencies, and other units. The goal of this advice is to help implement the principles of participation and inclusiveness to ensure fair and effective representation in the decision making of the church [G-9.0105].

The Committee on Representation plays such an important part in our church's quest for inclusiveness and diversity that the *Book of Order* was revised in 1998 to specify that "The Committee on Representation shall not, in any governing body, be merged with any other committee or designated as a subcommittee of any other committee" [G-9.0105f]. At the same time, G-9.0106 was revised to make it clear that every governing body above the session must elect a Committee on Representation and to set out the conditions under which a presbytery may claim an exemption to the provision that a majority of the Committee's members be selected from racial ethnic groups if it is unable to secure such persons to serve [G-9.0106a,b].

This committee acts as an advocate for persons of different age groups (youth and the elderly, for example), women, persons with disabilities, and racial ethnic group members within the structures of the governing body. The Committee on Representation is a resource for the Nominating Committee, suggesting names of qualified persons in these groups and working to locate such persons who are willing to serve. The Nominating Committee and the Committee on Representation are required to consult with each other at least annually toward these ends. The Committee on Representation also seeks to ensure that the hiring practices of the body are in line with what our Constitution says about inclusiveness in the church. It has no power to appoint anyone to an office or position or to require that certain quotas be filled; rather, it functions to monitor and promote inclusiveness. A majority of those on this committee are to be members of racial ethnic groups. One does not have to be an elder to serve.

The *Book of Order* allows for governing bodies to establish agencies as needed to carry out their work [G-9.0901]. These groups could include task forces, boards, and advocacy groups of various sorts. Every governing body above the session, with the exception of some synods [G-12.0102r], is required to have a council that oversees and evaluates the work of the body. One duty of such a council is to critique the structures of the governing body to make sure that they are appropriate to its mission and to the goals of the wider church. Councils also play an important function in coordinating all the various aspects of a governing body's work, making sure that business and mission are carried out wisely and well.

The system of related governing bodies that our polity provides draws Christians from far-flung locations into one denomination. Each presbytery, each synod, and the General Assembly exercises governance over and carries out mission in the particular part of the church that is under its jurisdiction. The relationships between these governing bodies enable a worldwide mission and express the essential unity of the church.

Chapter Eleven

STEWARDSHIP, FINANCE, AND PROPERTY

Ruth Diaz, a newly installed elder, has just attended her first session meeting. In talking with her family about it, she mentions that the agenda included a financial report and review of the church's budget, as well as a rather lengthy discussion about the stewardship campaign being planned for the fall. "I'm surprised that the session would spend all that time talking about money," comments her husband. "Aren't the trustees supposed to be responsible for that kind of thing?"

Offerings during the summer have been low at First Presbyterian Church, and there is not enough money in the church's bank account to pay the minister's salary for July. In the course of the session meeting called to discuss this problem, one elder mentions that several thousand dollars have been accumulated from special gifts toward the purchase of a new organ for the sanctuary. He suggests that this money be used to make up the shortfall in pledges. A motion to use these funds is made and seconded, but several elders are troubled by the idea. What is wrong with using these special gifts to pay the minister's salary?

Suburban Presbyterian Church has received an offer to buy five acres of its undeveloped property from a local builder who plans to put a shopping center on it. A congregational meeting is called to discuss this possibility. In the course of the meeting the minister announces that before the congregation can sell its property, the session must obtain the written permission of presbytery. Soon afterward a member of the congregation takes the floor to ask, "This property has belonged to our congregation for a long time. We paid for it, and we hold title to it. Why do we need to have presbytery's permission to sell it?"

The Grace of Stewardship

To many people, "stewardship" is a euphemism for church fund-raising. A stewardship sermon is a sermon asking for money. Stewardship visitation is a means of obtaining pledges to underwrite the church's budget. Stewardship Sunday is the day those pledges are collected. The whole business is seen as a necessary evil inflicted on the church once a year and somehow foreign to the real meaning of Christianity.

Underlying this attitude are two common, but faulty, ideas. The first is that what we earn or own is ours absolutely, by right of labor or inheritance, to dispose of as we see fit. The second is that money, being secular, is alien to the spiritual character of the church, an embarrassing necessity, perhaps, but far removed from the heart of the Christian life.

The Bible is full of declarations that God, as Creator, is the source of all our blessings and the ultimate owner of all things. Psalm 24 begins:

> The earth is the Lord's and the fullness thereof,
> the world and those who dwell therein;
> for he has founded it upon the seas,
> and established it upon the rivers.

Everything that is good and helpful is a gift from God, given not because we deserve it but because God's love toward us overflows into giving. Even our capacity to work and earn money is built upon gifts that we did not do anything to earn: intelligence, talent, health, and the opportunity for education. Real stewardship begins with the grateful acceptance of God's love and blessing. It is a grace born in response to what God has done for us. It is our love for God overflowing in practical ways into every area of life.

The idea that linking money to the spiritual life is somehow wrong finds very little warrant in Scripture. From the earliest days men and women brought things that were precious to them for sacrifice to Yahweh. Times of celebration, thanksgiving, and penitence were marked with gifts. Worship without sacrifice was unthinkable. The Old Testament prophets had no hesitation about taking the people to task about their stewardship. They preached that God's claim of life was total and absolute. It extended beyond the traditional rituals of religion to how one did business and earned and spent money.

Jesus' perceptive comment, "Where your treasure is, there will your heart be also," sets the tone for New Testament teachings on stewardship. It is interesting to note just how many of Jesus' teachings, sayings, and parables have to do with money and possessions. Again and again he stresses that faith cannot be separated from the affairs of everyday life. His parables are filled with the imagery of economics: a woman searching for a coin, a merchant buying a perfect pearl, a man leaving money with his servants to invest while he goes on a journey. In the vision of the Judgment Day found in Matthew 25, Jesus' identification with the poor is such that it must have direct economic impact on those who love him. Finally, the cross confronts us with the ultimate picture of sacrificial giving and calls us to commit all we are and have to the service of our Savior.

The book of Acts tells how the gospel influenced the first Christians in their use of possessions:

> Now the company of those who believed were of one heart and soul, and no one said that any of the things which he possessed were his own, but they had everything in common. . . . There was not a needy person among them, for as many as were possessors of lands or houses sold them, and brought the proceeds of what was sold and laid it at the apostles' feet; and distribution was made to each as any had need. (Acts 4:32–35)

The apostle Paul spent considerable time and effort during his ministry encouraging the grace of liberality among his congregations. He praised the churches in Macedonia who, though very poor themselves, gave freely to aid the Christians in famine-stricken Jerusalem. These passages echo the message of the whole Bible: God's love demands the best of ourselves and our possessions in response. They make it clear that stewardship is more than simply raising money to keep the church going. Rather it is a lifestyle of grace that

> should take the form, in part, of giving a worthy proportion of [our] income to the church of Jesus Christ, of giving [our]selves in dedication to God, of giving service to others in God's behalf, thus worshiping the Lord with all [we] have and are. Furthermore, all not given more directly to God should be used as a Christian testimony to God and to the world.[1]

Presbyterian Stewardship

To be a Presbyterian is to be in relationship with other Presbyterians all over the world. We are not individual congregations choosing to associate with one another in order to accomplish certain tasks; rather we are the body of Christ, unified and unbroken. The Presbyterian Church is

> a spiritual commonwealth bound together by a series of ascending [governing bodies] which are in subjection to one another in the Lord. . . . Although its members worship in local congregations in different places, these congregations are parts of one whole, elements of one church, organs of one body.[2]

It is because of this relationship that we send money collected in the congregation to presbytery, synod, and General Assembly. We are participating in the life and mission of the larger church through our gifts. This participation takes a number of different forms, including general mission giving, special offerings, and per capita assessments.

General Mission Giving. The *Book of Order* charges the session "to lead the congregation in participation in the mission of the whole Church in the world" [G-10.0102c]. As Presbyterians, our opportunities for ministry begin at our own doorstep, but they extend across the entire earth. It is because of these opportunities that sessions budget part of the offerings of the people for general mission giving.

Presbyteries and synods are responsible for a general mission budget to support the work of the church in their area [G-11.0304, 12.0303]. The general mission budget of the General Assembly supports the ministry of the church at the national and worldwide level. Money for these budgets comes from the gifts of each local congregation. Through giving to general mission budgets, Presbyterians on the local level have the opportunity to take part in the wider ministry of the church. They support, among other things, children's homes and retirement communities for the elderly. They fund the work of missionaries in dozens of countries. They provide for a denominational church school curriculum and resources for youth ministry. They provide food for the hungry, hospital care for the sick, and re-settlement help for refugees. General mission funds help support colleges and other educational institutions, not only in our country but also overseas. On the presbytery level, general mission money might be used to help operate a night shelter or soup kitchen. It might support a home for battered women or a presbytery camp or conference center. It also provides for resource people to staff the presbytery and to develop programs of nurture and mission. Participation in all these ministries through giving to general mission budgets makes our oneness in Christ a living reality.

Giving to general mission budgets falls into two categories: unified giving and selected giving. Unified gifts go into the general budgets of the governing bodies to support their whole mission and program. Selected giving is targeted by the donors to go toward specific objectives—the denomination's evangelism program and the Theological Education Fund, to cite two examples. Both types of giving have their place in the practice of Christian stewardship. Unified giving, normally the lion's share of an individual's or congregation's gifts, makes possible the day-to-day operation and ministry of the church as a whole. Without strong unified giving the church's worldwide ministry would cease. Selected giving, on the other hand, helps people get involved in and support a particular area of the church's work. It develops personal interest in mission and enthusiasm for stewardship. The session should promote strong unified giving while at the same time offering judiciously chosen opportunities for selected giving.

The *Book of Order* places the responsibility for determining the distribution of the church's benevolences on the session in G-10.0102i. This provision refers not only to deciding where such funds shall go but also to deciding what proportion of the congregation's offerings is allocated to mission beyond the local church. In allocating the amount to be distributed to benevolence causes, the session should take seriously the responsibility of the congregation for mission beyond itself. A ratio of one dollar of benevolence for every ten dollars of current receipts is a good goal for churches to work toward in distributing these funds.

Special Offerings, Emergency Appeals, and Campaigns. In addition to general mission funds, the governing bodies of the church also approve the taking of special offerings for specific purposes. These offerings are not counted toward fulfillment of one's pledge but are "over-and-above" gifts, focusing on a particular area of need or mission. Collections for support of racial-ethnic schools and those for ministerial relief, along with the One Great Hour of Sharing offering, are examples of special offerings approved by the General Assembly. A synod might authorize a special offering for the purpose of new church development. A presbytery might decide to finance its hunger program in this way. These offerings are usually received on a continuing basis at a particular time of year.

Occasionally emergency needs arise, and offerings are taken to meet these needs. These offerings are called emergency appeals. They are usually one-time collections for specific purposes, such as relief for a severe famine or for a disaster area. These offerings can be authorized by any governing body as necessary, and they also are over-and-above gifts.

Often institutions of the church such as seminaries and colleges will have special campaigns to build new buildings or create endowment funds. Before an institution can solicit such funds from congregations or sessions, it must have the approval of the presbytery. These campaigns are not special offerings per se, but they are collections over and above the general mission budget, for specific purposes. While supporting the mission thrust of the whole church through general mission funding, Presbyterians are able to become involved with particular aspects of the work through these special offerings, appeals, and campaigns.

Although most of the requests for special offering funds received by churches are for good, even denominational, causes, there are usually far too many to take offerings for all of them. It is the responsibility of the session to review these requests and to decide which offerings will be received by the congregation. In doing so, the session should give special consideration to requests from its own presbytery and synod and the General Assembly. After the offerings have been received, the session has the responsibility to see that the funds "are distributed to the objects toward which they were contributed" [G-10.0102h].

Per Capita Monies. This term, literally meaning "by heads," refers to a voluntary apportionment used to finance the meetings and ecclesiastical work of governing bodies above the level of the session. The General Assembly in particular depends upon per capita monies. Most presbyteries and synods also use this form of funding. Generally, governing bodies set the amount of the per person asking annually, and the money is received by presbyteries from local congregations.

Per capita funding pays for the expenses of presbytery, synod, and General Assembly meetings, including meals, housing, and travel expenses for commissioners. This allows all persons to participate in the government of the church regardless of their financial status, and thus helps implement the principle of broad participation. Per capita funds also enable the work of many of the administrative committees and commissions of the church. For example, on the General Assembly level these funds cover the expenses of the Nominating Committee and the Permanent Judicial Commission. The Office of the General Assembly, the General Assembly Council, and some of our denomination's ecumenical activities are also financed in this way.

Stewardship Development and the Session

The *Book of Order* places the responsibility for nurturing the grace of stewardship in the congregation squarely on the session. Over half of the duties of the session listed in G-10.0102 touch either directly or indirectly on this topic. Even in churches where part of this responsibility has been delegated to a board of trustees or to deacons, the session is still to provide "support, report, review, and control" as they do this important work [G-10.0102m].

The session is specifically charged "to challenge the people of God with the privilege of responsible Christian stewardship of money and time and talents, developing effective ways for encouraging and gathering the offerings of the people" [G-10.0102h]. The *Book of Order* also says that elders are to "strengthen and nurture the faith and life of the congregation committed to their charge . . . , encourage the people in the worship and service of God, and equip and renew them for their tasks within the Church and for their mission in the world" [G-6.0304]. The carrying out of these responsibilities depends directly on stewardship through general mission giving, just as the quality of a church's stewardship hampers or helps the mission of the local congregation. Without generous gifts of time, talents, and money, the work of the church cannot go forward. Without a constant outpouring of gratitude to God in practical form, faith grows stagnant and sterile. Stewardship development is a primary duty of the session as a whole and of elders as individuals.

There are many ways that the session can fulfill this responsibility, and two deserve particular mention. First, elders should be leaders in personal stewardship. The *Book of Order* [G-6.0304] states:

Those duties which all Christians are bound to perform by the law of love are especially incumbent upon elders because of their calling to office and are to be fulfilled by them as official responsibilities.

Elders should be role models to the congregation in the areas of stewardship and sacrificial giving. If the leadership of the session in this area is

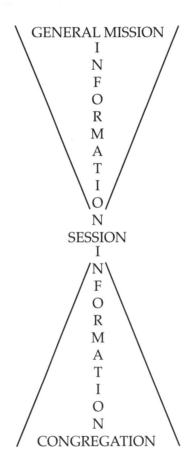

weak, if elders are "preaching" something they do not practice, the whole program of the church will suffer.

    Those approached about being nominated for the office of elder should give earnest consideration to the stewardship responsibilities of the position before they accept. Elders should be tithers or serious proportionate givers moving toward tithing. Their use of the rest of their possessions should reflect God's ownership of the whole. New elders should look upon their training period as a time to review their giving of money as well as time and talents to the church. They should take seriously the biblical teaching that God will provide for those who respond to the call to do God's will. The giving of a sacrificial proportion of one's income to God's church is as much a duty of elders as is serving communion or visiting the sick.

A second important responsibility of the session in the area of stewardship development is sharing information about the mission of the wider church with the congregation. The session is the vital link between the congregation and the rest of the body of Christ. As illustrated in the diagram on the opposite page, information flows through the session into the congregation. This information stimulates the giving that makes the mission of the wider church possible.

With the minister, elders should plan and carry out creative ways to "lead the congregation continually to discover what God is doing in the world" [G-10.0102j] and to share with its members "opportunities for witness and service in the world" [G-10.0102e]. The church budget should be set up in such a way that the mission of the church is clearly represented to the congregation. Announcements during worship or a regular Minute for Mission can be used to communicate information about the work of the wider church. Articles in the church newsletter, special programs using films or speakers, and subscriptions to denominational periodicals are all ways in which the session can help people understand what happens to their dollars beyond the local church.

It has been traditional in some areas for the session to delegate much of its financial and stewardship responsibility to the deacons or the board of trustees. Along this line, the *Book of Order* does provide that deacons "shall assume such other duties as may be delegated to them from time to time by the session" [G-6.0402]. It is clear, however, that the *Book of Order* intends stewardship development to be an important and primary duty of the session. This responsibility is so essential to the spiritual welfare and mission of the church that it deserves constant close attention.

Stewardship and Financial Management[3]

Once the job of stewardship development in the congregation has been accomplished and the offerings are received, it is up to the session to serve as steward or manager of these funds. The session is morally and legally responsible for the correct administration and disbursement of the people's gifts. The session must take its financial duties seriously, using all the means at its disposal to carry out this trust with integrity. Sloppy or unwise management of the congregation's offerings is poor stewardship on the part of the session.

The *Book of Order* touches on a number of points that relate to the fiscal responsibilities of the session. These include the church budget, supervision of the work of the treasurer, yearly audits, financial reports to the congregation, and correct handling of specified gifts.

The Church Budget. In simplest terms, a church budget shows how much money the church expects to receive in a given period of time or for a particular purpose and how it intends to spend that money. In a broader sense, however, a budget is a reflection of values, a statement of goals, an authorization to spend money, and a restraint on spending.

Every budget, whether of a family, a business, or a church, reveals the values of those who drew it up. A family that decides not to budget the cost of a new car this year in favor of putting the money into savings for future college costs is saying something about what is important. A business that budgets gifts to charitable and cultural organizations in the community is making a statement of values. In much the same way, the priorities of a congregation are revealed in its budget.

Try analyzing your congregation's budget in terms of the values it reflects. Compare the amount spent for operating expenses (utilities, supplies, and so on) with the amount spent for programs and ministries. Compare what the church gives for general mission with what it keeps for local use. How does your church budget speak to the needs of your community? How does it reflect the priorities and mission of the wider church? What budget item has the largest allotment of funds? Is this item really one that most people would consider a primary priority of the church? Budgets talk, and questions like these can help you hear what your church budget is saying.

Budgets are also statements of a congregation's goals. Goals are concrete and specific things that the church wants to accomplish. Building a new sanctuary, recruiting and training three new church school teachers, starting a shepherding program, or winning ten persons to Christ in the next year are examples of goals. While some of the work of the church can be done by volunteers with little expense involved, most goals require some sort of funding. Even if the goal is simply to keep the doors open and provide weekly services of worship, the minister must be paid and utility bills arrive regularly. A budget that reflects the stated goals of the congregation helps to focus attention on those goals and to make sure that the resources are available to accomplish them.

Budgeting should be preceded by an intentional process of evaluation and planning. What new opportunities for mission have arisen? What new needs have been discovered? Is the church growing or languishing? What programs have been successful in the past year? What programs have not? Where does the church want to be a year from now? What methods will it use to get there? Specific goals arise out of this kind of questioning. Once they have been arrived at, goals are then ordered according to priority, and funds are budgeted as necessary to accomplish them. If this kind of budget is shared with the congregation, they will have a clearer idea of where their church, and their money, is going.

The budget is also an authorization to spend money. If the session had to vote on every expenditure of funds, little else would get done around the church. On the other hand, there has to be some control over disbursements if the session is to be a responsible steward. The budget, duly approved by the session, permits specified persons to spend money on behalf of the church to carry out its programs on a day-to-day basis. For instance, if the worship committee has a budget item for music supplies, it can spend that money on printed music, choir robes, music folders, or any other music-related item without going to the session for approval. The original adoption of the budget gave them this authority.

The budget also serves as a restraint on spending. Many people have gotten into financial trouble because they did not keep track of how much they were spending. Churches too can get into difficulty when there are no clear financial limits. A budget provides a kind of fiscal safety net, helping to ensure that the funds provided by the congregation are being used as intended to carry out the church's program.

It is the session's duty to "establish the annual budget" [G-10.0102i]. In the Presbyterian Church, the congregation does not vote on the entire budget. The session prepares the budget and presents it to the congregation for information. Although the congregation may make recommendations to the session about various budget items, it votes only on changes in the minister's terms of call [G-7.0304a(3)]. These include increases or decreases in compensation and the addition or deletion of benefits. The session must present any changes in terms of call to the congregation so that they can exercise this right. Otherwise, all decisions relating to the budget, including the allocation of general mission monies [G-10.0102i], are the responsibility of the session.

Supervision of the Work of the Treasurer. G-10.0401 states of the treasurer that "his or her work shall be supervised by the session, or by specific assignment to the board of deacons or trustees. Those in charge of the various funds in the church shall report at least annually to the session, and more often when requested." Here again it is clear that the session is the steward of the gifts of the congregation. This section of the *Book of Order* goes on to say:

> The following minimum standards of financial procedure shall be observed:
> a. The counting and recording of all offerings by at least two duly appointed persons, or a fidelity bonded person;
> b. The keeping of adequate books and records to reflect all financial transactions, open to inspection by authorized church officers at reasonable times;

c. Periodic reporting of the financial activities to the board or boards vested with financial oversight at least annually, preferably more often.

These procedures do not reflect distrust of any person in the church. Rather, they protect those who handle the church's money and provide for orderly lines of accountability and communication.

The status of the current operating fund of the church should be reported to the session regularly. At the very least, these reports should include a statement of actual income for the period, in comparison with the anticipated budgeted income. They should include expenses in major program categories, compared with budgeted funds for those programs. They should also include the status of all ongoing benevolence commitments. A year-end statement of income and expenses should include budgeted figures for the year, actual figures for the year, and actual figures for the preceding year. Such statements can be very simple in form, but their purpose is to let the session gauge the financial health of the church and how far it has progressed toward meeting its goals.

Financial Reviews. A financial review is an examination of financial records for the purpose of verifying that all financial transactions have been properly carried out and recorded. The *Book of Order* [G-10.0401d] requires a

full financial review of all books and records relating to finances once each year by a public accountant or public accounting firm or a committee of members versed in accounting procedures. Such auditors should not be related to the treasurer (or treasurers).

Upon completion, the results of this annual review should be reported promptly to the session.

Larger churches with more complicated financial affairs will contract with professionals for their audit. Smaller churches may choose to have their members review the books. A church with several members who are knowledgeable about accounting (and not otherwise involved in keeping the church's books) could easily establish such a financial review committee.

The financial review serves "to certify the financial statements of the church, verify the propriety of the entries made throughout the year, and to make certain that all the items of income received and disbursed during the period have been recorded in the books of account."[4] As with financial reports, these review procedures are not meant to show suspicion of anyone; rather, they protect those who do the church's financial record keeping. Anyone can make a mistake, and a review simply brings any mistakes to light so that they can be corrected. This accepted practice in the world of business can help the church manage its money more correctly and efficiently.

Financial Reports to the Congregation. The *Book of Order* says that the session has the responsibility "to establish the annual budget, determine the distribution of the church's benevolences, and order offerings for Christian purposes, *providing full information to the congregation of its decisions in such matters*"(emphasis ours) [G-10.0102i].

While the congregation is not entitled to vote on the entire budget or many other financial decisions, it should still be kept informed as to the status of the church's finances. People want to know how their money is being handled, and regular reports can instill confidence and stimulate giving. They help inspire the feeling that the session is doing its best to be a good steward of the funds contributed by the congregation. Far too often a congregation is kept in the dark about money matters until a crisis arises and an appeal of some sort has to be made. This gives the impression that the church's money is being managed poorly. If the session informs the congregation of the church's ongoing financial situation, many of these crisis appeals can be avoided, and those that are necessary because of unusual circumstances will probably receive a better response.

There are any number of ways that the session can assure that full information about finances is provided to the congregation. In small churches a simple monthly report could be posted in the narthex or printed in the bulletin. Such a report should include income figures, both from pledged and from other sources, for the period and for the year to date. It should also include a summary of expenses and indicate what the balance is when expenses are subtracted from income. A statement of the total assets of the church, including any savings accounts or special funds, is helpful as well. The report should also indicate the amount received for any special offerings, with a statement that these have been sent to their appropriate destination. Larger churches could print such a monthly statement in their newsletter, perhaps in addition to a weekly report of how much income was received last week compared to how much is needed to meet the budget for that period. If pledged income begins to fall behind, the congregation should be informed promptly and specifically, either in terms of a percentage of budgeted income or of a dollar figure in comparison to budgeted income.

Congregations should also be given a year-end report that, in addition to the above information, indicates how far the church has progressed toward meeting the goals expressed in the budget. For instance, if one of the goals was to increase general mission giving by 5 percent of budgeted income, the congregation should be informed whether or not the goal was attained. Annual reports should also show a number of important ratios, such as the per member giving rate (gift income divided by church membership), the ratio of pledged income to giving units, and the ratio of benevolences (money used in mission beyond the membership) to program and operating expenses. These figures should be presented in comparison to those of other Presbyterian churches in the area of similar size, to give the congregation an idea of where they stand in stewardship. Just as this information is extremely helpful to the session as it evaluates and makes plans for the future, so it is helpful to the congregation's understanding of the work of the church.

Handling of Designated Gifts. In a very real sense, money given to the church is given in trust. In a trust agreement there are three parties involved: donor, trustee, and beneficiary. The trustee has the responsibility to make sure that the money is used by the beneficiary as the donor intended. In the situation where a church receives funds, the session is put in the position of being both beneficiary (on behalf of the church) and trustee. As trustee, it is the moral and legal duty of the session to see that the intention of the giver is carried out. In the case of a gift to the current operating budget of the church, the session has the responsibility to ensure that the program represented by the budget is carried out in the way that was indicated to the congregation when the gift was made. In the case of a gift designated or specified for a particular purpose, the session has clear responsibility to ensure that the gift is used as was intended. For instance, in the second example at the beginning of this chapter, the question was raised as to whether the session could use money that had been donated toward the purchase of a new organ to make up a shortfall in current operating income. Deficits of this kind are embarrassing and troublesome, and it is very tempting to use restricted gifts to make up the amount needed. However, this is a clear violation of the intent of the donors, who gave the money with the understanding that it would be used for a specified purpose. The session would be abusing its position as trustee of these funds if it used them to pay the minister's salary without the express permission of the donor.

Situations of unintentional abuse can be avoided by keeping specified gifts entirely separate from gifts to the current operating budget. A different bank account for these special gifts is strongly recommended. Into this account could be placed all specified memorial gifts, as well as the proceeds from special offerings for various causes. It is also a good practice to place a percentage of the weekly offering equal to the church's pledged benevolence commitments into this special account, for disbursement of benevolences either monthly or quarterly.

Good financial management is good stewardship by the session. Even though the church is a nonprofit corporation, appropriate business practices should be used to manage more effectively the gifts given by the congregation to the glory of God. The discussion above is only the briefest survey of church business management principles. Those assigned specific duties in regard to the church's finances should make a more detailed study of the subject.

The Session and Church Property

Among the responsibilities of the session listed in the Form of Government is "to provide for the management of the property of the church, including determination of the appropriate use of church buildings and facilities" [G-10.0102n]. Considering that a good part of the church's resources is invested in its buildings and property, this duty is an important one. It becomes even more important in light of the fact that this management is carried out not only on behalf of the local congregation but also for the wider church.

Property Held in Trust. Section G-8.0201 states:

> All property held by or for a particular church, a presbytery, a synod, the General Assembly, or the Presbyterian Church (U.S.A.), whether legal title is lodged in a corporation, a trustee or trustees, or an unincorporated association, and whether the property is used in programs of a particular church or of a more inclusive governing body or retained for the production of income, is held in trust nevertheless for the use and benefit of the Presbyterian Church (U.S.A.).

This means that while the congregation or governing body holds title to its property, it also accepts certain restrictions on the rights of ownership.

This view of the ownership of church property stems from our relational form of church government. As the *Book of Order* says, "The several different congregations of believers, taken collectively, constitute one Church of Christ, called emphatically the Church" [G-1.0400]. We are not separate churches with a voluntary affiliation with one another; we are all one church, bound together in unity by Jesus Christ. Each congregation of this one church is entrusted to manage its property for the good of the entire Presbyterian Church (U.S.A.).

This basic principle works itself out in a number of ways in relation to the property of congregations. If a congregation leaves the denomination, its property is received by presbytery (unless it has been dismissed to another denomination with its property), which continues to hold it or disposes of it for the benefit of the wider church [G-8.0301]. If a church is dissolved by presbytery or ceases to exist from some other cause, again the presbytery receives the property on behalf of the denomination [G-8.0401]. In the case of a schism or split in the church, the presbytery has the responsibility to decide which faction (if either)

> is entitled to the property because it is identified by the presbytery as the true church within the Presbyterian Church (U.S.A.). This determination does not depend upon which faction received the majority vote within the particular church at the time of the schism. [G-8.0601]

Further, a congregation cannot "sell, mortgage, or otherwise encumber" its land, buildings, or facilities without having presbytery's permission in writing. Permission is necessary when a congregation wishes to buy or otherwise acquire real property that has a mortgage or condition attached. This written permission must be secured before a closing may take place. Also when a church wishes to lease its sanctuary or to lease any of its property for more than five years, written permission from presbytery must be granted [G-8.0501–.0502].

The purpose of these provisions is not to hamper the congregation in its exercise of power granted in G-7.0304a(4) in relation to "buying, mortgaging, or selling real property." Neither is their intent to alienate the local church's property from the normal control of the congregation. They simply acknowledge the interest of the wider church in the property held in trust by the congregation. Presbytery is the agent of the Presbyterian Church (U.S.A.), which makes sure that what is being done with such property is not contrary to the interests of the denomination.

Exemptions. While the principle of property held in trust for the wider church holds true, the *Book of Order* allows some exceptions to the specific provisions stated above. These exceptions apply only to a congregation that was not bound by "a similar provision of the Constitution of the church of which it was a part" before reunion. Such congregations must have requested an exemption from provisions of G-8.0500 relating to selling, encumbering, or leasing church property within eight years after reunion (before June 10, 1991).

The congregation must have voted to be excused from the new provision at a regularly called congregational meeting.

The congregation must have notified its presbytery of this vote.

Such a congregation excused from specific provisions of G-8.0000 is instead able to buy, sell, mortgage, and lease its property without the approval of presbytery [G-8.0701].

After claiming such an exception, former PCUS congregations are now subject to Chapter VI of the Form of Government, *Book of Church Order, 1982–1983.* This chapter, as does the present Form of Government, upholds the principle that all church property is held in trust for the denomination.

A further exemption is outlined in Article 13 of the Articles of Agreement under which the two former churches reunited. This exemption applied to former PCUS churches that were not in union presbyteries and that wish to be dismissed with their property to another denomination. The Articles of Agreement state that no church shall be dismissed for a period of eighteen months after reunion (earliest date for dismissal was December 10, 1984) except with the permission of the General Assembly.

After that time a congregation may be dismissed with its property by following a series of procedures outlined in Section 13.3 of the Articles. These procedures include two congregational meetings and the involvement of a special committee of presbytery. To come under this exemption provision, the petition for dismissal must have been filed with presbytery by June 10, 1991.

Good Stewardship of the Church's Property. The session's responsibility to serve as a faithful steward of the church's resources extends beyond purely financial matters to the management of the property of the church. This stewardship is important because money saved in the operation of the church buildings and facilities can be used to increase ministry and mission.

It is not possible to include here a full discussion of the many areas involved in managing church property. There are, however, certain basics that deserve mention. The session should make sure that the church has adequate insurance coverage for its buildings and also adequate coverage for public liability. This coverage should be based on accurate professional advice and brought up to date on a regular basis. Any major improvements to the facilities increase their value, and this increase should be reflected in the valuation. Damage to a church by fire or other natural disaster is unfortunate; insurance coverage inadequate to repair the damage or to rebuild can be tragic.

Those responsible for managing the church's property should also be very sensitive to the use of energy. High electric or gas bills drain a church's budget of money that could be used for ministry and mission. Every church should have its buildings evaluated by the local utility company or other appropriate agency and implement as many energy-saving suggestions as possible. The session is responsible for "determination of the appropriate use of church buildings and facilities" [G-10.0102o]. Part of this responsibility is setting policies for the use of the church buildings by persons or groups outside the membership of the church. What will be the criteria for deciding if a group can use the church? Who will make that decision? What fee will be charged? Will nonreligious groups be permitted to meet there? Can nonmembers use the sanctuary and fellowship hall for weddings? Can alcoholic beverages be served at social occasions in the church buildings or on the grounds? Where is a "no smoking" rule in effect? All these questions should be considered in a comprehensive policy for the use of church facilities.

Along these lines, the session could also consider the possibility of letting community service organizations have access to unused space in the church during the week for a nominal fee sufficient to cover utilities and the costs of using the buildings. This is a way to broaden the contacts and ministry of the church in the community as well as to make better use of buildings.

Churches have been known to house counseling centers, health clinics, public welfare offices, religious broadcasting studios, and Planned Parenthood offices. A building that is full of people all week long, rather than just on Sunday, is a sign that the session is practicing good stewardship of its facilities.

Incorporation and Trustees. The *Book of Order* requires that a church form a corporation if the laws of its state allow it to do so. Incorporation is currently allowed in all states except Virginia and West Virginia. A corporation is a group of people who are legally authorized to act as a single person. The main characteristic of corporations that is of interest to churches is limited liability. This means that individual members of the church or of the session are not held responsible for the corporation's debts or other obligations.

Members on the active roll of the church are members of the church corporation and have the right to vote in corporation business meetings. The corporation has the power to

> receive, hold, encumber, manage, and transfer property, real or personal, for the church; to accept and execute deeds of title to such property; to hold and defend title to such property; to manage any permanent special funds for the furtherance of the purposes of the church, all subject to the authority of the session and under the provisions of the Constitution of the Presbyterian Church (U.S.A.), provided further that in buying, selling, and mortgaging real property, the trustees shall act only after the approval of the congregation granted in a duly constituted meeting. [G-7.0402]

Instructions for business meetings of the corporation are found in G-7.0403.

Trustees are the agents of the corporation who handle its business and carry out its orders. The Form of Government states that "the elders in active service in a church who are eligible under the civil law shall, by reason of their office, be the trustees of such corporation, unless the corporation shall determine another method for electing its trustees" [G-7.0401]. A committee of the session can also serve as a board of trustees. The pastor, not being an elder in active service elected by the congregation, cannot serve as a trustee. However, pastors may serve by virtue of office as advisors to the trustees. In unincorporated churches, trustees are elected from the active membership, are nominated by a committee elected by the congregation, and serve the same term of office as elders. Whether the church is incorporated or not, trustees function under the review and control of the session.

Laws governing incorporation and the functions of corporations vary from state to state. Churches should seek legal advice in all matters related to incorporation.

Stewardship involves almost every part of the church's life and work. It begins as a personal response of love and gratitude to God and flows outward to enable a worldwide witness in God's name. It is the duty of the session to challenge the congregation with the importance of stewardship, to nurture the grace of liberality in its people, and to serve as a responsible steward of the church's resources. Time and efforts invested in these tasks will bear rich rewards in the ministry and life of the church.

Chapter Twelve

MEETINGS
OF GOVERNING BODIES
AND OF THE CONGREGATION

A meeting of the session of Green Pastures Presbyterian Church had been called for the last Sunday in December to approve the budget for the new year. Because of heavy snow, only the pastor and two out of ten session members were able to attend the meeting. "Why don't we call the ones who couldn't get here," said one of the elders, "and if they give the budget their OK, let's go ahead and vote on it tonight. What would be wrong with that?"

Pastor Franklin had just left on a tour of the Holy Land when the clerk of session got a call from the leader of the youth fellowship. "We are planning to have communion at our retreat next weekend," she said. "Rev. Jones, the presbytery's youth consultant, will be with us to lead the service, but somebody just told me that the session has to approve it. Since Mr. Franklin is out of town, I guess that means that you are in charge. Would you call a session meeting this Sunday after church to approve our communion service?"

The Importance of Meetings

Many a weary elder, sitting in a session meeting that threatened to drag on into the late evening, has wondered if it would not be better to let the pastor make all the decisions and be done with it. Presbyterian polity, however, has always insisted that church government is best exercised by groups of people who meet together to seek the guidance of the Holy Spirit on matters before them. The church's power "is a shared power, to be exercised jointly by presbyters gathered in governing bodies" [G-4.0301h]. Therefore, the power to make most decisions in the Presbyterian Church is assigned to governing bodies of elected officers. The congregation also retains the right to make decisions in certain areas [G-7.0304]. This power is exercised in meetings.

The power of governing bodies to make decisions is not an unlimited one, however. Governing bodies are not allowed to do everything they wish. Instead, they are bound by the church's Constitution, particularly by the provisions in the *Book of Order*, as they make decisions. The Constitution seeks to set limits of power and to ensure that all decisions reached are fair and in accord with Presbyterian beliefs and practice.

An important part of the duty of an elder is to function as a decision maker in meetings of governing bodies. This is done through an orderly process of prayer, discussion, and voting. Through this process the life, mission, and program of the congregation are shaped. In order to function effectively as a decision maker, the elder must know the rules by which meetings of governing bodies operate. This chapter will focus on the constitutional provisions for meetings of session, presbytery, synod, and the General Assembly, as well as those particular rules governing meetings of the congregation. It will also touch briefly on some general considerations relating to effective functioning in meetings.

Consensus and Conflict

In the ideal situation, there would be one perfect answer to every issue, and everyone would recognize it as such. In such a situation debate and voting would be unnecessary, because all those involved would be in agreement. Many times, particularly where small numbers of people are involved, a group can come to an agreement fairly easily. In session meetings, for example, much routine business can be disposed of by common consent. But such is not always the case. As the historic principles of church order state: "There are truths and forms with respect to which persons of good characters and principles may differ" [G-1.0305]. Differences of opinion are to be expected whenever people gather to make decisions. Conflict is a natural by-product of this process.

The hoped-for goal of decision making is to come to a consensus on an issue, that is, to find an answer to which the whole group can give its consent. To this end the group engages in discussion and debate. Persons who feel strongly about the issue try to persuade others to see things their way. Compromise answers are proposed to try to bridge the gap between differing positions. It often happens that through the process of debate an answer is produced that is better than any of the original suggestions. The group has agreed on an action, and a vote on the matter (often unanimous) simply affirms its common judgment. Presbyterians believe that this process is one of the ways the Holy Spirit works in the life of the church.

There are times, however, when it is not possible to find an answer on which everyone can agree. After debate and discussion, there are still conflicting opinions. In this situation, the purpose of the vote is to determine the will of the majority, for in our Presbyterian polity "a majority shall govern" [G-1.0400]. The decision of the governing body binds all its members to act accordingly, regardless of their personal opinion or vote on the matter. If a member thinks that the body has acted in a manner contrary to the church's Constitution, he or she may protest or dissent [G-9.0303ff]. In cases of extreme disagreement, a case of process may be brought against the governing body (see the Rules of Discipline).

Types of Meetings

The *Book of Order* mentions two types of meetings of governing bodies, stated and special. *Stated meetings* are those that are scheduled in advance and generally held on a regular basis (the second Tuesday of the month, for example). At these meetings the governing body can act on any business, including new business, that arises. The bylaws of the governing body usually specify how many stated meetings the body shall have in a year and may specify when they shall be held. The Constitution specifies a minimum number of stated meetings per year for each governing body. Notice for these meetings generally goes out through the governing body's normal channels of communication.

Special meetings are held to deal with special matters requiring more time and attention than a stated meeting provides or with business that cannot wait until the next stated meeting. A session, for instance, may call a special meeting to receive new members into the church if the next stated meeting of the session is too far in the future. A presbytery might have a special meeting to examine candidates for ordination, in order to give this important business extra attention. Special meetings of synods and the General Assembly are rare, but they may be held if the constitutional provisions are met.

Whenever a special meeting of a congregation or governing body is called, the intended business must be stated clearly in the notice. No new business, or business other than that stated in the call, can be transacted [G-7.0302b]. There should be no surprise items on the agenda of special meetings. Other provisions relating to these meetings will be dealt with later in this chapter in the sections devoted to each governing body and the congregation.

Moderators and Clerks

The stated officers that all governing bodies from session to the General Assembly must have are moderator and clerk [G-9.0201]. These offices are functional, not honorary, and their rather modest titles reflect the clear teaching of our polity that Christ alone is head of the church. Officers of governing bodies (other than moderator of the session) are usually elected for limited periods of time, again reflecting our reluctance to invest inappropriate authority in any individual.

Officers of governing bodies are elected by the governing body itself. The moderator is the presiding officer of the governing body. It is his or her responsibility to see that meetings are orderly and that the business of the body is conducted with efficiency and fairness. Moderators should be quite familiar with the Constitution of the church, especially the Form of Government, and with the most recent edition of *Robert's Rules of Order*. The moderator convenes and adjourns stated meetings as directed by the group, except in emergency situations when such meetings may be otherwise convened by written notice [G-9.0202]. Moderators carry out any duties assigned to them by the body, including those of assigning members to standing committees and making appointments to certain offices or functions.

Clerks (called stated clerks in more-inclusive governing bodies) record and preserve the minutes of meetings and keep rolls of membership and attendance. They present all minutes to the governing body for approval and submit all records and reports requested by more inclusive governing bodies. The clerk works closely with the moderator to make meetings run smoothly. The clerk presents the minutes of the body annually for review by the next more inclusive governing body. Most official communications to a governing body come to it through its clerk. Clerks are responsible for conveying these communications to their governing bodies and for recording their disposition.

The moderator of the session is always the pastor of the congregation unless there is no installed pastor. The session cannot convene in the absence of the pastor except in cases of sickness or other unusual circumstance. In these cases the *Book of Order* makes provision for another minister or elder to preside temporarily [G-10.0103].

The pastor-moderator, as presbyter and member of the session, is entitled to vote on all questions that come before the body [G-10.0101]. Although there is some difference of opinion on this point, it is our opinion that it is wise for the moderator to make it a practice to vote. In so doing the moderator not only exercises his or her right as a member of the session, but also defuses potential charges of favoritism when controversial issues arise and close votes occur.

Elders, whether actively serving on the session of their particular church or not, are eligible to serve as commissioners to and officers of more inclusive governing bodies. An elder elected moderator of presbytery "shall be enrolled as a member of the presbytery for the term of office, whether or not commissioned by his or her session" [G-11.0101c]. Further, an elder elected to some other office in the presbytery, to serve as chairperson of a standing committee, to serve as a member of council, or called to serve in certain staff positions may be enrolled as a member of the governing body for the term of office, whether or not the session has elected him or her to be a commissioner [G-11.0101c].

The clerk of session may also be an inactive elder elected by the session to serve in this capacity for a specified period of time. In this situation the clerk cannot vote, because he or she is not a member of the session. However, it would be wise to grant such a clerk the privilege of the floor so that he or she can ask questions, in order to ensure that the record of the meeting is complete and accurate.

The term for a moderator of presbytery is one year or such shorter period of time as the presbytery shall decide [G-9.0202b]. Some presbyteries elect a different moderator for each stated meeting, allowing several persons a year to hold the office. Others prefer the continuity that can come with having one moderator for all the meetings within a twelve-month period. Either practice is allowed by the *Book of Order*.

The moderator of synod is elected to serve a term as specified by the governing body, of at least one year and not more than two years. The moderator of the General Assembly is elected at each stated meeting [G-9.0202b]. The moderator of a presbytery, a synod, or the General Assembly convenes all stated meetings during his or her term of office and presides until the governing body elects a new moderator [G-9.0301a].

While the moderator and the clerk are the two stated officers required by the *Book of Order*, governing bodies may also elect other officers as necessary [G-9.0201]. These might include assistant or associate stated clerks and vice-moderators.

Parliamentary Procedure

In order to help the decision-making process go forward in a fair and orderly manner, most groups adopt a set of rules to govern their procedure. The *Book of Order* specifies that "meetings of governing bodies, commissions, and committees shall be conducted in accordance with the most recent edition of *Robert's Rules of Order*, except in those cases where this Constitution provides otherwise" [G-9.0302].

The underlying ideas of general parliamentary procedure are:

1. Everyone is treated with courtesy.
2. One item is dealt with at a time.
3. The majority rules.
4. The majority respects the rights of the minority.
5. Justice for all.
6. No partiality.[1]

These principles are very much in accord with Presbyterian polity and Christian principles. The purpose of parliamentary procedure is to move the business of the body along as swiftly and efficiently as possible while ensuring that everyone is treated fairly.

A group may also adopt special rules that apply particularly to that body. Constitutions, bylaws, and standing rules fall into this category. These special rules take precedence over the general rules when they come into conflict. For example, a group's constitution may specify that a two-thirds vote is required on certain items of business, while the general parliamentary rules require only a majority. The group's constitutional provisions would govern in this case. Any provision of the Presbyterian

Church (U.S.A.)'s Constitution, particularly the *Book of Order*, overrules any provision of *Robert's Rules of Order* or of any group's bylaws or standing rules with which it may be in conflict.

It is hard to overestimate the helpfulness of a knowledge of parliamentary procedure to those participating in the meetings of governing bodies. For moderators of meetings, it is essential. Ignorance of the rules of order results in much confusion and wasted time and endangers the rights of individuals and the welfare of the group. Unfortunately, a survey of parliamentary procedure is beyond the scope of this book. Elders should obtain a copy of whatever general and special rules have been adopted by their governing bodies and make a careful study of them. Further, it is helpful for each governing body to have a parliamentarian whose job it is to know these rules in detail and to offer suggestions about procedure to the group when asked.

The rest of this chapter will survey briefly the provisions in the *Book of Order* relating to meetings of each of the governing bodies and of the congregation. A chart containing this information in condensed form will be found on pages 156–157.

Congregational Meetings

Participants. When the congregation gathers for a business meeting, all members on the active roll who are present are eligible to speak and to vote. No proxy or absentee voting is allowed in congregational meetings or in any meeting of a governing body, except in meetings of church corporations where required by civil law. The pastor, as moderator, may speak as necessary to provide information or clarification but, not being a member of the congregation, should refrain from engaging in debate and shall not vote. The *Book of Order* specifies that, as the moderator may not vote to break a tie, after two successive votes resulting in a tie the motion shall be lost [G-7.0308]. Visitors at a congregational meeting are not entitled to speak unless the congregation votes to grant them this privilege. The only exception to this rule is for representatives of the presbytery under certain circumstances [see 13.3b,e in the Articles of Agreement].

Officers. The officers serving at a congregational meeting are the moderator and secretary. Just as the pastor is the moderator of the session, so is she or he the moderator of the meetings of the congregation. When a church is without a pastor, the person serving as moderator of the session by appointment of presbytery shall moderate congregational meetings. In cases where circumstances are such that the pastor cannot or should not preside, he or she (with session's approval) shall invite another minister of the presbytery. Also, when appropriate, a member of the session may be invited to preside at the congregational meeting. The approval of both the moderator of the session and the session itself are necessary for this to take place [G-7.0306]. Again, as with session meetings, co-pastors preside at alternate meetings of the congregation.

Congregational meetings also require a secretary whose job it is to record the minutes of the meeting and to see that they are entered in the session's minute book. Ordinarily, the clerk of the session shall serve as the secretary of the congregational meeting. If the clerk is absent or otherwise prevented from serving, one of the very first items on the agenda must be to elect someone to serve as secretary of the meeting.

Required Meetings. The *Book of Order* requires that congregations meet at least once a year [G-7.0302a]. If the church is incorporated, state law may also require that certain meetings be held to conduct the business of the corporation. These may be held in conjunction with a regular meeting of the congregation, if state law allows [G-7.0304b].

Many churches have made good use of the required annual meeting to draw together and celebrate the life of the congregation over the past year. This is an excellent opportunity for groups in the church to make reports on program and mission. It can be an opportunity to evaluate strengths and weaknesses. It is a chance for members of the congregation to express their thoughts and feelings about how things are going in the church and to share ideas about directions for the future. The meeting should be held at a time that will encourage a large attendance. At the very least, the annual meeting of the congregation should be a time to count the blessings that God has poured out upon the people and to give thanks.

Called Meetings. The *Book of Order* asserts [G-7.0303a] that special meetings of the congregation shall be called

(1) By the session whenever it determines such a meeting is necessary,
(2) By the presbytery whenever it determines such a meeting is necessary,
(3) By the session when requested in writing by one fourth of the members on the active roll of the particular church.

When any congregational meeting is to be called, the congregation must be given prior notice on two successive Sundays [G-7.0302a, 7.0303b]. This means, for instance, that if the session wishes to have a congregational meeting on the second Sunday of the month, notice must be given on the first and second Sundays to fulfill this requirement. The meeting can then be held after the notice given on the second Sunday. Ten days' notice including two successive Sundays is required for a congregational meeting

for the purpose of calling a pastor [G-14.0502a]. All the general requirements for special meetings mentioned earlier in this chapter apply to special meetings of congregations.

Quorum. This term refers to the minimum number of eligible voters
required to be present in order for business to be transacted. Actions taken
in the absence of a quorum are subject to challenge, as specified in *Robert's
Rules of Order.* It is the duty of the secretary of the congregational meeting
to make sure that a quorum is present and to report this fact to the moderator at the beginning of the meeting. Normally the quorum for a meeting of the congregation is one tenth of the members. Churches may ask
presbytery for permission to set a smaller one, but in no case can a meeting of less than three people be considered a congregational meeting. A
congregation does have the right to set a higher quorum by its own vote
[G-7.0305].

Business. A congregation is not a governing body. Therefore it can transact
only those items of business specifically given to it by the Constitution. The
Book of Order [G-7.0304a] lists five kinds of business that can be transacted
by congregations:

(1)   matters related to the electing of elders, deacons, and
      trustees;
(2)   matters related to the calling of a pastor or pastors;
(3)   matters related to the pastoral relationship, such as changing
      the call, or requesting or consenting or declining to consent
      to dissolution [of the call];
(4)   matters relating to buying, mortgaging, or selling real prop-
      erty; (G-8.0500)
(5)   matters related to the permissive powers of a congregation,
      such as the desire to lodge all administrative responsibility
      in the session, or the request to presbytery for exemption
      from one or more requirements because of limited size.

While, on the one hand, the Constitution limits the congregation's decision making to the matters listed above, at the same time it protects the
congregation's right to decide these matters free from interference by any
governing body. A session, for instance, cannot buy any property on behalf of the church without the consent of the congregation voting as a
corporation, if the church is incorporated. The presbytery cannot insist that
a certain person be installed as pastor against the wishes of a congregation.
Only under the most extreme conditions and only as specified by the Constitution may a governing body interfere with the right of a congregation
to decide the matters listed above.

Meetings of the Session

Participants. All elders installed in active service, plus the pastor, co-pastors, and associate pastors are members of the session. They are all entitled to speak in meetings and to vote. Assistant pastors are not members of the session. They may be given the privilege of the floor, but they may not vote. Other members of the congregation and staff members may be invited to attend session meetings, and if the session votes to allow them to speak, they may do so. However, the session has the right to exclude nonmembers from the meeting place and to "meet in executive session whenever circumstances indicate the wisdom of doing so" [G-10.0201]. Such circumstances might include discussion of personnel or disciplinary matters.

Required Meetings. Stated meetings of the session must be held at least quarterly [G-10.0201].

Special Meetings. Special session meetings can be called in any of three ways. If two members of the session ask the moderator of session in writing to convene a meeting, a special meeting must be called. The pastor or moderator also has the power to call a meeting whenever he or she thinks one is needed. Third, presbytery can direct the session to convene a meeting for some special business. The *Book of Order* does not specify exactly how much notice is required before a special session meeting can be held. It simply says that "reasonable notice of all special meetings must be given when other than routine business is to be transacted" [G-10.0201].

Quorum. The pastor or other authorized moderator and one third of the elders in active service, but no fewer than two, constitute a quorum. The moderator and two elders can make a quorum for the reception and dismissal of members. Since the quorum indicates the minimum number required to do business, the session may vote to set the number of its quorum at a greater number [G-10.0202].

Meetings of Presbytery

Participants. Ministers who are continuing members of presbytery in the active-member or member-at-large categories (see pages 78–79) and elders commissioned by their session may vote in meetings of presbytery. Also, an elder who is elected to serve as moderator of presbytery and elders elected to redress an imbalance between ministers and elders may vote. Further, the presbytery may enroll as a member any elder currently serving as an officer other than moderator, as a chairperson of a standing committee, as exempt staff of presbytery or as a member of the presbytery's council [G-11.0101c]. G-11.0203 provides that visiting ministers, members in good standing of other presbyteries, can be enrolled as corresponding members. They may speak, but they cannot vote. A presbytery may vote to allow someone other than a commissioner or corresponding member to speak, but unless this is done, visitors must be silent.

The *Book of Order* states that the balance between ministers and elders should be as nearly even as possible. In order for this to be so, the presbytery shall invite sessions to send additional elder commissioners to the meeting or find some other way acceptable to the presbytery if they are needed to balance the composition of the governing body. In doing this, presbyteries should pay particular attention to *Book of Order* provisions relating to inclusiveness [G-11.0101b].

The number of elder commissioners a church is entitled to send to presbytery depends on the size of the church. Representation is as follows:

> 1–500 members—1 elder commissioner
> 501–1000 members—2 elder commissioners
> 1001–1500 members—3 elder commissioners
> 1501–2000 members—4 elder commissioners
> 2001–3000 members—5 elder commissioners

Churches with more than 3000 members send an additional elder for each 1000 additional members [G-11.0101a].

Required Meetings. The presbytery is required to have at least two stated meetings a year [G-11.0201].

Special Meetings. Special meetings of the presbytery may be called in a number of ways:

a. The moderator may call a meeting if he or she can get the agreement of two ministers and two elders, the elders representing two different churches.
b. The moderator must call a meeting if requested by ministers and elders as specified in (a) above.
c. The stated clerk shall call the meeting with two ministers and two elders from different churches if the moderator is unable to act.
d. Three ministers and three elders (from different churches) may call a meeting if both moderator and clerk are unable to act.
e. The synod may direct the presbytery to meet.

Notice of such a special meeting must be sent out to all ministers and sessions in the presbytery not less than ten days prior to the meeting [G-11.0201].

Quorum. While a presbytery may fix its quorum at a higher number if it wishes, the minimum number required to transact business is three ministers and the elder commissioners present, provided that the elders represent at least three different churches [G-11.0202].

Meetings of Synod

Participants. Those entitled to vote in synod meetings are commissioners elected by the presbyteries. The commissioners from each presbytery in the synod shall be divided equally between ministers and elders. The basis of electing these commissioners and the ratio of representation is proposed by the synod and must receive the consent of a majority of its constituent presbyteries [G-12.0101]. Synod may also invite those who are members in good standing in other governing bodies of our church or in other Christian churches to sit as corresponding members. They may then speak, but they may not vote [G-12.0203].

Required Meetings. Synods must hold at least one stated meeting every other year [G-12.0201].

Special Meetings. Special meetings of the synod:

    a. May be called if the moderator can get the concurrence of ten ministers and ten elders, the elders representing at least three presbyteries, all of whom must have been commissioners at the preceding stated meeting of the synod.

    b. Must be called by the moderator at the request of the ministers and elders in (a) above.

    c. Must be called by the stated clerk in conditions mentioned in (a) above if the moderator is unable to act. If under these conditions both the moderator and the stated clerk are unable, the most recent moderator must call the meeting.

    d. Must be called when so directed by the General Assembly. [G-12.0201]

If a special meeting is called, the presbyteries shall send the commissioners elected for the last preceding meeting of synod, unless death or change of residence makes it necessary to replace them [G-12.0201].

Notice for the special meeting must be sent out not less than fifteen days before the meeting. The notice goes to commissioners elected to the last previous meeting and to the stated clerks of all presbyteries in the synod [G-12.0201].

Quorum. In order to have a quorum for a synod meeting, twenty commissioners must be present. Further, these commissioners shall include at least ten elders and at least ten ministers representing three or more presbyteries [G-12.0202]. Synod may raise its quorum if it so desires.

Meetings of the General Assembly

Participants. Commissioners to the General Assembly are elected by the presbyteries and must include ministers and elders in equal number. Each presbytery is eligible to send one minister and one elder commissioner to the General Assembly for each 10,000 members, plus one additional pair for any fraction of 10,000 that is at least 5,000. For example, a presbytery with 35,000 members would send eight commissioners, four minister-elder pairs [G-13.0102].

The General Assembly also has the power to designate who shall sit as corresponding members. As in other governing bodies, these corresponding members may speak but do not have a vote [G-13.0106].

Required Meetings. As with the synod, the General Assembly must have at least one stated meeting every other year [G-13.0104].

Special Meetings. Special meetings of the General Assembly are extremely rare, and the procedure for such a call is set out in G-13.0104. Not less than sixty days' notice must be given for a called meeting of the General Assembly.

Quorum. One fourth of the synods must be represented in a quorum of not less than one hundred commissioners, evenly divided between ministers and elders [G-13.0105].

Decision making is an important part of the responsibility of the ruling and teaching elders. Much of this decision making takes place in meetings. Presbyterians believe that the Holy Spirit works in and through meetings to shape the life and mission of the church. To be effective participants in these meetings, elders and ministers need not only knowledge of parliamentary procedure and the church's Constitution but also a prayerful willingness to know and do God's will.

TABLE OF RULES FOR MEETINGS OF GOVERNING BODIES AND THE CONGREGATION

	CONGREGATION	SESSION	PRESBYTERY	SYNOD	THE GENERAL ASSEMBLY
WHO MAY CALL MEETINGS	(a) session (b) presbytery (c) session must call when requested by $\frac{1}{4}$ members on active roll	(a) pastor (b) presbytery (c) pastor must call upon request of two elders	(a) moderator with 2 ministers and 2 elders (see G-11.0201) (b) stated clerk with 2 ministers and 2 elders if moderator unable to act (c) 3 ministers and 3 elders in accordance with G-11.0201 (d) synod	(a) moderator with 10 ministers and 10 elders (see G-12.0201) (b) stated clerk and then former moderators next in line if moderator unable to act (see G-12.0201) (c) General Assembly	(a) moderator with 25 ministers and 25 elders from 15 presbyteries and 5 synods (see G-13.0104) (b) stated clerk if moderator unable to act; if stated clerk unable, then the most recent moderator
REQUIRED NOTICE OF SPECIAL MEETINGS	prior notice on two successive Sundays	"reasonable" when other than routine business is on agenda	not less than 10 days	not less than 15 days	not less than 60 days
QUORUM	At least $\frac{1}{10}$ of active members or smaller number set by presbytery	usually pastor and $\frac{1}{3}$ of elders (see G-10.0201)	3 ministers plus elders representing at least 3 churches, or higher if set by presbytery	20 commissioners (10 ministers and 10 elders) representing at least 3 presbyteries, or higher if raised by synod	100 commissioners ($\frac{1}{2}$ ministers, $\frac{1}{2}$ elders) representing at least $\frac{1}{4}$ of its synods
REQUIRED STATED MEETINGS	once a year	quarterly	twice a year	biennially	biennially

	CONGREGATION	SESSION	PRESBYTERY	SYNOD	THE GENERAL ASSEMBLY
WHO IS ELIGIBLE TO VOTE	all members listed on active roll who are present at meeting	pastors, co-pastors, associate pastors, and elders in active service	ministers who are active members or members-at-large, commissioned elders, moderator, and any other elders enrolled by presbytery while holding office at presbytery level	commissioners elected by presbyteries	commissioners elected by presbyteries
OFFICERS	moderator secretary (usually clerk of session)	moderator clerk	moderator stated clerk	moderator stated clerk	moderator stated clerk
BUSINESS	matters related to: (a) electing officers (b) calling pastors (c) changing pastoral relationship (d) property (buying, selling, etc.) (e) permissive powers of the congregation	all matters related to G-10.0102	all matters related to G-11.0103	all matters related to G-12.0102	all matters related to G-13.0103

Chapter Thirteen

PRESERVING
PEACE
AND PURITY

John Harper is a commissioner to the meeting of Sealand Presbytery. During the meeting, candidates for ordination to the ministry are examined. As the examinations proceed, it becomes clear
that one of the candidates does not believe in the baptism of infants and does not intend to teach this doctrine or to administer
the sacrament to children. John is very disturbed when the presbytery votes to ordain the candidate anyway. What can he do to
correct what he feels is an error committed by his presbytery?

Clearview Presbyterian Church is in turmoil. A small group in the
church, led by a well-respected elder, has decided that the pastor
is not a "born-again Christian" and that she should be fired. At the
request of the pastor a meeting of the session is called to discuss
the issue. The session gives the pastor a vote of confidence. However, the elder is not satisfied. In various ways he continues to dis-
rupt session meetings, to verbally abuse the pastor and undermine
her work, and to spread gossip about her in the community. What
can the session do to help restore order in the church?

Conflict in the Church

From the earliest days of the church, believers have clashed over issues of
faith and how to live out that faith in the world. The infant church was often
rife with controversy, as a reading of the book of Acts will show. Conflict in
the church often arose over things that seem quite trivial to us today, such as
the issue of whether Christians should eat meat that had been offered first to
idols (1 Cor. 8; 10:23–33). In the early decades of the church's life there were
squabbles over whether Gentiles should be allowed to convert to Christianity without being circumcised first, whether Christians should marry, and
whether Christians were bound to keep the Jewish law, among other questions. Even personalities got involved, causing dissension in the church at
Corinth as "disciples" of various evangelists split the church into factions.

These conflicts must have been quite painful to those early Christians. It
may have seemed to them that the church was coming apart at the seams.

Yet, in many cases, something positive emerged from these dark experiences to the benefit of the church. Some of the key doctrines of our faith were forged in the fire of these early controversies. In fact, almost every important facet of Christian belief, from the nature of Christ to the hope of life after death, was a matter for conflict in the ancient church at one point or another.

The book of Acts could almost be read as a manual for conflict resolution in the church. Time and time again differences of opinion and practice arose in the fledgling community. Yet the church was not destroyed by conflict; to the contrary, it often grew stronger because of it. A good example of this is the problem described in Acts 6:1–6. It was the practice of the Christians to provide food for the widows among them who were destitute. The Greek-speaking church members complained that the Greek-speaking widows were being neglected in the distribution of food while the Hebrew-speaking widows were well fed. This conflict put pressure on the apostles, who already had all the work they could handle preaching the gospel and making disciples of new converts. The outcome of this discord was an office similar to what we today call the office of deacon, and in an epilogue to the story, the Scripture notes that "the word of God increased; and the number of the disciples multiplied greatly in Jerusalem" (Acts 6:7).

Considering human nature and the fact that human beings make up the church, we should not be surprised when conflict arises. People with perfectly good motives and intentions may have conflicting goals. Sincere Christians may confess the same doctrines yet have radically different ideas about how those doctrines should be interpreted and lived out. In these situations, our goal as Christians is reconciliation—restoring harmony and fellowship among those who differ. We believe that today, as in the early church, the Holy Spirit works through the process of conflict to bring about the will of God. Painful though it may be, conflict can help the church grow and become more creative in its life and ministry.

One of the finest things about our Presbyterian system of government is that it provides fair and efficient means to deal with conflict in the church. Our polity is realistic about life in community: It takes for granted that differences will exist and helps us to deal with those differences in ways that are constructive rather than destructive. Before getting into the particulars of how the system works, it will be helpful to understand some of the underlying principles on which it is based.

Ground Rules for Dealing with Conflict

Our Form of Government makes several important assumptions about how churches and their governing bodies should go about their business. Elders and other officers are expected to give assent to these basic principles.

Freedom of Conscience. The Declaration of Independence names liberty as one of the inalienable rights of human beings. This, of course, refers to our political freedom. The Bible tells us about another kind of freedom, which belongs to Christians through the death and resurrection of Christ. Christian freedom is freedom from many things, but it is also freedom for a new kind of life. Part of our Christian birthright is a freedom of the mind, a liberty to think freely, to question, even to doubt. This kind of liberty grows out of a loving and obedient relationship to God. Reformed theology has called this intellectual freedom "freedom of conscience," and it is one of the important principles of our system of government. "Freedom of conscience" means that we are freed from demands for slavish, unquestioning obedience. God does not want us to be robots who act according to programmed instructions. God wants us to respond freely in love, to give God our trust, and to follow God's way in willing faith and gratitude. If God does not demand mindless submission from us, neither should the church demand it. The Westminster Confession (XXII, 2) puts it like this:

> God alone is Lord of the conscience, and hath left it free from the doctrines and commandments of men [sic] which are in anything contrary to his Word, or beside it in matters of faith or worship. So that to believe such doctrines, or to obey such commandments out of conscience, is to betray true liberty of conscience; and the requiring an implicit faith, and an absolute and blind obedience, is to destroy liberty of conscience, and reason also.

We are bound by the Word of God and by the authority of the church as it flows from the Word. However, within these bounds we have the right to interpret the Scriptures for ourselves. The door is always open for honest doubt and questioning; we are called to respect the right of others to see things their own way. The Presbyterian system of government always allows room for a "loyal opposition."

Power of Governing Bodies and the Constitution. Freedom of conscience, like any other freedom, has its limits. In tension with the Christian's freedom is the power of the church to govern itself and its members. One of the questions asked of elders at their ordination is, "Will you be governed by our church's polity, and will you abide by its discipline?" [G-14.0207e]. Another question asks if the officer is willing to adopt the confessions of the church as "reliable expositions of what Scripture leads us to believe and do" [G-14.0207c]. To say yes to these questions is to make a commitment to be Presbyterian in the way we express our faith and do our business.

The *Book of Order* [G-6.0108a] states:

So far as may be possible without serious departure from [the essentials of the Reformed faith expressed in our church's Constitution], without infringing on the rights and views of others, and without obstructing the constitutional governance of the church, freedom of conscience with respect to the interpretation of Scripture is to be maintained.

This means that we can study the Bible for ourselves and come to our own conclusions about what it means. We are free to have our own opinions on matters of faith and practice. We are free to speak our minds on the floor of church meetings and to seek to persuade other people to see things our way. We can vote as our consciences tell us on any matter. However, when the vote has been taken and the matter decided by a majority, we are bound to follow the decision of the governing body. We are still entitled to hold opinions that do not agree with the decision, but our actions, including teaching, must be in line with the Constitution of the church and the decision of the governing body. This tension between the freedom of the individual and the authority of the church maintains the possibility of creative conflict, while assuring that order will be preserved and that the work of the church will go forward. Ours is a system of church government that lets people read the Scripture and interpret it for themselves in freedom before God, but it is also a system that binds us together in a community marked by humility and loving submission.

Mutual Forbearance. The key to making the system work is recognizing that we may not always be right. One of the historic principles of church order as stated in our Form of Government is "that there are truths and forms with respect to which men [sic] of good characters and principles may differ" [G-1.0305]. Christians can agree to disagree at times without sacrificing their integrity or that of the faith. It is this willingness to bow to the decision of the majority that lets conflict be resolved and the work of the church go on.

Our form of church government is based on the idea that God's Spirit moves in and through the actions of the church's governing bodies. Debate, discussion, and orderly decision making are some of the ways we explore the will of God and hear God's voice. We take seriously the idea that "where two or three are gathered in my name, there am I in the midst of them" (Matt. 18:20), and we apply it to meetings of church committees, sessions, presbyteries, and other governing bodies. When we participate in these meetings, we translate our beliefs into action through discussion and the vote. This theology requires that we respect the decision of the group, even though we may disagree with it. We bow to the will of the majority, believing that even if the decision is wrong, God can still bring something good out of our failure.

In times of conflict, it is well to remember that no one has a monopoly on the Spirit of God. The business of the church should always be carried out in a spirit of humility. An open mind and a willingness to be shown where we are in error will do much toward smoothing a troubled situation. The Form of Government states that "it is the duty both of private Christians and societies to exercise mutual forbearance toward each other" [G-1.0305]. This means that we should be patient with those who disagree with us and slow to express resentment or to retaliate. This kind of tolerance and respect oils the wheels of our Presbyterian system of government and helps it to work well, even when conflict arises.

Options for Disagreement—Dissent and Protest

There are times when, for conscience' sake, it is necessary to speak out against the decision or action of a governing body. The Form of Government offers several ways to express disagreement with the majority without beginning judicial process.

A *dissent* is a means of having it recorded in the minutes of a meeting that one voted against a certain decision. Dissenters are listed by name in the official record of the proceedings. The request to dissent must be made during the same session as the objectionable action. A person who wants to dissent should address the moderator of the meeting and say something like: "I dissent from this decision and request that my negative vote be recorded." Only those who voted against a motion, except the moderator if unable to vote [G-9.0305] can dissent.

A *protest* is a means for expressing more serious disagreement. While a request for a dissent is simply spoken before the group, a protest is presented to the clerk of the meeting in written form. It should state the date and place of the meeting, the governing body that took the action being protested, and the reasons for disagreement. The names of those protesting are signed at the bottom. A protest, like a dissent, can only be made by those who voted against an action, except the moderator if unable to vote, and it must be filed before the session of the governing body is adjourned [G-9.0304a].

The language of a protest should reflect forbearance and respect for the governing body. If a protest is orderly and respectful, it shall be included in the minutes of the meeting. The value of entering a protest, other than simply for conscience' sake, is that it will draw the objectionable action to the attention of those in more inclusive governing bodies who are reviewing the minutes of the lower body. The more inclusive governing body has the power to investigate the situation and to correct any errors of the lower body. This power of more inclusive governing bodies is called "administrative review." After a protest has been entered in the minutes, the governing body has the right to prepare an answer to it and to enter the answer in the minutes. This is the end of the protest. Making a protest in no way gives one permission to act counter to the action of the governing body. Neither dissents nor protests "justify disobedience" [D-4.0304b]. These two options for expressing disagreement with a decision of a governing body are not means to have the decision changed; they simply register one's disapproval in the minutes of the meeting.

What Is "Discipline"?

One of the sections of our *Book of Order* is called Rules of Discipline. Yet few church members, or even officers, are clear about what discipline is and how it works in the church. The word "discipline" comes from the Latin word *discere*, to learn. A disciple is one who learns and lives by the teachings of another. To be a disciple of Jesus, a member of the body of Christ, is to agree to live by the example and the teachings of Jesus. Not only our individual lives but also the internal life of the church should reflect Christlike qualities. "Church discipline," simply put, is the church's power to help us live as disciples of Christ.

Discipline has many facets. When we make mistakes or fall into sin, the church has the power to point out what we have done wrong and to call us to repent and to change our ways. When we have neglected our duties as Christians, the church has the power to correct us. When conflict arises, discipline is one of the ways the church restores peace. When scandal threatens, discipline helps to preserve the good name of Christ in the world. Discipline protects the rights of the minority and makes sure that people are treated fairly in the church. Discipline provides for orderly resolution of differences in ways that are "just, speedy, and economical" [D-1.0101]. Discipline is the church's use of power given to it by Christ to guide, control, and nurture its members, as well as to offer constructive criticism to those who do wrong [D1.0101].

Several centuries ago, especially in Scotland, it was not uncommon for sessions to take church members to task about their conduct. To miss worship regularly was to risk being called before the session and censured in public. This kind of encounter is rare today, but the idea of discipline still leaves a bad taste in the mouths of some. Our polity stresses that discipline is more a positive, loving concern for people than a vengeful system for punishing wrongdoers. Our rules for discipline focus on bringing people to reconciliation with God and one another. Their purpose is to build up the body of Christ. They do this by making sure that people are treated fairly, that conflicts are resolved in an equitable way, and that everyone has a chance to speak and to be heard. Discipline is also a witness to the fact that it means something to be a Christian. It reminds us of our commitments and calls us to live up to them. When our conduct does not measure up to the standards required of disciples, it is the church's duty to correct us in a spirit of love and mercy.

On July 6, 1996, a newly revised Rules of Discipline went into effect. The purpose of the revision was primarily to simplify and clarify procedures and make the Rules easier to use. This revision also provided for the use of mediation in remedial cases and gave a definition for sexual misconduct to be used in disciplinary cases.

Judicial Process

From time to time there arises in the church a disagreement so severe or an error so harmful that a dissent or protest is not enough to deal with it. In this case our Rules of Discipline offer the option of solving the problem through judicial process. The Rules of Discipline [D-2.0101] defines judicial process as

> the exercise of authority by the governing bodies of the church for:
>
> a. The prevention and correction of irregularities and delinquencies by governing bodies or by a council or an agency of the General Assembly (remedial cases, D-6.0000);
> b. The prevention and correction of offenses by persons (disciplinary cases, D-10.0000).

An irregularity is an action or decision of a governing body that is in error. A delinquency is the neglect of duty or the refusal to carry out responsibilities by a governing body [D-2.0202b]. Judicial cases that attempt to correct irregularities or delinquencies on the part of governing bodies or the General Assembly Council or an agency of the General Assembly are called *remedial cases* [D-2.0202a].

An offense is an action or failure to act on the part of an individual—member, elder, deacon, or minister—that is in opposition to the Scriptures or to the Constitution of the church. Cases that aim at correcting or censuring the offenses of individuals are called *disciplinary cases*.

For example, in the situations at the beginning of the chapter, John Harper could have complained against the action of his presbytery in accepting the candidate for ministry, in an attempt to correct the irregularity. This would involve a remedial case. The session of Clearview Presbyterian Church, in the second situation, could have brought charges against the troublesome elder in an attempt to make him stop damaging the peace of the church. This would involve a disciplinary case.

Judicial process in the church is a very serious matter. As stated in D-1.0101, its purpose is

> to honor God by making clear the significance of membership in the body of Christ, to preserve the purity of the church by nourishing the individual within the life of the believing community, to correct or restrain wrongdoing in order to bring members to repentance and

restoration, to restore the unity of the church by removing the causes of discord and division, and to secure the just, speedy, and economical determination of proceedings.

Judicial process should not be undertaken lightly or be used to further personal causes. Its sole purpose is to build up the body of Christ by ensuring that people are treated fairly, that correct doctrine and practice are preserved, and that scandal is not allowed to damage the church's reputation. As with all discipline, its function is to correct in a spirit of love and concern, not to punish. Those considering beginning a judicial case are required to exhaust every other option for reconciliation and correction before taking this step.

Above the level of the session, judicial cases are heard and decided by permanent judicial commissions. The Rules of Discipline directs each presbytery, synod, and the General Assembly to elect a permanent judicial commission from among its ministers and elders, membership being divided evenly between the two, as much as possible. The presbytery commission has no fewer than seven members, with no more than one elder member from the same church. Synod's commission has no fewer than eleven members, usually no more than one from the same presbytery. The General Assembly's commission is made up of one member from each of the synods. Members of permanent judicial commissions serve a term of six years, and their expenses for the meetings of the commission are paid by the governing body that elected them.

Judicial commissions act on behalf of their electing bodies to try the cases brought before them. They are serving the functions of judge and jury in secular courts—they hear and decide questions of fact and interpret the "law" (Constitution) of the church when trying a case. If a judicial commission finds that an irregularity or a delinquency exists, it has the power to order the less-inclusive governing body or the General Assembly Council or an agency of the General Assembly to correct its mistake or to do its duty. It can also order that body to "conduct further proceedings in the matter" [D-7.0402b]. If the commission finds that an offense has been committed by an individual, it can impose certain censures on the person (see section below on disciplinary cases). The decision of a case by a permanent judicial commission becomes the decision of the body that elected it. This means, for instance, that while the decision of a presbytery's judicial commission can be appealed to the synod, the presbytery itself cannot overturn the decision or set it aside.

In understanding how judicial process works in the Presbyterian system, it is helpful to know something about standing and jurisdiction, or who has authority to bring cases or to hear cases. Basically, in remedial cases standing is as follows [D-6.0202]: church members have standing to complain against the session to presbytery; sessions and members of presbytery have standing to complain to synod against their presbytery; also a governing body may complain against another governing body on the same level under the provisions of D-6.0202a(5).

When a case has been initiated, it is then heard by the appropriate governing body. Presbytery hears complaints against its sessions; synod hears complaints relating to presbyteries. The General Assembly hears complaints from members of synod against synod, complaints from presbyteries against synod, complaints from one synod against another synod, complaints from individuals who claim to have been injured by a General Assembly agency, and complaints from any less inclusive governing body against the General Assembly Council or an agency of the General Assembly. In disciplinary cases

> The session of a church has original jurisdiction . . . involving members of that church including elders and deacons, with the exception of commissioned lay pastors.
>
> The presbytery has original jurisdiction . . . involving commissioned lay pastors and ministers who are members of the presbytery [D3.0101].

In rare cases, a governing body will give up its jurisdiction and pass the case on to the next higher governing body. This is called "reference" [D-4.0000]. A governing body may also lose its jurisdiction by its failure to act.

Remedial Cases. The process of correcting an error in the church through a remedial case begins with the filing of a complaint. Any member of a governing body at the time that an objectionable action has occurred can complain to the next higher governing body concerning that action. John Harper could complain to the synod, for example. Individual members of local churches can file complaints against their session but not against the actions of higher governing bodies unless they are members of those bodies. (The exception to this rule is that employees of General Assembly entities who have suffered injury or damage to themselves or their property from the General Assembly Council or a General Assembly agency can complain to the General Assembly.) Sessions, presbyteries, and synods can file complaints against the actions of the General Assembly Council or one of the Assembly's agencies. The party bringing the complaint is called the complainant. The governing body being complained against is called the respondent.

A "complaint" is a written statement that contains basic information about the problem as outlined in D-6.0301. Complaints should be concise and specific. They must be filed within ninety days of the time that the error occurred or, in the case of a delinquency, of the refusal to act on the part of the respondent after written request. A copy of the complaint must be delivered to the respondent, and proof of delivery must accompany the filing of the complaint with the clerk of the more-inclusive governing body [D-6.0301f].

A party that is involved in judicial process, either as respondent or complainant, is represented before the more-inclusive governing body by a committee of no more than three persons, called the committee of counsel. They represent the party until the case is finally settled, including all appeals. The function of this committee is much like that of lawyers in secular courts. They defend or prosecute the case before the judicial commission. The *Book of Order* specifies that all parties in remedial and disciplinary cases are entitled to appear at trial and to be represented by professional attorneys, provided that all such attorneys must be members of the Presbyterian Church (U.S.A.).

After a complaint has been filed against a governing body, the General Assembly Council, or a General Assembly agency, that body's committee of counsel must file an answer to the complaint with the stated clerk of the more inclusive governing body within thirty days, also sending a copy to the complainant. Contents of this answer are outlined in D-6.0303. Also within thirty days, the clerk of the respondent governing body may be requested to send all the materials relating to the case to the clerk of the more inclusive governing body and copies thereof to the complainant. After giving the complainant ten days to request that more materials be submitted, the clerk must pass these materials on to the stated clerk of the more inclusive governing body. After the judicial commission has received the papers, the moderator and clerk of the permanent judicial commission must notify the parties that the materials are in its hands and give them an estimated date when the trial will be held. The judicial commission may also ask the parties to prepare and file briefs outlining their evidence and arguments, much as in the secular courts.

These comments are meant to give a brief overview of the procedures involved in a remedial case. They are in no way exhaustive; anyone who is involved in such a case should make a careful study of D-6.0000 and D-7.0000.

Disciplinary Cases. Cases involving the offenses of members against the Scriptures or our church's Constitution tend not to be as prevalent as remedial cases. However, there are times when the Rules of Discipline must be used to preserve the peace and purity of the church. Disciplinary cases could arise out of a conflict in the church, such as that at Clearview Presbyterian, in our opening vignette. Open scandal in the church, damaging its reputation, could also call for disciplinary charges. Someone who feels that gossip is undermining his or her good name could use this process as a means of vindication. False teaching or heresy in the church may be corrected by disciplinary action.

Full instructions for this kind of case are found in D-10.0000 and D-11.0000, and those involved in disciplinary cases should take great care to conform to the procedures in these chapters. It should be noted that the *Book of Order* provides for time limitations on the filing of disciplinary charges. The exception to these rules on limitations is an accusation of sexual abuse against another person. Such charges may be brought no matter how long it has been since the offense is alleged to have taken place [D-10.0401a].

When an accusation has been made against an individual, a special disciplinary committee investigates the accusation to see if the evidence warrants the filing of official charges. This committee also prosecutes the charges before the judicial commission or session at all hearings and appeals. The prosecution in a disciplinary case is always a governing body of the church, even when the charge originated in one individual's accusation against another. It is the duty of the special disciplinary committee to work with the accused to see if the filing of charges can be avoided by use of alternative forms of resolution [D-10.0202g]. If the situation can be corrected in any other way, judicial process should not be used.

The accused person in a disciplinary case has rights similar to those of persons in secular criminal court proceedings: the right to remain silent, the right to call witnesses in his or her defense, the right to be represented by counsel, and the right to have counsel provided if the accused person is not able to afford it. Our system of church government makes a special effort to see that accused persons are treated fairly and given every chance to defend themselves.

If one is found guilty of an offense against the Scripture or the Constitution of the church, censures can be imposed against him or her. A censure is a kind of punishment. As outlined in D-12.0000, censures include rebuke (verbal criticism), rebuke with supervised rehabilitation, temporary exclusion from membership in the church or office, and removal from membership or office. Temporary exclusion is suspension from being a member or officer for a limited period of time. In 1998, the Rules of Discipline added a fourth level of censure called "rebuke with supervised rehabilitation." This censure allows the governing body that has jurisdiction over the offender to order and oversee a process of rehabilitation while the person continues to hold and exercise office in the church. Specifics on this new censure are found in D-12.0103. Removal from membership or office is permanent unless the person is later restored as outlined in D-12.0200. One's name is stricken from the rolls of the church and/or one's ordination to office is annulled.

Trials and Appeals

Detailed instructions for trials in remedial cases are found in D-7.0000 and for disciplinary cases in D-11.0000. These sections will be of special interest to sessions or permanent judicial commissions involved in hearing cases or to individuals who are bringing remedial complaints or defending themselves against disciplinary charges.

After a case has been heard and a verdict has been given, the verdict or decision can be appealed to the next more inclusive governing body. The exceptions to this rule are that decisions of synod permanent judicial commissions are final in all cases except those in which synod is exercising original jurisdiction and those affecting the doctrine of the church or the interpretation of the Constitution of the church [D-5.0100a]. Decisions of the Permanent Judicial Commission of the General Assembly are final in all cases. In appeals, jurisdiction is as follows:

> Presbytery permanent judicial commissions hear appeals from disciplinary decisions of sessions, synod permanent judicial commissions hear appeals from the decisions of presbytery permanent judicial commissions in both remedial and disciplinary cases,
> the General Assembly's Permanent Judicial Commission hears appeals from remedial and disciplinary decisions of synod permanent judicial commissions.   [D-8.0000, D-13.0000]

All appeals are heard and decided by permanent judicial commissions. Their task is to review the way the case was handled by the lower commission or session and to make sure that the proceedings were fair and correct according to the Constitution. The commission that hears an appeal has the power to "correct, modify, set aside, or reverse" the proceedings and judgment of the less inclusive body [D-8.0101]. Only those people or governing bodies who were first involved in the case, the original parties, are eligible to appeal the decision to a more inclusive governing body.

Written notice of appeal must be filed and received by the clerk of the governing body that elected the permanent judicial commission whose decision is being complained against within thirty days after the decision is delivered to the parties. The content of this notice of appeal is listed in D-8.0202. It is very important to observe the deadlines given for complaints and appeals and for the filing of all necessary papers in a judicial case; to miss a deadline is to risk having the case or appeal dismissed.

The judicial commission hearing an appeal is not to retry the case. It does not go back and hear the evidence again in order to make its own decision on the facts. The job of the commission is to decide whether the proceedings were fair and were carried out according to the Constitution of the church. Grounds for appeal as listed in the Rules of Discipline [D-8.0105] include the following:

a. Irregularity in the proceedings;
b. Refusing a party reasonable opportunity to be heard or to obtain or present evidence;
c. Receiving improper, or declining to receive proper, evidence or testimony;
d. Hastening to a decision before the evidence or testimony is fully received;
e. Manifestation of prejudice in the conduct of the case;
f. Injustice in the process or decision;
g. Error in constitutional interpretation.

Stay of Enforcement. If a decision of a governing body or General Assembly Council or agency or the verdict of a judicial commission is being appealed or complained of to a more inclusive body, anyone who is eligible to appeal or complain can keep the decision from being carried out until the appeal or complaint has been decided finally. The means for this is called a "stay of enforcement" [D-6.0103]. In the example at the beginning of the chapter, by filing such a stay John Harper could have prevented the candidate from being ordained and installed until a complaint on the matter could be heard by the synod. Basically, a stay of enforcement holds everything "as is," until an appeal can be filed and heard. There are three ways to get a stay of enforcement. For a stay against the action of a governing body, the signatures of at least one third of the members of the body who were recorded as present when the objectionable action was taken are required. To get a stay of enforcement against the decision of a permanent judicial commission, one third of the members who decided the case must sign.

Another alternative is to have three members of the judicial commission to which the action or decision would be appealed certify that in their opinion there are grounds for upholding a complaint against the decision or action and that it may have been in error. In order to certify this, they must have in hand a complaint or the substance of a complaint that is to be filed. A stay of enforcement is in effect until the time has run out for filing a complaint or appeal or until the matter has been decided by the permanent judicial commission that has jurisdiction.

Our system of church government recognizes that conflict may occur even within the Christian community, and it gives us the means to deal with it fairly and efficiently. If wisely used, the Rules of Discipline can do much to preserve the peace and purity of the church.

Chapter Fourteen

LEADING
THE CHURCH
IN WORSHIP

John Dowler, chair of the worship committee at Sunshine Presbyterian Church, was changing the paraments before worship one Sunday morning when he was cornered by an angry church member. Waving the worship bulletin in John's face, the member all but shouted, "I am sick and tired of these awful hymns we sing every Sunday! Ever since that new music director came, we have not sung a hymn I recognize, and I've been a Presbyterian all my life. Who's in charge of picking the hymns for the service? And why can't those of us in the pew have something to say about what we sing?"

The regular monthly session meeting of the Downtown Presbyterian Church was drawing to a close when an elder rose to present a piece of new business. "I have gotten several calls this week," he began, "about the guest preacher we had last Sunday. A number of people were very upset by what she said about capital punishment. In fact, the members of one family were so angry they were talking about leaving the church! I would like to make a motion that in the future all guest preachers and the topics of their messages must be approved by the session before they are invited to fill our pulpit." Several other elders nodded approvingly, but one session member turned to the pastor and said, "Does the *Book of Order* give us the power to do this?"

A New Thing

Even before the United Presbyterian Church in the United States of America and the Presbyterian Church in the United States reunited in 1983, groups in both churches were working on various parts of a new directory for worship. After reunion, a task force was created to pull these efforts together and incorporate them into a comprehensive guide for Presbyterian worship.

The task force to write a new directory for worship spent five years carrying out this commission. It held hearings and had consultations with a wide variety of groups across the denomination. During this period all overtures for changes in the *Book of Order* relating to worship were referred to the task force.

In 1985 the task force to write a new directory for worship made public the principles that would guide their work. They stated that the new directory would:

1. Reflect Biblical understandings of the human response to God's presence and action in the life of the world
2. Be guided by the faith and practice of the church through the ages
3. Be guided by that heritage which frees us to resist imposed forms but constrains us to obey God's Word in matters of worship
4. Be informed by our Reformed confessions
5. Be in scope and orientation catholic rather than sectarian
6. Be open to the richness of traditional and cultural ways of responding to God's grace
7. Assure an openness to the Holy Spirit's creativity, which is spontaneous yet orderly
8. Emphasize worship as the work of all the people, whose different gifts are expressed through different functions and offices
9. Recognize that as we faithfully worship God, the Holy Spirit calls and sends us to bear witness to Jesus Christ in the world through grateful and obedient service, and
10. Be the product of reflection, debate, and consideration by the whole church.

The new Directory for Worship, after approval by the General Assembly of 1988, was sent out to the presbyteries. A majority of the presbyteries must vote in favor of any proposed change in the *Book of Order* before it goes into effect. After receiving affirmative votes by a large majority of the presbyteries, the new Directory was published in the 1989–90 edition of the *Book of Order*. It has now become part of the standards of our church. It contains the theology and polity that shape the worship and ministry of the church. It is not, however, a service book with detailed instructions for actual services of worship, or a prayer book. True to our "free church" tradition, the Directory for Worship lays the foundation and draws the outlines for worship in the church without prescribing liturgies. It does not contain required prayers or rituals. Such tools with which to build on the Directory's foundation can be found in the *Book of Common Worship* published by our denomination.

There is a distinctive emphasis in the new Directory for Worship that merits notice: It recognizes and makes allowances for the diversity of the

church. The Presbyterian Church (U.S.A.) contains all kinds of congregations, some large and some small, some considering themselves theologi-
cally liberal and some who see themselves as conservative, some with a
large, trained staff, and some with no paid staff persons. Churches also differ according to the part of the country in which they are located and according to the racial or ethnic backgrounds of their members. The new
Directory attempts to leave room for all kinds of churches to build a worship
life that meets their needs while being faithful to the Reformed tradition.

What Is Worship?

When God touches our lives, we feel the call to worship. Worship is a response to the experience of the presence of God in our midst. The gathered
people of God worship in answer to the call of God that brings them into
existence. God is both the creator and the object of our worship. Without
the Spirit of God moving among us, worship is impossible. Worship oc-
curs whenever we respond to God with praise, repentance, obedience, and
service.

The experience of worship never leaves us unmoved or unchanged. It
impacts the will as well as the mind and the emotions. "The Spirit of God
quickens people to an awareness of God's grace *and claim upon their lives.*
The Spirit moves them to *respond* by naming and calling upon God, by re-
membering and proclaiming God's acts of self-revelation in word and
deed, and by committing their lives to God's reign in the world" [W-
1.1002a, italics added].

The Directory for Worship points to the life of Jesus as the perfect human response to God. Jesus' whole life was an offering of worship. His
obedience to God, his healing presence, his inspired teaching, his service
to those in need, and his sacrifice for our sin on the cross all illustrate an
existence perfectly focused on the divine reality. "Jesus Christ is the living God present in common life" [W-1.1003c]. The story of Jesus bears out
the truth that worship is not something separate from everyday life; worship *is* life.

The Elements of Worship

The Directory identifies six essential elements of worship in the Christian
community. All these elements may not be present in each worship experience; yet, taken together, they form the fabric of the church's worship life.

Prayer. Listening to God and speaking to God are at the center of the
Christian life and, therefore, at the center of worship. While prayer may
commonly include expressions of adoration, thanksgiving, confession,
intercession, and petition, no expression of honest human thought or

feeling is inappropriate for prayer. Prayer can reflect doubts and struggles of faith. It can involve an offering of self and possessions. Prayer may take the form of an act of commitment to God's will. Even the anger and pain of the people of God can be lifted up in the form of a lament. The goal of prayer is perfect love of God and perfect obedience to God's holy will.

The new Directory draws music into the context of prayer: "Song unites the faithful in common prayer wherever they gather for worship whether in church, home, or other special place" [W-2.1003]. Thus music is never to be used in worship to entertain. The aesthetics of music must always be in the service of the purpose of worship: to draw us closer to God and help us to respond to God's grace and demands.

In order to experience the fullness of prayer, worship contains prayerful actions as well as speech and song. In worship, "it is appropriate," the Directory states,

> a. to kneel, to bow, to stand, to lift hands in prayer;
> b. to dance, to clap [but not applaud as at a performance!], to embrace in joy and praise;
> c. to anoint and to lay on hands in intercession and supplication, commissioning and ordination. [W-2.1005]

Scripture Read and Proclaimed. If prayer is at the heart of worship, Scripture is its lifeblood. Scripture is the Word of God in written form. The Directory for Worship states that "where that Word is read and proclaimed, Jesus Christ the Living Word is present by the inward witness of the Holy Spirit" [W-2.2001].

It is the duty of the session to ensure that Scripture is read and proclaimed regularly to the congregation in a language that the people can understand. It is the responsibility of the pastor to select the Scripture to be read, making sure that a wide range of biblical readings are covered over the course of time. The pastor (or minister of the Word and Sacrament invited to preach by the pastor or by the session if there is no pastor) also selects the version of Scripture to be read.

The Directory does not limit the proclamation of the Word to preaching and the reading of Scripture. Creeds and confessions are also ways to hear and express response to the Scriptures. Other creative possibilities for proclaiming the Word include appropriate dramas, cantatas, oratorios and anthems, hymns, spirituals, and other songs. If these means of setting forth the message of Scripture are used, care shall be taken to make sure that the gospel message is clearly expressed in ways that are appropriate to worship.

Baptism and the Lord's Supper. The sacraments could be called the gospel in active form. The session bears significant responsibility in seeing that both sacraments are offered to the congregation. A full discussion of baptism and the Lord's Supper follows under the section headed "The Font and the Table."

Self-offering. The emphasis on the offering of one's self as an act of worship is a distinctive facet of the new Directory. Self-offering includes, but goes far beyond, the giving of money and/or possessions. In fact, the Directory declares that the whole "Christian life is an offering of one's self to God" [W-2.5001].

The giving of material offerings in the context of a service of worship is an act of self-dedication by the whole worshiping community. This is why we take up the offering at the service of worship rather than having people mail in their checks or charge their contributions on their credit cards.

Along with the offering of material gifts of the people, worship should also include opportunities for people to dedicate themselves to the mission of the church in the world. Presentations such as the Minute for Mission and special worship emphases throughout the year hold faith and works together before the people. Worship should include invitations to deepen discipleship, to join the church, and to make a commitment to particular Christian ministries.

Relating to Each Other and the World. We do not worship in isolation. Even when one worships alone, one is bound up in the mystic communion of the worshiping saints of all times and places. Times in the service of worship that are particularly appropriate for expressing our concern for each other include the gathering at the beginning of worship, during the confession and after the declaration of pardon, in times of greeting during the service, and in preparation for the prayers of the people. We can also share and support our individual and common ministries during worship, giving witness to the work of the church in the world.

The Order of Worship

Presbyterians do not have prayer books with required prayers or liturgies; in this sense we fall into what has historically been known as the "free church" tradition. The Presbyterian way of structuring the service of worship does strive to be faithful to the witness of Scripture. Outside of the Scriptures, however, there is no absolute standard governing the ordering of services.

The Directory offers a suggested rationale for the ordering of worship that takes Scripture, contemporary needs, and the traditions of the church into account. All the parts of congregational worship on the Lord's Day are presented in terms of five actions relating to the Scripture:

1. Gathering around the Word
2. Proclaiming the Word
3. Responding to the Word
4. The sealing of the Word (Sacraments)
5. Bearing and following the Word into the world

The Directory contains helpful suggestions as to specific elements of worship appropriate for each of these parts of the service.

While placing primary emphasis on the Service for the Lord's Day, the Directory also discusses the ordering of worship at other times [W-3.4001–.6205]. These occasions include daily prayer, services on Sunday other than in the morning, worship in the church school, prayer meetings, services of prayer for healing, services for evangelism, times of mission emphasis, and other regular meetings of church groups. Governing body meetings, retreats, camps, and conference centers are also the setting for very significant worship experiences. If worship is held in a setting other than the Service for the Lord's Day (especially if Communion is involved), the governing body having jurisdiction over those involved in the gathering shall authorize it and take note that it is ordered in an appropriate way.

The Context of Worship

Another distinctive feature of this Directory is that it pays special attention to the setting of worship. Beginning with the subject of time, the Directory says that while "Christians may worship at any time . . . God set aside one day in seven to be kept holy" [W-1.3011(1)]. This day (usually Sunday, in celebration of the resurrection of Jesus) is known as the Lord's Day. The Directory also commends daily public worship as an expression of our Reformed heritage and of our roots in the Jewish worship tradition.

Just as the time of worship is not essential to its nature, neither is a particular space necessary for worship. Worship happens wherever believers commune with their risen Lord. Whatever space is used for worship, it should be arranged in such a way that it promotes ease of gathering for all people, a sense of being in community, and openness to the presence of God, who is holy. The place should contain furnishings for the sacraments of baptism and the Lord's Supper. The close relationship between Word and sacraments suggests that the font and table should be near the place where Scripture is read and preached.

While we worship a God whose nature is spiritual, we must never forget that this God created our world and called it good, and that God also became incarnate in Jesus Christ. We believe that the created world belongs to God and reflects God's glory. Therefore, the spiritual and the material are closely intertwined in worship. The Old Testament tells of the use of "Ark, showbread, woven and embroidered linens, basins, oil, lights, musical instruments, grain, fruit, and animals" to worship and praise God [W-1.3031]. Jesus himself made use of physical objects in his ministry. We remember his taking water and a towel to wash the disciples' feet. We remember his breaking bread and pouring wine. We remember his parables about trees, pearls, coins, and sheep. We remember that he accepted worship in the form of a jar of ointment poured over his body.

The worship of the early church gave prominence to three physical elements as signs of the gospel: water, wine, and bread. We are heirs of this sacramental tradition. We believe that these material things as they are used in worship express the gospel in physical form. "Sacraments are signs of the real presence and power of Christ in the Church, symbols of God's action. Through the Sacraments, God seals believers in redemption, renews their identity as the people of God, and marks them for service" [W-1.3033(2)].

Along with the sacraments, worship is enriched by the creative offerings of the people of God. These might include artwork, vestments, sanctuary furnishings and accessories, banners, preaching, vocal and instrumental music, drama, and dance. Even the architecture of the buildings and rooms used by the congregation can be an offering of worship to God [W-1.3034]. In all these things, care shall be taken to see that the focus remains on God and not on the offerings or those making them.

Along with time, space, and matter, language is an essential element of worship. Worship takes place within the context of the Word. The speaking, hearing, and understanding of the Word are crucial to drawing us closer to God and to our neighbors. The Directory gives considerable attention to the place of language in worship.

First, it is important to understand how symbols are used in the language of the church. Two realities are held in tension here: on the one hand, no human symbol can express the fullness of God's being; on the other hand, because of the limitations of our human nature we must use symbols to talk about God. Symbolic language and actions used in worship are acceptable and useful as long as they point to the reality of God expressed in the life, death, and resurrection of Jesus [W-1.2002].

When we talk about God as the Rock of Ages, for instance, we know that God is not really a rock. But there is something about the solidness and the enduring qualities of rock that remind us of God's faithfulness. When we use masculine or feminine words to talk about God, we are not saying that God is either physically male or female, but rather that the qualities we find often in men or in women remind us of how God acts toward us.

Along with the use of symbols, the Directory raises the issue of using appropriate language in worship. Such language

   a. is more expressive than rationalistic,
   b. builds up and persuades as well as informs and describes,
   c. creates ardor as well as order,
   d. is the utterance of the whole community of faith as well as
       the devotion of individuals. [W-1.2005]

The inclusive nature of the gospel also requires that the language of worship be language that does not exclude people on the basis of such things as gender or race.

The Font and the Table

Baptism. This sacrament is "the sign and seal of incorporation into Christ" [W-2.3001]. In baptism we

> "participate in Jesus' death and resurrection" [W-2.3002],
> "die to what separates us from God and are raised to new-
>   ness of life" [W-2.3002],
> are bound, with the whole church, in covenant to our Cre-
>   ator and Lord [W-2.3003],
> are united with the people of God of every place and time
>   in a way that calls all barriers between individuals and
>   peoples into question [W-2.3005],
> receive our identity as God's people and our commission
>   for service [W-2.3006].

"Baptism enacts and seals what the Word proclaims: God's redeeming grace offered to all people" [W-2.3006].

In the Presbyterian Church we baptize people one time only. It is true that persons baptized as infants or children may have no conscious memory of their baptism. However, the effectiveness of baptism does not depend on our memory or appreciation of it at the time of its administration. Later experiences of conversion or spiritual growth do not invalidate our earlier baptism; instead these experiences are the natural fruit of baptism. "Baptism signifies the beginning of life in Christ, not its completion" [W-2.3007].

While the Directory emphatically denies the possibility of a person's being baptized more than once, it does encourage all baptized Christians to renew their baptism frequently. This involves a recommitment to Christ and to his service. Renewal of baptismal promises can take place each time we see another baptized and each time we celebrate the Lord's Supper. Suggestions for a more formal renewal of baptism can be found in the *Book of Common Worship.*

In our churches we baptize infants, children, and adults. Whatever the age of the person being baptized, the sacrament is the same. However, with adults the symbolism focuses on our decision to follow Jesus and our response in faithfulness to God's gracious call. With children and babies the symbolic emphasis is on the unconditional grace that claims us before we know anything about it or can respond in any way. Whether persons have been baptized as adults or as children, our denomination recognizes as valid all Christian baptisms with water in the name of the Trinity.

The form of baptism does not affect its validity, although each of the three commonly used methods has a different symbolic thrust. Pouring water over the one to be baptized reminds us of the pouring out of the Holy Spirit at Pentecost. Sprinkling reminds us of the cleansing power of the blood of Jesus. Immersion reminds us that through faith we have died with Christ and have been raised to walk in newness of life.

While a minister or commissioned lay pastor always does the actual baptizing, the Directory for Worship places primary responsibility for baptism in the hands of (1) the session, (2) the congregation, and (3) the parents of children being baptized. The session (of which the pastor is a member) bears the responsibility to see that parents are encouraged to present their children for baptism at the appropriate time. We do not believe that children who die unbaptized go to hell or to limbo; therefore, we do not rush to baptize children immediately upon birth. However, delaying baptism of children is discouraged. The session also is responsible to instruct and examine those adults who desire to be baptized upon profession of their faith. After the baptism the session will enter the baptized persons on the appropriate rolls of the church and make sure that the newly baptized persons and the parents who may have presented them for baptism are nurtured and encouraged in the life of faith [W-2.3012].

The congregation bears the responsibility to do the actual nurturing in the faith, to draw the baptized into the church family, and to make sure that they have all things necessary for growth in the faith. Special responsibilities in this area may be delegated to persons such as church school teachers, children's workers, and sponsors appointed by the session [W-2.3013].

The parents who are presenting children for baptism ordinarily are active members of the congregation. Members other than parents may also present children for baptism if they exercise parental responsibility for them. Sessions may choose to allow parents who are active members of another congregation to present children for baptism, but they are not required to do so.

The Directory also provides for baptism under unusual circumstances outside the normal worship of the congregation. The celebration of baptism may be authorized, for example, by chaplains or ministers serving "hospitals, prisons, schools, or other institutions," armed forces, and new church developments [W-2.3011b]. However, in all such cases the baptism must be entered in the records of some congregation.

In W-3.3602–.3608 the Directory gives detailed suggestions and in-structions as to the ordering of the baptismal service. It is most important to note that the sacrament shall be set in the context of reading and pro-claiming of the Word. This must be done in such a way that the meaning of baptism will be understood and the responsibilities of candidates for baptism, parents presenting children for baptism, session, and congrega-tion will be made clear.

The Lord's Supper. If baptism is the sign and seal of our entry into the com-munity of faith by grace, the Lord's Supper is the sign and seal of our con-tinued experience of this renewing grace. In Communion we

> give thanks to God;
> remember the life, death, and resurrection of Jesus;
> anticipate the coming of God's Kingdom in all its fullness,
>   and offer ourselves to work toward the day when
>   God's will shall be done on earth as it is in heaven;
> are nourished in our faith and strengthened in our com-
>   mitment;
> call on the Holy Spirit to be present among us in power
>   and join in "communion with Christ and with all who
>   belong to Christ"
> [W-2.4003–.4006].

Because of this communion, all faithful baptized persons are welcome at the Lord's Table in a Presbyterian church, regardless of their denomina-tion or any other human condition. The invitation is extended to baptized children who are being nurtured in the faith as well as to confirmed believers.

The Directory states that it is appropriate to observe Communion in worship as frequently as every Sunday. A minimum of once a quarter is required [W-2.4012a]. The best situation is for Communion to be cele-brated often enough so that it seems like a normal part of the congrega-tion's worship, not an unusual event.

While Communion is generally celebrated during public worship, the Directory also specifies that "the Lord's Supper may be observed in con-nection with the visitation of the sick and those isolated from public wor-ship as a means of extending the church's ministry to them" [W-2.4010]. In the same way that the Word is always read and proclaimed when Com-munion is celebrated in public worship, so is it when the Lord's Table is laid in the sick room or living room. In order to show forth the communion of the saints and the unity of the body of Christ in these special circum-stances, the pastor shall be accompanied by one or more church members authorized by the session to represent the congregation [W-2.4010]. This is a change from the former Directory for the Service of God, which required that the persons accompanying the minister be elders. A session or governing body always authorizes the celebration of the Lord's Supper. A group wishing to observe the sacrament shall seek the permission of the governing body having jurisdiction over that group. For instance, if the Presbyterian Women of a particular church want to celebrate Communion at a retreat, the session would be requested to authorize it. If a presbytery youth council wanted to have Communion at the close of its youth rally, presbytery would be requested to authorize the sacrament.

In W-3.3609 and following, instructions for the ordering of Communion are given. This section mandates that at least one week's notice be given before Communion in order to allow for personal and communal preparation for the sacrament. First Corinthians 11:23–26 or one of its gospel parallels is specified for use during the breaking of the bread and pouring of the cup or in the prayer of thanksgiving. No particular way of distributing the elements is mandated, but a number of possibilities are mentioned. The session is responsible for deciding what form of grape product will be used in Communion; if wine is used, however, unfermented grape juice must also be provided and clearly identified as such.

Worship on Special Occasions

Although the Word and Sacraments are always the focus of Christian worship, Chapter IV of the Directory deals with nine special circumstances that bear recognition in the life of the congregation and individuals. A number of these occasions, such as receiving new members, welcoming children to the Lord's Table, welcoming new members into the church, renewal of baptism and other commitments, and commissioning for service in the church and world are generally incorporated into the Service for the Lord's Day. Also in this category might be included the marking of transitions in ministry; the recognition of one or more members' service outside the church; the ordination and installation of elders, deacons, and ministers; services expressing repentance and reconciliation; and services imposing the censures of the church [see D-12.0000].

Two special occasions for worship are dealt with at greater length. These are services at the time of marriage and of death. The Directory states that "as a service of Christian worship, the marriage service is under the direction of the minister and the supervision of the session" [W-4.9003]. All things relating to the service, including music and decorations, should reflect its character as a service of worship. When Communion is celebrated along with the marriage service, it requires authorization by the session. All baptized persons present must be invited to partake of the sacrament.

The section on funerals specifies that ordinarily the service will be held in the church "in order to join this service to the community's continuing life and witness to the resurrection" [W-4.10003]. The pastor is in charge of this service. The Christian service of worship takes precedence over fraternal or other rites, which should be conducted separately from worship. Whatever the specifics of the service, the focus should be on the hope of resurrection that Christians share in Christ and the comforting of those who grieve [W-4.10001].

Worship and Personal Discipleship

The Directory for Worship not only gives instructions for ordering the worship life of the congregation, but also offers help in developing rich worship experiences for individuals, families, and small groups. Worship is never private. Even when we worship by ourselves, we are still bound up in the communion of the saints that transcends all limits of time and space. Yet one who is committed to growing in the faith will make time during the day for worship, either alone or with small groups of other believers. This is part of being a disciple of Christ: to take advantage of the means of grace that God has placed at our disposal. The more we commit ourselves to ministry and serious discipleship, the more we will need frequent worship and sacraments.

The Directory says that daily personal worship may take place when we are assembled in groups, in households and families, or when we are alone [W-5.2001]. The emphasis is on "finding the times and places where one can focus on God's presence, hear God's Word, and respond to God's grace in prayer, self-offering, and commitment to service" [W-5.2001]. The key elements of daily personal worship are Scripture and prayer. The Directory reminds us that "one may read Scripture for . . . guidance, support, comfort, encouragement, and challenge" [W-5.3002a]. Study of the Scriptures as historical and literary documents is commended, along with meditation, memorization, reflection, and analysis of Scripture. Using imagination to enter into the world of the original hearers is another helpful method of approaching Scripture. When we are confronted with the challenges of the Word, we may find ourselves wrestling with its demands and being led to offer ourselves in obedience to God in response [W-5.3002]. The use of a journal in the study of Scripture is recommended, along with some kind of systematic tool such as a lectionary for covering the whole message of the Scriptures.

Prayer is another essential part of the discipline of personal worship. Prayer can take many forms, and one committed to Christian growth will do well to explore a wide variety of such forms. The Directory lists a number of possibilities, including conversation with God, waiting before God in silence, meditation, communion with God beyond words, praying in tongues, and acting out prayer in various kinds of movement. What is commonly called intercessory prayer is commended, and we are encouraged to hold the events and peoples of the world, as well as those close to us, before God. Prayer is learned through the discipline of praying, and the use of a wide variety of aids, such as Scripture, prayer books, hymnals, and literature and visual art, is helpful in prayer education.

Other disciplines commended by the Directory are the keeping of the Lord's Day, public worship, cultivating the habits of rest and recreation, and taking part in ministry in Christ's name [W-5.5001]. Acts of fasting and keeping vigils (not sleeping, in order to pray through the night) may also be helpful means of personal discipleship related to prayer. Any serious disciple will sooner or later be brought to deal with issues of stewardship in his or her life. The use of property in the name of God is an important facet of discipleship. "Tithing is a primary expression of the Christian discipline of stewardship. . . . Those who follow the discipline of Christian stewardship will find themselves called to lives of simplicity, generosity, honesty, hospitality, compassion, receptivity, and concern for the earth and God's creatures" [W-5.5004–.5005].

Worship and Ministry

Worship of the true God never leaves the worshiper unchanged. Those who truly worship will be drawn into the service of God. The Directory for Worship talks about the various ministries of the people of God, dividing them into those carried out within the community of faith and those carried out in the world.

The church is engaged in a number of activities aimed at meeting the needs of its members. The Directory speaks of these in terms of nurture and pastoral care. Nurture includes the cultivation of faith in persons at all stages of their life, from baptism to the deathbed. The nurture of the church prepares persons for baptism, leads them to a profession of Jesus Christ as Lord and Savior, and gives them training and resources to enable them to live as disciples of Christ in ministry to the world [W-6.2001].

The issue of vocation is mentioned several times in the Directory, especially in terms of the church's duty to guide, support, and provide resources for those who are living active lives of witness in the world. The idea that worship and the service of God in the world are inseparable is stressed. Therefore, the church bears the responsibility of connecting the worship life of the congregation with the vocation of Christians to serve God at home and in the school, workplace, neighborhood, nation, and world [W-6.2003].

The various stages of human life, and the losses and challenges connected with these stages, also offer opportunities for growth in faith. The Directory has a section on the ministry of pastoral care as an aid to such growth. Occasions such as illnesses, death, grief, loss of employment, divorce or separation, and children leaving home are mentioned as important times for pastoral care. The church often shies away from getting involved in delicate situations involving broken relationships and sin, but the power of the gospel extends even to these situations. A congregation that wishes to minister to people in the whole of life will find sensitive ways of being present even to those caught up in painful circumstances [W-6.3008 and .3009]. Such care might involve prayer, sacraments, and the sharing of Scripture and of familiar parts of the service of worship such as the Lord's Prayer, creeds, and psalms [W-6.3011].

The Directory concludes with a chapter on the ministry of the church in the world. Worship is closely linked with serving God's purposes in the world because "worship presents the reality of the divine rule which God has promised in Jesus Christ" [W-7.1001]. Worship and mission feed each other. In worship we are called into mission; as we engage in mission we find ourselves ever returning to God with our praise and our need for renewal.

The ministry of the church in the world has a number of facets. Proclamation of the Word and sharing the good news are placed in the context of worship, where the Word is regularly read and proclaimed. In worship, ministries of compassion to persons in need are encouraged "as the faithful respond in prayers of confession and intercession, in acts of self-offering, and in offering material goods" to be used in these ministries [W-7.3002]. Another facet of the church's mission in the world involves working for peace and justice. This is a ministry of reconciliation that draws on the Scriptures' call for holiness and justice in our personal dealings with others and in our larger society. The stewardship of life and creation is another facet of the mission of God's people. In worship, our thanksgiving is coupled with commitment to live on the earth in ways that do not tend toward destruction.

All these ministries are called forth and empowered by the Holy Spirit, whose presence enables all the ministry and worship of the church. Through the presence and working of the Spirit "the Church's ministries of evangelism and caring for creation, of compassion and reconciliation are signs of God's reign and offer hope in the midst of life-denying situations. That hope is not dependent on the success of the Church's ministries or the effectiveness of its worship, but is sustained by the power of God present with the Church as it ministers and worships" [W-7.6002]. Quite appropriately, the Directory ends with a statement of hope for the coming of the reign of God (Phil. 2:9–11) and ascriptions of praise to God (Jude 24 and Rev. 7:12).

Responsibilities for Worship

It is the duty of the session in each church to make sure both that opportunities to worship are made available to the congregation and that people are encouraged to take full advantage of these opportunities. The Directory places oversight of the worship of the congregation squarely in the hands of the session [W-1.4004].

Specifically, the session is responsible to see that the

    a. preaching of the Word,
    b. celebration of the Sacraments,
    c. corporate prayer, and
    d. offering of praise to God in song

occur regularly in the congregation [W-1.4004]. In this regard, the session is authorized

    e. to oversee and approve all public worship in the life of the particular church with the exception of those responsibilities delegated to the pastor alone [W-1.4005]
    f. to determine occasions, days, times, and places for worship [W-1.4004].

The Directory also gives the session direct responsibility to determine where worship shall be held and how the space is to be arranged and furnished. This responsibility includes exercising its discretion about the use of flowers, banners, candles, and other such things in worship. The music program of the church, as well as other activities involving the arts, are under the oversight of the session. The session also supervises the persons who are involved in leading worship "through music, drama, dance, and other arts" [W-1.4004j].

There are two duties mentioned in the Directory [W-1.4006] that the session and pastor share. Primary responsibility for deciding the order of worship lies with the pastor, but this shall be done in consultation with and with the agreement of the session. Primary responsibility for the choice of pew Bibles, hymnals, and other such aids to worship lies with the session, but they must consult with and secure the concurrence of the pastor. In choosing these worship aids, the Directory also specifies that other persons involved in leading the congregation (such as educators and church musicians) should also be consulted.

The second vignette at the beginning of this chapter raises the question of whether the session has the right to approve guest preachers. This is another area of worship planning in which the pastor and the session must work with each other. The Directory specifies that "a minister of the Word and Sacrament or other person authorized by presbytery may be invited by the pastor with the concurrence of the session or, when there is no pastor, by the session" [W-2.2007]. This means that the pastor and the session must come to agreement before a particular person is invited.

The pastor of the congregation has certain duties in connection with choosing the contents of services of worship "which are not subject to the authority of the session" [W-1.4005]. These include

    (1) the selection of Scripture lessons to be read,
    (2) the preparation and preaching of the sermon or exposition of the Word,

(3)   the prayers offered on behalf of the people and those pre-
      pared for the use of the people in worship,
(4)   the music to be sung,
(5)   the use of drama, dance, and other art forms. [W-1.4005]

A wise pastor will confer with the session, other professionals on the
church staff, and if possible a worship committee as she or he makes these
important choices in the planning of worship.

Because of the emotional connections people have with familiar hymns,
choosing hymns to be sung in worship is a particularly sensitive area of pastoral responsibility. In the first vignette at the beginning of the chapter, John
Dowler could have explained to the irate church member that the pastor is
responsible for the music sung in worship. He could then have suggested
to the member that he share his concern about the hymns with the pastor.
Perhaps the pastor should consult with the session and members of the congregation to see if the irate member's concern is generally shared. If so, the
pastor might consult with the music director on this matter, making the
congregation's preferences known. If the pastor has delegated the selection
of hymns entirely to the music staff, he or she might want to consider taking a more active role in this part of planning the congregation's worship.

By far the largest part of the responsibility for the congregation's worship lies with the session. Aside from the general oversight of the congregation's worship and its specific duties as discussed above, the session is
also charged with providing worship education for the congregation. This
shall be done for different age groups in ways that are appropriate to them.
Worship is something we learn how to do. Therefore, learning to participate fully in worship is an important part of Christian education for persons of all ages. Along with this general education for worship, the
Directory specifies that it shall be used as a regular part of the training of
officers of the church.

Following is a reference chart showing the places in the Directory where
the session is mentioned in connection with worship.[1]

Accountability to presbytery for congregation's worship	W-1.4008
Authorizing services of worship other than the Service for the Lord's Day	
Daily prayer	W-3.4005
On Sunday	W-3.5101
Prayer meetings	W-3.5301
Services for wholeness	W-3.5402
Services for evangelism	W-3.5501
Services for mission interpretation	W-3.5601
Baptism	
General responsibilities	W-2.3012

In extraordinary circumstances W-2.3011a
Of children whose parents are not members of the congregation W-2.3014

Children and worship W-3.1004

Counsel about manifestations of the Spirit W-3.1002b

Discipline of personal worship, encouraging W-5.1004

Education for worship W-1.4007

Guest preachers, concurrence, in pastor's invitation to W-2.2007

Lord's Supper
  Authorizing the sacrament W-2.4012a
  Authorizing at retreats, etc. W-3.6204
  Disposition of elements W-3.3619
  Services on the occasion of death (funerals) W-4.1003
  Manner of distribution decided by session W-3.3616
  On occasions other than worship on the Lord's Day W-2.4010
  Use of wine at communion W-3.3611
  Welcoming children to the Lord's Table W-4.2002

Marriage services
  Under the supervision of session W-4.9003
  If requested, counsel with minister on decision not
    to marry a couple W-4.9002b

Meetings of pastor and choir director, responsibility to see that
  they occur regularly W-1.4005(b)

Nurture
  Approval of resources W-6.2006
  Responsibility for educational program W-6.2005

Ordering worship on the Lord's Day W-3.3201

Provide for reading and preaching of the Word W-2.2007
                                                       W-2.2001

Reception of new members W-4.2003
                                                       W-4.2004

Sense of personal renewal shared with session W-4.2006

Services on occasion of death W-4.10002

Worship at session meetings W-3.6101

The worship of the Triune God is at the core of the church's identity. A church without worship is a church without life. Therefore, the session's responsibilities to encourage, nurture, and order the worship of the congregation are among the most important given to it by the *Book of Order.*

NOTES

Chapter 1. A Polity for the Church

1. Stuart R. Oglesby, *Presbyterianism in Action* (Richmond: John Knox Press, 1949), pp. 34, 35.
2. Ben Lacy Rose, *Confirming Your Call* (Richmond: John Knox Press, 1967), p. 27.
3. Ibid., p. 19.

Chapter 2. Calling to Office in the Church

1. Robert Clyde Johnson, ed., *The Church and Its Changing Ministry* (Philadelphia: Office of the General Assembly, The United Presbyterian Church in the United States of America, 1961), p. 26.
2. "Church Membership and Discipline" (Atlanta: Office of the Stated Clerk, Presbyterian Church in the United States, 1979), p. 11.
3. "The Nature and Practice of Ministry" (Atlanta: Office of the Stated Clerk, Presbyterian Church in the United States, 1981), p. 5.
4. "Ordination to the Ministry of the Word" (Atlanta: Office of the Stated Clerk, Presbyterian Church in the United States, 1976), p. 6.
5. Robert W. Henderson, "Concerning the Eldership," *Reformed World* 1 (December 1973): p. 365.

Chapter 4. The Office of Elder

1. Janet G. MacGregor, *The Scottish Presbyterian Polity* (Edinburgh: Oliver and Boyd, 1926), p. xiv.
2. Ibid., p. xvi.
3. Ibid., p. 51.
4. Ibid.
5. Ibid., p. 112.
6. Ibid., p. 122.
7. Ernest Trice Thompson, *Presbyterians in the South* (Richmond: John Knox Press, 1963), vol. 1, p. 12.
8. Ibid., p. 20.
9. Ibid., p. 23.
10. Samuel Miller, *An Essay on the Warrant, Nature, and Duties of the Office of the Ruling Elder* (Philadelphia: Presbyterian Board of Publication, 1832), p. 4.
11. Ibid., p. 175.
12. Ibid., p. 194.
13. Ibid., p. 201.
14. Ibid., p. 207.
15. Ibid., p. 213.
16. Ibid., p. 214.
17. In 1984 excerpts from Miller's book on the elder were reprinted in booklet form under the title, *The Ruling Elder,* by Presbyterian Heritage Publications,

P.O. Box 180922, Dallas, Texas 75218. The text was made more readable by changing to contemporary spelling, grammar, and word usage. A second edition was published in 1994. This booklet is a valuable resource for understanding the significance of the office of elder.

18. Miller, *An Essay on the Warrant, Nature, and Duties of the Office of the Ruling Elder*, p. 302.
19. Ibid., p. 253.
20. Thompson, *Presbyterians*, vol. 1, p. 516.
21. Ibid., p. 517.
22. Ibid.
23. *Minutes*, General Assembly, 1844, p. 370; Thompson, *Presbyterians*, vol. 1, p. 518.
24. Ralph E. Prime, *A Sermon or Address on the Elder Moderator and the Ruling Elder* (Philadelphia: MacCalla & Company, Inc., 1895), pp. 10ff.
25. James E. Andrews, "We Can Be More Than We Are," article included in the Joint Committee on Reunion's resource packet, p. 5.

Chapter 5. The Office of Deacon

1. John Calvin, *Institutes of the Christian Religion*, vol. II, ed. John T. McNeill (Philadelphia: Westminster Press, 1960), iv.iii.9, p. 123.
2. Janet G. MacGregor, *The Scottish Presbyterian Polity* (Edinburgh: Oliver and Boyd, 1926), pp. 108, 123.
3. *Minutes*, General Assembly, 1841, p. 418, quoted in Samuel J. Baird, *A Collection of the Acts, Deliverances, and Testimonies of the Supreme Judicatory of the Presbyterian Church* (Philadelphia: Presbyterian Board of Publication, 1856), p. 38.
4. James B. Ramsey, *The Deaconship* (Richmond: Presbyterian Publishing Company, 1879), p. 17.
5. Ibid., pp. 17–18.
6. Ibid., p. 19.
7. Ibid., p. 23.
8. Ibid., p. 25.
9. Ibid., pp. 26–27.
10. *The Deacon: His Work and How to Do It* (Roanoke, Va.: The Stone Printing and Mfg. Co., 1895).
11. C. E. Vaughan, *The Deacon's Office* (Richmond: Presbyterian Committee of Publication, 1897), p. 16.
12. Paul M. Penick, *The Deacon's First Responsibility* (Louisville: Executive Committee of Christian Education and Ministerial Relief, c. 1917 or 1918), p. 3.
13. Edward Mack, *The Office of Deacon* (Richmond: Presbyterian Committee of Publication, 1923), p. 8.
14. Ibid., p. 21.
15. Ibid.
16. Ibid., p. 29.
17. *The Scriptural Office of Deacon* (Philadelphia: Presbyterian Board of Publication, 1860–1870), pamphlet #95, p. 7.
18. Ibid., p. 11.
19. William Henry Roberts, *A Manual for Ruling Elders and Church Sessions* (Philadelphia: Presbyterian Board of Publication and Sabbath-School Work, 1912), p. 366.
20. Ibid., p. 363.

21. *Minutes,* General Assembly, PCUSA, 1892, p. 52, quoted in *Minutes, 1896,* General Assembly, PCUSA, p. 183.
22. UPNA *Book of Government and Worship,* printed in Milligan, Ohio, *The Digest of the Principal Deliverances of the General Assembly of the U.P.C.N.A.* (Pittsburgh: United Presbyterian Board of Publication and Bible School Work, 1942), p. 27.
23. Ibid.
24. Robert W. Gibson, *The Place of the Deacon in the Life of the Church* (Pittsburgh: United Presbyterian Board of Publication and Bible School Work, 1938).
25. *A Proposal for Considering the Theology and Practice of Ordination in the Presbyterian Church (U.S.A.),* The Theology and Worship Ministry Unit, Presbyterian Church (U.S.A.), Louisville, Kentucky, 1992, pp. 101–102.
26. Ibid., p. 102.

Chapter 6. A First Look at the Session

1. Presbyterian Church (U.S.A.), Directory for the Service of God, S-6.0200, 1983.

Chapter 8. Officers and Staff Working Together

1. *Guidelines for a Session Personnel Committee,* 3rd ed. (Atlanta and New York: The Vocation Agency in consultation with the General Assembly Mission Board, Presbyterian Church (U.S.A.), 1984).
2. *Toward Inclusiveness in Employment: A Churchwide Plan for Equal Employment Opportunity, Presbyterian Church (U.S.A.)* (New York: The General Assembly Council, Presbyterian Church (U.S.A.), 1985).
3. *Presbyterian Church (U.S.A.) Churchwide Compensation Policy Guidelines* (Louisville, Ky.: Church Vocations Ministry Unit, 1988).

Chapter 9. Leading the Church in Mission

1. Directory for the Service of God, S-4.0600a.
2. See Robert McAfee Brown, *Making Peace in the Global Village* (Philadelphia: Westminster Press, 1981), p. 20.
3. Directory for the Service of God, S-6.0500.

Chapter 10. Presbytery, Synod, and the General Assembly

1. Janet G. MacGregor, *The Scottish Presbyterian Polity* (Edinburgh: Oliver and Boyd, 1926), p. 137.

Chapter 11. Stewardship, Finance, and Property

1. Directory for the Service of God, S-2.0900.
2. Ben Lacy Rose, *Confirming Your Call* (Richmond: John Knox Press, 1967), pp. 16, 17.
3. In this section we are heavily indebted to John C. Bramer, *Efficient Church Business Management* (Philadelphia: Westminster Press, 1960).
4. Ibid., pp. 76, 78.

Chapter 12. Meetings of Governing Bodies and of the Congregation

1. Sarah Corbin Robert et al., *Robert's Rules of Order* (Glenview, Ill.: Scott Foresman & Company, 1981), pp. xxxi, xlii.

Chapter 14. Leading the Church in
                Worship

1. This chart is adapted from un-
   published materials compiled by
   Dr. C. Benton Kline and dated
   November 30, 1989. In writing
   this chapter on the Directory for
   Worship, the authors drew on
   these and other such unpub-
   lished materials and are heavily
   indebted to Dr. Kline for his re-
   search and his generosity in sharing its fruits.

INDEX OF *BOOK OF ORDER* REFERENCES

Book of Order subsections marked with a lowercase letter (for example, 14.0701a) are not included in this index, but may be found by referring to the pages listed under the appropriate numbered entry.

The authors' citations of *Book of Order* sections are indexed; cross-references within quoted *Book of Order* sections are not.

Preface	8	G-1.0501	6
D-1.0101	163, 164	G-2.0100	6
D-1.0102	xiii	G-3.0101–.0103	99
D-2.0101	164	G-3.0200	106
D-2.0202	164	G-3.0300	63, 103, 105, 106
D-3.0101	166	G-3.0400	108
D-3.0400	110	G-3.0401	24, 28, 107
D-4.0000	166	G-4.0101–.0102	8
D-5.0100	169	G-4.0201	99, 108
D-6.0000	167	G-4.0301	6, 144
D-6.0103	170	G-4.0400	111
D-6.0202	165	G-4.0403	24, 26, 28, 69, 83
D-6.0301	166, 167	G-5.0000	64
D-6.0303	167	G-5.0101	64
D-7.0000	167, 169	G-5.0102	13, 102
D-7.0402	124, 165	G-5.0103	64
D-8.0000	169	G-5.0201	65
D-8.0101	169	G-5.0202	20, 64
D-8.0105	169	G-5.0203	65
D-10.0000	168	G-5.0204	65
D-10.0202	168	G-5.0402	66
D-10.0401	168	G-5.0403	66
D-11.0000	168, 169	G-5.0501	15, 71
D-12.0000	168, 181	G-5.0502	72
D-12.0103	168	G-6.0100	77
D-12.0200	168	G-6.0102	19
D-13.0000	169	G-6.0106	16, 17, 18
		G-6.0107	5, 16
G-1.0100	4, 5	G-6.0108	21, 160–61
G-1.0305	145, 161, 162	G-6.0200	77
G-1.0307	10	G-6.0201	76
G-1.0308	10	G-6.0202	77, 86, 87, 89, 91, 92, 166
G-1.0400	8, 9, 139, 145	G-6.0203	76
G-1.0500	6	G-6.0302	110

G-6.0303	18	G-10.0101	147
G-6.0304	89, 91, 131	G-10.0102	5, 9, 63, 64, 67, 68, 72, 73,
G-6.0401	18, 104		90, 92, 94, 95, 101, 104, 107,
G-6.0402	46, 57, 104, 133		108, 125, 129, 130, 131,
G-6.0403	57, 58, 92		133,135, 137, 139, 141, 157
G-6.0405	92	G-10.0103	79, 147
G-7.0302	146, 150	G-10.0201	152, 156
G-7.0303	150	G-10.0202	152
G.7.0304	135, 140, 144, 150, 151	G-10.0301	110
G-7.0306	150	G-10.0302	65, 67, 71, 72, 73
G-7.0308	149	G-10.0401	135, 136
G-7.0401	142	G-11.0000	111
G-7.0402	142	G-11.0101	9, 113, 147, 152, 153
G-7.0403	142	G-11.0103	33, 70, 80, 87, 108, 111,
G-8.0000	114, 140		112, 113, 114, 115, 116,
G-8.0201	139		117, 157
G-8.0301	139	G-11.0201	153, 156
G-8.0401	139	G-11.0202	154
G-8.0500	140	G-11.0203	152
G-8.0501–.0502	140	G-11.0304	129
G-8.0601	139	G-11.0402	32
G-8.0701	140	G-11.0403	77, 78, 114
G-9.0101	9	G-11.0406	77, 78, 79
G-9.0102	10, 11, 111	G-11.0408	78
G-9.0103	10, 110	G-11.0501	124
G-9.0104	26, 94, 111	G-11.0502	31, 33, 80, 113, 114, 116
G-9.0105	125	G-12.0000	111
G-9.0106	125	G-12.0101	9, 118, 154
G-9.0201	146, 148	G-12.0102	102, 111, 112, 118, 119,
G-9.0202	147, 148		120, 125, 157
G-9.0301	148	G-12.0201	154, 156
G-9.0302	148	G-12.0202	155
G-9.0303	145	G-12.0203	129, 154
G-9.0304	162	G-13.0000	111
G-9.0305	162	G-13.0101	9
G-9.0400	10, 107	G-13.0102	155
G-9.0403	123	G-13.0103	108, 111, 112, 121, 122,
G-9.0404	9, 114		123, 157
G-9.0501	124	G-13.0104	155, 156
G-9.0502	123	G-13.0105	155
G-9.0503	80, 124	G-13.0106	155
G-9.0702	83	G-13.0108	124
G-9.0704	83	G-13.0111	45, 124
G-9.0801	45, 124	G-13.0112	124
G-9.0901	125	G-13.0200	122
G-9.0902	124	G-13.0201	83, 94
G-10.0000	60	G-13.0202	45

G-14.0102	70	W-1.1003	173
G-14.0201	24, 25, 26, 28	W-1.2002	177
G-14.0202	25, 27, 28, 114	W-1.2005	178
G-14.0203	21	W-1.3011	176
G-14.0204	29	W-1.3031	177
G-14.0205	29	W-1.3033	177
G-14.0206	30	W-1.3034	177
G-14.0206–.02009	19	W-1.4004	11, 184, 185
G-14.0207	7, 20, 73, 160	W-1.4005	87, 185, 186, 187
G-14.0208	20	W-1.4006	185
G-14.0300	70, 124	W-1.4007	187
G-14.0301	115	W-1.4008	186
G-14.0303	70	W-2.1003	174
G-14.0305	31, 70	W-2.1005	174
G-14.0306	70	W-2.2001	174, 187
G-14.0309	71	W-2.2007	185, 187
G-14.0310	31, 87	W-2.3001	178
G-14.0314	33	W-2.3002	178
G-14.0400	70	W-2.3003	178
G-14.0402	78	W-2.3005	178
G-14.0406	73	W-2.3006	178
G-14.0501	76, 79, 80, 93	W-2.3007	178
G-14.0502	30, 31, 151	W-2.3011	179, 187
G-14.0503	33	W-2.3012	66, 179, 196
G-14.0505	33	W-2.3014	65, 187
G-14.0506	32	W-2.4003–.4006	180
G-14.0507	33, 116	W-2.4010	180, 181, 187
G-14.0508	9	W-2.4011	9
G-14.0513	79, 80, 81, 82, 83	W-2.4012	180, 187
G-14.0515	84, 93	W-2.5001	175
G-14.0600	115	W-3.1002	187
G-14.0601	80	W-3.1004	68, 187
G-14.0702	97	W-3.3201	187
G-14.0703	97	W-3.3602–.3608	180
G-14.0704	97	W-3.3609	181
G-14.0705	97	W-3.3611	187
G-14.0801	85, 87	W-3.3616	21, 187
G-15.0101–.0103	108	W-3.3619	187
G-15.0202	9	W-3.4001–.6205	176
G-15.0204	9	W-3.4005	186
G-15.0300	122	W-3.5101	186
G-15.0302	108	W-3.5301	186
G-18.0000	116	W-3.5402	186
G-18.0201	117	W-3.5501	186
G-18.0301	117	W-3.5601	186
		W-3.6101	187
W-1.1002	173	W-3.6204	187

W-4.2002	66, 187	W-5.5004–.5005	183
W-4.2003	187	W-6.1002–.1003	68
W-4.2004	187	W-6.2001	66, 183
W-4.2006	187	W-6.2001–.2004	68
W-4.9002	187	W-6.2003	183
W-4.9003	181, 187	W-6.2005	187
W-4.10001	182	W-6.2006	68, 187
W-4.10002	187	W-6.3008	184
W-4.10003	182, 187	W-6.3009	184
W-5.1004	187	W-6.3011	184
W-5.2001	182	W-7.1001	184
W-5.3002	182	W-7.3002	184
W-5.5001	183	W-7.6002	184

INDEX OF TOPICS

administration, 112
administrative review, 9–10
agencies, 123–125
Amendment A, 18
Amendment B, 18
Andrews, James E., 45
Anglican Church, 3
apostolic succession, 3
assistant pastor, 79
assistant stated clerks, 148
associate pastor, 30, 31, 33, 79–80, 84
   responsibilities of, 93
   role after loss of pastor, 81
associate stated clerks, 148

baptism
   baptized church members, 65
   commissioned lay pastors adminis-
     tering, 85, 87
   emphasis on infant, xii
   forms of, 179
   meaning of, 12–13
   one time only, 178
   ordering of service, 180
   outside worship settings, 179
   as part of worship, 174–175, 176, 178–
     180
   participation of elders in, 90
   preparation for, 66
   symbolism of, 178–179
Baptist churches, 2–3
bishop, 3, 4, 113
Book of Common Worship, 172, 178
Book of Confessions, 6–7
Book of Order, 7–8
Breckinridge, Robert J., 42–43

call
   to church membership, 12–14
   as concept, xii

knowledge of, 16–17
   to office, 15–17
   to office in the church, 12–22
   of a pastor, 30–32, 79
   presbytery's refusal to accept, 5
   responsibilities in church resulting
     from, 13–14
   to serve, xiv
Calvin, John, xvi
   concept of church officers, 21, 35–36
   on covenant, xi
   on God's grace, xii
   scriptural basis for office of deacon,
     47
   on sin, xiii
   on theological understanding and
     form of government, xi
campaigns, 130
censure, 168
Christian education, 67–68, 95–97
Church and Its Changing Ministry, 14
church budget, 134–135
"Church Membership and Discipline,"
   14
church membership, as ministry, 14–
   15
church officers
   election of, 23–34
   freedom of conscience and, 21–22
   limit on terms of office, 24–25
   ordination to office, 19–21
   perpetual nature of, 21
   qualifications of, 17–19
   session's responsibility for, 73–74
church property, 139–142
   exemptions, 140–141
   good stewardship of, 141–142
   property held in trust, 139–140
church staff, 93–94
"church universal," 8–9

Churchwide Compensation Policy Guidelines, 95
"clergy" vs. "clerical," 41
clerks, 146–148
commissioned lay pastor, 85
commissioners, 6
commissions, 123–125
Committee on Representation, 124–125
committees, 123–125
compensation
    for minister, 135
    for staff, 95
complaint, 166–167
confessional statements, 6
conflict in church, 158–170
    discipline, 163–164
    dissent, 162
    in early church history, 158–159
    freedom of conscience, 160
    ground rules for dealing with, 159–162
    judicial process, 164–168
    levels of censure, 168
    mutual forbearance, 161–162
    power of governing bodies and the Constitution, 160–161
    protest, 162–163
    stay of enforcement, 170
    trials and appeals, 169–170
congregation
    affirming election of new officers, 20
    budget of as indicator of values and goals of, 134
    financial reports to, 137–138
    inability of to instruct officers how to vote, 5–6
    limitations on governing authority of, 5
    meetings of, 149–151, 156–157
    presbytery's relationship to, 113–114
    protected from interference by governing body, 151
    role in Baptisms, 179
    role in calling a pastor, 30
    role in dissolving pastoral relationship, 80

    role in observing Lord's Supper, 180–181
congregational care, responsibilities for, 91
congregational meetings, 149–151, 156–157
    business allowed to transact, 151
    called meetings, 150–151
    officers, 149–150
    participants, 149
    quorum, 151
    required meetings, 150
congregational polity, 2–3
    difference from Presbyterian polity, 5
consistory, 37
Constitution
    amendments to, 116
    parts of, 6–8
co-pastor, 30, 31, 33, 79, 150
    determination of responsibilities for, 93
councils, 123–125
covenant, xi–xii

Deacon's First Responsibility, 51–52
deacons
    changes in understanding office of, 50–51
    commitment to inclusiveness in election of, 23–25
    under congregational polity, 2
    election, examination, ordination, and installation of, 29–30, 73
    encouraging churches to institute office of, 48–50
    function of, 46–47, 50–51, 56–58, 104
    liturgical function of, 58
    nominating committee and, 25–26
    operating under jurisdiction of the session, 92, 104
    in Presbyterian Church U.S., 51–53
    in Presbyterian Church U.S.A., 53–54
    qualifications for, 18–19
    recovering essence of office of, 56–59
    in Reformed tradition, 47
    scriptural basis for, 4
    under 1788 Constitution, 47–48

in United Presbyterian Church of North America, 54–55

in United Presbyterian Church in the U.S.A., 55–56

working with elders and pastors, 92

See also church officers

delegates, 6

delinquencies, 164, 165

designated gifts, 138

designated pastor (co-pastor), 80–81

designated pastoral relationships, 80–81

Directory for Worship, 7–8, 171–185 *See also* worship

Disciples of Christ, 3

disciplinary cases, 164, 166, 167–168

discipline, 163–164

dissent, 162

Dutch Reformed Church, xiii

ecumenical relations, 112

elders, 4

advocacy for office of, 40–42

commitment to inclusiveness in election of, 23–25

debates surrounding office of, 42–45

decision making responsibilities of, 145

distinction between corporate and individual duties, 40–41

early emphasis on, 35–40

election, examination, ordination, and installation of, 29–30, 73

lack of governing power as individuals, 109

as leaders in personal stewardship, 131–133

in more inclusive governing bodies, 147

office of, 35–45

participation in higher governing bodies, 109–110

qualifications for, 17–18

as representatives and commissioners, 21

responsibilities for governance, 91

responsibilities for pastoral care, 91

responsibilities of, 89

scriptural support for office, 39

working with pastors, 89–90

working with pastors and deacons, 92

See also church officers

emergency appeals, 130

envelope system, 51

episcopal polity, 3

difference from Presbyterian polity, 5

Essay on the Warrant, Nature, and Duties of the Office of the Ruling Elder, 40–42

Evangelical Lutheran Church in America, 122

evangelism, 100–102

fasting, 183

fellowship, 69

financial reports to the congregation, 137–138

financial reviews, 136

First Book of Discipline, 37, 47

Form of Government, 7

"free church" tradition, 175

freedom of conscience, 21–22, 160

General Assembly, 9–10, 110, 111–112

call/referral system, 31

Christian educator certification, 97

committees of, 124

makeup of under 1788 form of government, 39–40

meetings of, 155, 156–157

moderator of, 148

power to receive or unite with other ecclesiastical bodies, 122

relating to whole church, 121–122

relationship to presbytery, 115–116

relationship to synod, 119–120, 121

responsibilities of, 120–123

sphere of mission for, 121

General Assembly Council, responsibility for church personnel policies, 94–95

General Assembly meetings, 155, 156–157

general mission giving, 129–130

governance
    parity in, 45
    responsibilities for, 91
governing bodies, 5
    authorization of Lord's Supper, 181
    decision making power of, 144
    delinquencies, 164, 165
    discipline in, 164–170
    dissent and protest against, 161–162
    election of officers to, 146–147
    irregularities, 164, 165
    more inclusive structure of, 109–112
    powers and responsibilities of, 10–11
    reliance on per capita monies, 131
    responsibilities in common, 111–112
    structure of, 9
    See also General Assembly, pres-
        bytery, session, synod
guest preachers, 185
Guidelines for a Session Personnel Com-
    mittee, 94

Hodge, Charles, 43
hymns during worship, 186

inactive members, 71–72
inclusiveness, 23–28, 69, 178
    exceptions for certain congregations,
        27–28
    in governance, 91
    governing bodies' responsibilities for,
        111
    nominating committee and, 25–26
    picking a pastor and, 30, 31
incorporation, 142
interim associate pastor, 79, 82
interim co-pastor, 79, 82
interim pastor, 79, 81–82
irregularities, 164, 165

judicial commissions, 165
judicial functions, governing bodies' re-
    sponsibilities for, 111
judicial process, 10, 164–168

law, xii–xiii
lay-elder, 41

laying on of hands, 3
    during ordination, 19, 41–43, 44
"Life and Mission Statement of the
    Presbyterian Church (U.S.A.)," 103,
    106
limit on terms of service, 24–25
Lord's Supper, 9, 66, 122
    authorization for, 180–181
    commissioned lay pastors serving, 85
    frequency of, 180
    governing bodies' authorization of,
        111
    inclusiveness of, 180
    officers serving, 21, 87
    ordering of service, 181
    as part of worship, 174–175, 176,
        180–181
    participation of elders in, 90
Luther, Martin, xii, xiii

Mack, Edward, 52–53
Makemie, Francis, 38
Manual for Ruling Elders and Church Ses-
    sions, 54
meetings, 144–157
    congregational, 149–151, 156–157
    consensus and conflict in, 145
    General Assembly, 155, 156–157
    importance of, 144–145
    moderators and clerks, 146–148
    parliamentary procedure, 148–149
    presbytery, 152–154, 156–157
    session, 152, 156–157
    special, 146
    stated, 146
    synod, 154–155, 156–157
    types of, 146
membership in church, categories of, 64
    active, 64
    affiliate, 65
    baptized, 65
    inactive, 64–65
membership, members reviewing, 71
Methodist Church, 3
Miller, Samuel, 40–42, 44
minister of the Word and Sacrament, 4
    commissioned lay pastors and, 85

daily life of, 86
designated pastoral relationships, 80–81
dissolving permanent pastoral relationships, 80
election, ordination, and installation of as pastors, 33, 73
lack of governing power as individual, 109
as members of presbytery, 76–79
office of, 76–77
organizing pastor, 83–84
overcommitment of, 77
parish associate, 84
participation in higher governing bodies, 109–110
pastoral relations with congregation, 79
permanent pastoral relationships, 79–80
relationship of presbytery to, 114–115
role of, 86–87, 89
serving congregations, 75–87
session and candidates for, 70
as staff member, 93
temporary pastoral relationships, 81–83
transferring name from church roll to presbytery, 73
See also church officers, pastor
ministry, 14–15, 103–105
worship and, 183–184
mission
evangelism, 100–102
governing bodies' responsibilities for, 111
nature of, 98–100, 107–108
prophetic witness, 105–107
scriptural basis for, 99
service, 102–104
sphere of for General Assembly, 121
Mission Yearbook for Prayer and Study, 104
moderators, 146–148
voting rights of, 147, 149
mutual forbearance, 161–162

"Nature and Practice of Ministry," 15
nominating committee, 25–27

Old School General Assembly, 48
order of worship, 175–176
ordination of women, xv
ordination to office, 19–21
constitutional questions asked during, 19–20
differences between ministers and elders/deacons, 33
participation of elders in, 90
purpose of, 20–21
service of, 19
organizing pastor, 79, 83–84
Orthodox churches, 3
overture, 10, 115–116

parish associate, 79, 84
as staff member, 93
parity, 45
parliamentary procedure, 148–149
pastor
calling, 30–32, 79
relationships of, 79–83
responsibilities for governance, 91
responsibilities for pastoral care, 91
responsibilities for worship, 90, 174, 185–186
as session moderator, 147, 149
working with elders, 89–90
working with elders and deacons, 92
See also minister of the Word and Sacrament
pastor nominating committee, 30–33, 81–82
Pentecostal churches, 3
per capita monies, 131
permanent pastoral relationships, 79–80
polity, 1–11
congregational, 2–3
defined, 1
episcopal, 3
Presbyterian, 4–10
power of governing bodies and the Constitution, 160–161

prayer, 173–174
  forms of, 182–183
Presbyterian Church U.S.
  deacons in, 51–53
  emphasis on ministry, 14
  exemptions from inclusiveness re-
    quirements, 27–28
  standards for Christian educators, 96
  standing of elders in, 43–44
Presbyterian Church U.S.A., deacon in,
    53–54
Presbyterian polity, 4–10
  allegiance ultimately to Jesus Christ,
    11
  basis for, 4
  constitutional nature of, 6–8
  fundamentals of, 5–10
  necessity of elections in, 16
  power exercised by groups, 4–5
  relational nature of, 8–10
  representative nature of, 5–6
  Scottish influence on, 36–38
  in 17th- and 18th-century America, 38
presbyters, 4
  church governed by, 5
  envisioned by Calvin, 36
  lack of hierarchy among, 4
  responsible to Christ, 6
presbytery, 9–10, 110, 111–117
  active member of, 78
  approval of special giving cam-
    paigns, 130
  of call, 32
  candidates for ministry and, 70
  committee on ministry, 31
  committees of, 125
  corresponding members, 153
  discretionary powers, 116
  inactive member of, 71, 78–79
  interdependence among, 32–33
  involvement in calling a pastor,
    31–33, 79–86
  jurisdiction over ministers, 76–77
  meetings of, 152–154, 156–157
  member-at-large status in, 78
  members of, 113
  ministers as members of, 33

  moderator of, 148
  of preparation, 32
  property of congregations and,
    139–140
  purpose of, 112–113
  relation to congregations, 113–114
  relation to ministers, 114–115
  relation to synod and General As-
    sembly, 115–116, 118–120
  responsibilities of, 113–117
  role in dissolving pastoral relation-
    ships, 80
  support of Christian educator certifi-
    cation, 97
  veto power of, 5
presbytery meetings, 152–154, 156–157
Prime, Ralph E., 44–45
professional service, candidates for,
    70–71
prophetic witness, 105–107
protest, 162–163

quorum
  for congregational meetings, 151
  for General Assembly meetings, 40,
    44, 155
  for presbytery meetings, 43–44, 154
  for session meetings, 39, 152
  for synod meetings, 44, 154–155

Ramsey, James B., 49–50
rebuke, 168
rebuke with supervised rehabilitation,
    168
Reformed Church in America, 122
remedial cases, 164, 165–167
removal from office, 168
required meetings
  of congregation, 150
  of General Assembly, 155
  of presbytery, 153
  of session, 152
  of synod, 154
review and control, 112
Robert's Rules of Order, 146, 148–149, 151
rolls, deleting names from, 72–73
Roman Catholic Church, 3, 35

rotation system, 24–25
Rules of Discipline, 7

Scottish Reformed Church, 36–38, 120
Scripture in worship, 174
Second Book of Discipline, 37–38, 47
secular matters, church's right to speak on, 105–106
selected giving, 129
self-offering, 175
Sermon or Address on the Elder Moderator and the Ruling Elder, 44
service, 69, 102–104
Service for the Lord's Day, 68
session, 9, 60–74
    candidates for professional service, 70–71
    Christian education, 67–68
    church property and, 139–142
    deleting names from rolls, 72–73
    evaluating approaches to evangelism, 101–102
    fellowship and service, 69
    financial management by, 133–138
    inactive members, 71–72
    inclusiveness, 69
    maintaining accurate church rolls, 67
    meetings of, 152, 156–157
    membership, members reviewing, 71
    moderator of, 147
    pastoral care, 67
    personnel responsibilities, 93–95
    receiving members of the church, 63–67
    responsibilities for church members, 67–73
    responsibilities for church officers, 73–74
    responsibilities and powers of, 60–63, 90
    responsibilities for worship, 184–187
    review of special offerings requests, 130
    role in Baptisms, 179
    stewardship development and, 131–133

session meetings, 152, 156–157
1788 form of government, 38–40
sin, xiii–xiv
    evangelism and, 101
    relation to decision making, xiv
Smyth, Thomas, 43
sovereignty of God, xiv–xvi
Special Committee on Church Temporalities (1896), 54
special meetings, 146
    of congregation, 150–151
    of General Assembly, 155
    of presbytery, 153
    of session, 152
    of synod, 154
special offerings, 130
staff of church, 93–94
staff relationships, 93–94
stated clerks, 147
stated meetings, 146
stated supply, 79, 82–83
stay of enforcement, 170
stewardship, 126–138
    campaigns, 130
    church budget, 134–135
    of church property, 141–142
    designated gifts, 138
    development and the session, 131–133
    emergency appeals, 130
    financial management and, 133–138
    financial reports to the congregation, 137–138
    financial reviews, 136
    general mission giving, 129–130
    grace of, 126–128
    per capita monies, 131
    Presbyterian, 128–131
    special offerings, 130
    treasurer, work of, 135–136
synod, 9–10, 110, 111–112, 118–120
    committees of, 12
    meetings of, 154–155, 156–157
    moderator of, 148
    relationship to General Assembly, 119–120, 121

synod (*continued*)
  relationship to presbytery, 115–116, 118–119
  responsibilities of, 118–120
  synod's council, 119
synod meetings, 154–155, 156–157

temporary exclusion from office, 168
temporary pastoral relationships, 81–83
temporary supply, 79
Thornwell, James Henley, 42–43
tithing, 183 *See also* stewardship, grace of; stewardship, development and the session
treasurer, supervision of work of, 135–136
trials and appeals, 169–170
trustees, 142

unified giving, 129
United Church of Christ, 3, 122
United Presbyterian Church in the U.S.A. (UPCUSA)
  deacons in, 55–56
  emphasis on ministry, 14
  exemptions from inclusiveness requirements, 27–28
  standards for Christian education, 96
United Presbyterian Church of North America (UPNA), 53
  deacons in, 54–55

validated ministries, 78
vice-moderators, 148
vigils, 183
vocation, 183

warning against error, 112
"We Can Be More Than We Are," 45
Wesleyan Church, 3
worship
  baptism, 174–175, 178–180
  context of, 176–178
  creative offerings, 177
  daily personal, 182
  on days other than the Lord's Day, 175
  description of, 173
  elements of, 173–175
  funerals, 182
  guest preachers, 185
  hymns during, 186
  leading the church in, 171–187
  Lord's Supper, 174–175, 180–181
  marriages, 181
  ministry and, 183–184
  order of, 175–176
  personal discipleship and, 182–183
  responsibilities for, 90, 184–186
  Service for the Lord's Day, 175
  session and, 184–187
  on special occasions, 181–182
  worship education, 186